Smart Baseball

Smart Baseball

THE STORY BEHIND THE OLD STATS THAT ARE RUINING THE GAME,
THE NEW ONES THAT ARE RUNNING IT,
AND THE *RIGHT* WAY TO THINK ABOUT BASEBALL

◆

Keith Law

WM
WILLIAM MORROW
An Imprint of HarperCollins *Publishers*

HarperCollins books may be purchased for educational, business, or sales promotional use. For information, please email the Special Markets Department at SPsales@harpercollins.com.

FIRST EDITION

Designed by Joy O'Meara

Library of Congress Cataloging-in-Publication Data has been applied for.

ISBN 978-0-06-249022-3

17 18 19 20 21   DIX/LSC   10 9 8 7 6 5 4 3

To my wife, Christa, and my daughter, Kendall Joy

Contents

PART THREE: Smarter Baseball

Introduction

Like many of you, I imagine, I grew up in a Pleasantville-esque world of baseball statistics, where everything you might want to know about a baseball player was displayed in tabular form on the back of his baseball card (until you destroyed it by flipping it against a brick wall or sticking it in the spokes of a bicycle tire). A hitter's home runs, average, and RBI were right there, along with the obscure and intimidating OBP and SLG. A pitcher's won-lost record, saves, and ERA were shown, along with strikeouts, innings, and the undefined GS, which for a few of my elementary school years I could only assume meant "grand slams," which never made mathematical sense to me. (It means games started.) I was born in 1973 and the eighties were my formative years as a fan. For most of that time, it didn't even occur to me that there might be more information out there to learn about players' performances, or that the stats were birthed from the *sanctum sanctorum* of baseball accounting. This was what there was, and if it was good enough for Topps and *Newsday* and WPIX, it was good enough for me.

Of course, there came a point where I realized that these stats weren't doing a particularly good job of telling me what was happening on the field or helping me predict what players might do in the future. I played fantasy baseball for thirteen years, from my senior year of high school (1990) until my first year as a front office employee of the Toronto Blue Jays, and in the first few years of playing, I was awful at it. I founded the league and finished dead last. I thought being good at math gave me some kind of advantage at the game, but it turned out it gave me a lot of false confidence and nothing else.

Eventually, the desire to be better at a frivolous endeavor—we never played for money—drove me to seek out some new perspectives on baseball, which led me to the small but active online sabermetrics community of the time, and eventually to books like *Baseball Prospectus* and works by Bill James and Eddie Epstein. None of these were specifically guides to statistics, but they all looked at the game a different way, often incorporating new stats—James was a sort of Thomas Edison of the field, generating new stats as easily as most of us breathe—to tell the reader something new about a player. The more I read, the more I wanted to read. Baseball had always been my favorite sport, likely because it was my parents' favorite and my grandmother's as well, but now I could watch and follow the sport with a totally new set of eyes.

In the twenty years since I first wrote my first public piece on baseball, in 1996, the field of baseball analysis has undergone a quantum-state change, going from one or two consultants providing statistical insight to a handful of interested teams to all thirty clubs employing departments of full-time quants. Where media coverage of baseball in the 1990s was homogeneous in people and in content, today it is exploding with diversity of faces, voices, and opinions. This revolution has had, at its heart, the rising adoption of statistical analysis within and around the game. If you said OBP was better than batting average in 1996, you'd be looked at as if you were a little strange. If you say it now, you'll be asked why you're not looking at wOBA or wRC+ instead.

Why has baseball as an industry, including the media covering it and the fans who follow it, stuck with outdated statistics for so long? The answer is largely a giant appeal to tradition, a common type of fallacious argument that says we should keep doing it this way because we've always done it this way. Baseball has always suffered from a sort of inertia. Whether it's about the rules of the game, replay, or the unwritten code of player behavior, old ideas are hard to unseat. For too long people have put faith in old numbers and stats precisely because they're old; these are the numbers that the baseball gods graced us with all those years ago, so we must follow them—even if there are numbers out there that actually work better. A game with a century and a half's worth of history has a hard time escaping the gravitational pull of that past.

The fact that baseball's irrational reliance on tradition, gut instinct, and flawed stats continued even as better stats became widely available to everyone isn't just an academic concern. Because allegiance to these old stats is not rooted in accuracy or success, people who've repeatedly failed at their jobs are often given new opportunities to fail some more. Using the wrong measurements has resulted in bad decisions on contracts, playing time, trades, and draft picks. It's led the voters in the Baseball Writers' Association of America (BBWAA) to pick the wrong players for MVP, Cy Young, and Rookie of the Year awards, and often to screw up even obvious stuff like which players to put in the Hall of Fame. It drives conversations around teams and players—often driving the conversations right off a cliff. Even now, in 2017, you will still hear broadcasters refer to and rely on outdated or flat-out useless statistics to try to analyze what's happening on the field, to advocate bad strategies, or to praise a player for doing something that actually wasn't very good. This isn't just an issue for Major League Baseball (MLB)—it's a problem at all levels of the game. Just go to a college or high school baseball game and watch the bench empty as players rush to congratulate a hitter who just advanced a runner via a bunt or an out. "Yay! We're in worse shape than we were a few pitches ago!"

But even as commentators, managers, writers, and talking heads have resisted the statistical sea change of the last decade, most front offices around the league have long recognized that these and other numbers lie at the heart of the game precisely because they work better. They describe in-game events with greater accuracy and they predict what players will do in the future with greater accuracy. Baseball might be a sport fueled by nostalgia and adherence to the past, but no team wants to go back to a time when they used to lose more often.

As such, teams evaluate players substantially differently today than they did in 2000, and it's time that we as journalists, bloggers, and fans adapt. For that to happen, the conversation has to go beyond merely pointing out that batting average and the pitcher win are bad, into a discussion of what stats are better, allowing us to reframe how we discuss player performance. Communicating that is my main goal in writing this book. (Also money. But mostly communicating that.)

The world of baseball is changing, and has been for some time now, but the mainstream discussion and coverage of the sport has lagged behind the changes within major-league team operations. You'll still read elegies to the pitcher win in your local paper, arguments that poor defenders are actually great because they don't make errors, and managers are brilliant for employing "small ball" tactics that lead to fewer runs. There's no reason on earth for any baseball fan to cling to old, anachronistic, or disproven notions like these. I coined the Twitter term #smrtbaseball a few years ago, an homage to a *Simpsons* joke, to refer to managerial moves and executive comments that were, in fact, the opposite of smart. I've restored the "a" to smart here because the point of this book is to try to educate the reader on the way front offices look at player statistics and valuation today, and where their thinking is likely to head in the future.

As 2016 drew to a close, Major League Baseball was coming off one of its most successful postseasons ever, one full of drama, narratives, and rising young stars, where the Chicago Cubs managed to end the longest championship drought in US professional sports, and did so in no small part because they went from also-rans in the stats department to industry leaders. You couldn't watch or follow the 2016 playoffs without noticing, reading, or hearing about the statistical revolution—players' Wins Above Replacement values, defensive positioning, advanced fielding metrics like Ultimate Zone Rating, and the use of leverage to determine when to use your best reliever. This was unthinkable when I first started dabbling in baseball analysis in my early twenties. It's now standard, with every MLB owner who wasn't already on board looking at the most successful teams the last few seasons and realizing that if they didn't add this capability in-house they'd only fall further behind their direct competitors.

You don't have to understand FIP or dRS or exit velocity to enjoy a baseball game or follow a team. Granted, there are folks out there who'll make you feel like you have to—I'm sure I've been guilty of that a few times—but the truth is you don't need to know all this. It will make you a more educated fan, and to me, becoming educated makes me enjoy the game even more. It will help you when you hear your team made a trade or a signing and you don't immediately get why they did it. It will help you understand a pitching change or a decision to bunt or bring the infield in—or maybe help you question it. And with coverage of every aspect of the sport, from games to transactions to postseason awards to the Hall of Fame, now suffused with the vernacular of sabermetrics, it'll help you keep up with all of the great content being written and spoken about our national pastime.

Smart Baseball is, more than anything else, a book for the reader. If we were sitting at a game together—something I've done with a handful of fans over the years—and you asked me why the save statistic is a travesty on the order of the Alien & Sedition Acts, or what I'm looking for when I scout a player in person, this book gives you the monologue version of the conversation we'd have.

I try to build up from zero here, assuming you come into this book without knowledge of advanced statistics, or that you come into it knowing some stats are bad and some are good but would like a rational explanation of why. In Part One, I cover most of the traditional statistics that just don't tell us what they purport to tell us. RBI, batting average, wins, saves—they're a bunch of filthy liars, really, and they've been lying to us for decades now. In Part Two, I work my way up through some better traditional statistics, like on-base percentage (OBP), on my way to discussing entirely new stats that show how teams and analysts try to value a player's production.

If you want to pay for a player, first you have to know what he's worth, and to do that, you have to know how much baseball value he produced. In Part Three, I apply these concepts to Hall of Fame debates, explain how traditional scouting works and is changing in light of new data, and discuss the MLB Statcast product, an entirely new stream of data that dwarfs anything teams have worked with previously. The future of baseball analysis revolves around Statcast, which has the potential to change the way teams look at everything from contracts to scouting to player development to keeping players (especially pitchers) healthy.

Sabermetrics is baseball math, but I've tried to keep the math in this book to a bare minimum. This isn't a manual to build your own, better sabermetric mousetrap, although I won't discourage you from trying; this is about a new way of thinking about the game, a general philosophy of player valuation and evaluation that over the last fifteen years has gone from the lunatic fringe to the predominant way of thinking. Every MLB team has made or is making statistical analysis a core part of its baseball decision-making process, and the effects of this revolution were all over the 2016 postseason, from Cleveland's unconventional use of closer Andrew Miller to the World Champion Chicago Cubs exploiting new data to become defensive wizards. Even if you just want to follow the conversation around the game, it will help to know where we came from and where the world of baseball statistics is going. This book will take you there.

PART ONE

◆

Smrt Baseball

1

Below Average:

The Fundamental Flaws
of Batting Average

The language of baseball is built around some of its most basic statistics. Batting average, the simple division of a hitter's hits recorded by the number of at bats he had, is the foundation of baseball's "batting title." The player in each league with the highest batting average is named the "batting champion." When hitters retire, we count their batting titles and compare them to other batting champions' totals. We revere the "lifetime .300 hitter" as if he ascended to a higher plane of existence than the mere .299 hitter. But the batting title and the stat behind it are both guilty of telling us half-truths, giving us a less-than-complete story of the hitter's performance.

Consider the descriptions found on the plaques for these Hall of Famers:

> *An artisan with a bat whose daily pursuit of excellence produced a .338 lifetime batting average, 3141 hits, and a National League record–tying **eight batting titles** . . .*
>
> —Hall of Fame plaque for Tony Gwynn

A five-time batting champion who also led the league in on-base percentage and intentional walks six times each . . .
                              —Hall of Fame plaque for Wade Boggs

Led American League in batting twelve times . . .
                              —Hall of Fame plaque for Ty Cobb

Accomplished as these players were, their lionization in Coopers-town ignores a crucial question: If you're only leading the league in batting average, one flawed and incomplete stat, should we really say you led the league in "batting"? Are you the "batting champion" if other players hit better than you did?

Batting average has been at the top of the heap of hitter stats for as long as hitters have been putting bat to ball. The English-American statistician Henry Chadwick is credited with creating batting average (among many other common baseball stats) in the late 1800s, designing it along the lines of cricket's version of batting average, which is runs divided by outs. Baseball in the nineteenth century resembled today's game, but had several significant differences, such as times when batters could tell the pitcher where they wanted the ball thrown, or periods where the number of balls required for a walk or strikes required for a strikeout varied from today's 4 and 3. Hitting the ball over the fence for a home run was rare—in 1895, the National League leader in home runs had 18—as most hitters were just trying to put the ball in play. So, at the time, Chadwick's idea had merit: when batters rarely walk and are focused on making contact, hits divided by at bats probably is a good measure of their performance.

Batting average today still has some value, albeit a limited one; batting average's primary problem is one of marketing. If batting average were content with second-tier statistical duty, to impart some small amount of information, without claiming to be the be-all and end-all of hitting statistics, then it would probably fly under the radar without attracting much notice from traditionalists or statheads.

Ah, but when you claim to be the King of All Stats and fail to deliver, then you have earned my ire—and that of analysts and executives around the sport, who now recognize that you can get all the information batting average is supposed to give you in other, more complete, less flawed statistics. So while we still celebrate the player who "won the batting title" or "led the league in hitting" for having the highest batting average in the league, the stat itself has been falling out of favor for twenty years already—and its decline is only accelerating.

All this history may be impressive, but it obscures what batting average actually tells you. Batting average is a simple calculation any third grader could do—take a player's hits, divide it by that player's at bats, and round to three digits. That's batting average, and while in tiny samples it can range from .000 to 1.000, in the modern era batting averages have typically fallen in the .200 to .400 range. In the five seasons from 2011 to 2015, no player qualified for the "batting title" with an average above .350, and only two players even cracked .340 (Jose Altuve once, Miguel Cabrera twice).

Did you notice that odd phrase in there—qualified for the batting title? Because batting average is a rate stat, a statistic that measures something per something else—in this case, hits per at bat—MLB sets a minimum threshold to appear on its leaderboards, in this case a reasonable 3.1 plate appearances per team game played. Since a full season for most teams is 162 games played, that means a player must have 503 plate appearances on the year to qualify for the league's batting title or appear anywhere on the leaderboard.

Yes, but weren't we talking about at bats a moment ago? What's this with plate appearances? Indeed, that bait-and-switch exposes batting average's first major flaw. Batting average doesn't tell you how often a player gets a hit, but how often he gets a hit *ignoring times he draws a walk, gets hit by a pitch, hits a sacrifice fly, makes a successful sacrifice bunt, or reaches via catcher's interference.* Those scenarios don't count as at bats, but do count as plate appearances.

(The first three count for the purposes of on-base percentage, a stat so valuable it will get its own chapter later in the book.)

So why does batting average ignore all of these other events, which in some extreme cases can account for more than a third of a player's trips to the plate? (Barry Bonds did this twice, in 2002 and 2004, the only MLB player in history whose plate appearances were more than 50 percent higher than his at bats.) Because . . . well, there's no really good explanation for this. I mentioned above the most likely theory, that when Chadwick created the stat, those other events were rare or just weren't considered the result of a hitter's skill or effort, so he chose to omit them. This alone should tell you why using batting average by itself, or even just as your primary metric, to evaluate a hitter leaves out far too much crucial information. Leaving walks drawn, an important skill for a hitter, out of the numerator (just hits) and denominator (at bats), only gives you a portion of the hitter's season.

The sins of batting average, though, are not just of omission. The numerator is even more flawed than you'd think, because it treats all hits as equal—a single and a home run both carry the same weight in batting average, even though we know they carry substantially different weights in the game.

So what does batting average really tell us about what a hitter did over some period of time? It tells us how often he got a hit in trips to the plate where he didn't walk or get hit by a pitch or hit a sac fly or bunt or have some other very rare thing that isn't actually an at bat happen, and it only tells us that he got a hit but not what kind of hit. (Hence the old baseball axiom, often heard after a weakly hit infield single, "It'll look like a line drive in the box score.") It's a bad tradition, but it has stuck with us for well over a century and still carries undue importance in discussions and evaluations of hitters, especially those who lead the league in batting average because we say they "won" something. It's often confusing because hitters who hit for high batting averages are generally good hitters, period; we're not getting totally false information from the stat, but we're misled by its false precision, acting as if going to the third decimal place is a summary judgment on the player. To see the full extent of the flaws in batting average, it helps to compare it to stats that are better equipped.

One basic statistical tool I'll use often in this book is correlation analysis, where I compare two columns of data to each other and get a number between 0 and 1 that tells us how strongly correlated the two are—that is, how much the two columns move together, 0 meaning no correlation at all, 1 meaning perfect correlation. The higher the number, the greater the correlation between the two stats, meaning that when stat A moves, stat B moves more with it. This does not mean A causes B or B causes A; you've probably heard someone say "correlation does not prove causation" at some point, because all a correlation analysis can tell is whether two statistics appear to be related. It could be a direct cause and effect, and it could be coincidence, but this tool only tells us to what extent the two numbers move together. In this book, I will often refer to a correlation between two statistics by saying that one "predicts" the other.

In the table below, I used MLB team stats from the five seasons from 2011 through 2015 to show the correlations between four commonly used hitter-rate stats at the team level and those teams' runs-scored-per-game figures:

Team Stat	Correlation to Team R/G
Batting average	0.749
On-base percentage	0.833
Slugging percentage	0.903
OPS	0.936

Batting average correlates pretty well to runs scored, at about 75 percent—while this doesn't show causation, it stands to reason that if a team as a whole is getting more hits during its (arbitrarily, narrowly defined) at bats, it will score more runs. But batting average fares worse compared to the two other common rate stats used for evaluating hitters: on-base percentage and slugging percentage.

On-base percentage, or OBP, does just what it claims to do, taking the times a hitter reached base safely, dividing it by all plate appearances other than sacrifice bunts and times reached on interference, and giving the frequency with which the hitter gets on base. A hitter with a .400 OBP, which would put him above the league leaders, reached base in 40 percent of those plate appearances, meaning he made an out of some sort in the other 60 percent. Of all basic batting stats—those you might find on the back of a baseball card or on the stats you find in a game program—OBP is probably the most important for telling you about a hitter's ability to produce.

Slugging percentage is calculated like batting average but no longer treats all hits as equal. The denominator (the bottom of the fraction) remains at bats, but the numerator changes from hits to total bases. A single counts for one total base, a double two, a triple three, and a home run four. This isn't an accurate reflection of their relative values; a home run isn't worth four times as much to an offense as a single, but something like twice as much. It does create some needed separation between hit types, however, and you can see that it correlates extremely well to runs scored at the team level. If you hit for more power, you're going to score more runs. (In fact, home runs per plate appearance all by itself has a coefficient of correlation of 0.623 with runs scored over this same sample—ignoring absolutely everything else a team does, home runs still drive a substantial fraction of run-scoring.)

OPS, which stands for "On-base Plus Slugging," is a kludge stat, a brute-force addition of OBP and slugging percentage that is deeply flawed at a basic math level, yet it has gained momentum in popular discussions of the sport, including media coverage, because it kind of works: you can see it correlates better with run-scoring than either OBP or slugging do individually. OPS is popular and problematic enough to merit its own section later in the book, but for now, its purpose here is to show how much information is missing from batting average. If these other rate stats correlate better to team run-scoring, and they're all easily available at the individual player level, what, exactly, is batting average actually good for?

*   *   *

Despite the deficiencies of batting average, the "batting champion" tag still matters quite a bit within baseball circles, especially where fans and the media are involved. The title features prominently on several Hall of Fame plaques, including the three players cited at the top of the chapter, and becomes a talking point in Hall of Fame elections, but perhaps most important, it's a primary focus for postseason award balloting and often used as a justification for voting for players who were not in fact the best hitters in the league.

In 2007, Detroit Tigers outfielder Magglio Ordoñez led the American League in batting average at .363, but he wasn't the best offensive player in the league because he didn't do enough besides hitting for average. The best offensive player in the league was Alex Rodriguez of the New York Yankees, who led the AL with 54 homers and a .645 slugging percentage, so while he "only" hit .314, he produced more total value with the bat. He had 26 more home runs than Ordoñez and drew 19 more walks, so the total value of all of his contributions—considering the values of all those hits, walks, and extra bases, compared to the number of outs he produced—exceeded that of Ordoñez, even before we consider things like defense. Rodriguez did win the AL MVP award that year, although two Detroit-based writers, Tom Gage and Jim Hawkins, made the absolutely-not-biased-at-all decision to list Ordoñez, the local player, first on their ballots. Gage specifically cited Ordoñez's batting average in defending his vote, dismissing home runs as "a glamour stat."

Similarly, the Miami Marlins' Dee Gordon led the National League in batting average in 2015 at .333, but the statistics site Baseball-Reference.com doesn't list Gordon among the top ten in the National League in "Adjusted Batting Runs" (ABR) an advanced metric that does just what I described above: assigns weights to different offensive events and adds 'em up. Bryce Harper led the NL in just about everything else, winning the NL MVP award unanimously. (Gage and Hawkins are no longer active award voters, and wouldn't have voted on a National League award as members of the Detroit chapter.) You can see below just how large the gap between Gordon and Harper was, even though Gordon led Harper in batting average:

	AVG	OBP	SLG	2B	HR	BB	Outs	ABR
Harper	.330	.460*	.649*	38	42	124	372	78.1
Gordon	.333*	.359	.418	24	4	25	447	10.9

ABR = Adjusted Batting Runs

* = led National League

Harper got on base more, hit for far more power, and made 75 fewer outs. Gordon's .003 advantage in batting average turns out to be not just meaningless but outright misleading: these two players were nowhere close to each other in offensive production, so exactly what good is batting average doing for us?

In 1991, Barry Bonds was the best player in the National League by a wide margin, and should have walked away with his second straight NL MVP award. He led the NL in on-base percentage that season, ranked fourth in slugging percentage, and even finished second in runs batted in, a statistic that at the time was a major criterion for MVP voters. But Bonds lost the award to Atlanta's Terry Pendleton, whose primary achievement that year was leading the league in batting average at .319. Bonds was by far the more valuable hitter; he reached base 29 more times than Pendleton did, despite having 10 fewer plate appearances. They hit for almost identical slugging percentages. Bonds had 3 more homers and stole 33 more bases. Both were excellent defenders. Pendleton didn't do anything better than Bonds except hit for average, but that was enough to carry him to the MVP award by a slim margin, as he received 12 of the 24 first-place votes as opposed to 10 for Bonds. Had the writers gotten it right, Bonds would have won four straight MVPs from 1990 to 1993, something no player had done before, and no player would do until Bonds himself did it in 2001–04.

Some of the statistics I discuss in Part One are quite useless for evaluating a player's performance or the value he delivered to his team. Batting average isn't useless, but it does not do what it has long been supposed to do. It doesn't tell us how good a hitter Joey

Bagodonuts is. It doesn't let us compare one hitter to another and say one is better than the other at anything specific. It doesn't tell us that someone is a better hitter for contact or for power, or better at getting on base. Whatever batting average does give us, we can get that same information, and more, from other, equally simple metrics.

So if the appeal of batting average as the lord of hitting stats isn't accuracy, or ease of calculation, then what is it? In many ways, the adherence to batting average isn't easy to explain, because it just isn't that logical. Batting average is emblematic of how the weight of baseball history can be the largest impediment to success on the field. The emphasis on batting average when smarter stats are out there embodies the false dichotomy we've seen in baseball coverage over the last fifteen years, whether it's pitched as "scouts versus stats" or traditional versus modern: the writers and fans who profess to disdain statistical analysis in fact rely very heavily on their own statistics—the ones they've used their whole lives. These statistics, like batting average, pitcher wins, and others I'll cover, are simpler to calculate or count, but they give us an incomplete or sometimes plain inaccurate picture of what a player did to help his team. Yet because they've been around forever, many fans don't want to let them go.

There's no such respect for tradition here: if the old stats don't work, throw them out and get new ones. But first we have to take the rest of the trash out.

2

Pitcher Wins:

One Guy Gets the Credit for Everyone Else's Work

"In pitching, the only thing that really matters is wins."

—headline of Paul Hoynes's Rant of the Week, *Cleveland Plain Dealer*, September 11, 2010

For as long as you've been a baseball fan, you've been inundated with the message that a pitcher—or at least a starting pitcher—is his win total. So-and-so is a 20-game winner. What's-his-face has a low ERA but "only" went 12-13. Until fairly recently, other metrics that might give us some sort of indication of how well he actually pitched paled in comparison to the mighty won-lost record; preventing runs wasn't enough, but somehow, the pitcher had to will his teammates to score more runs while he was in the game while simultaneously exhorting his relievers to pitch well after his departure.

This line of thinking, of course, is dumber than a sack of hair. In baseball, team victories matter, but the idea of a single player earning full credit for a win or blame for a loss exposes a deep ignorance of how the game actually plays out on the field. If you've ever watched an actual game of baseball, you know that the sport doesn't function this way: even a pitcher who throws a perfect game gets some help somewhere—from his defense, from his catcher, and of course from the offense that scored at least one run so he didn't have to go out and pitch the tenth inning—which happened to Pedro Martinez in 1995 while he was still a Montreal Expo. Pedro threw nine perfect innings against the Padres, but the Expos couldn't push a run across until the tenth inning; only after that did he qualify for the win despite retiring all 27 batters he'd faced to that point. As the pitcher, Martinez couldn't have done any more to help his team win the game, but he didn't "earn" the victory until his teammates scored. This is because the entire thought process that led us to this point, where a starting pitcher gets that credit or blame, is both out of date and very, very stupid.

Once upon a time, when men were men who ate giant hunks of raw meat for sustenance, the job of the starting pitcher was vastly different from what it is today. Starters in the late nineteenth century and well into the early twentieth century typically threw complete games, and might pitch every third day or, in some extreme examples from premodern baseball, every other day. (Check out Old Hoss Radbourn's career stats for some seasons that look like they came from a different sport entirely—which, in practical terms, they did.) Relievers would enter the game to clean up only after a starting pitcher had struggled and the game's outcome was probably already determined.

Before 1920, offensive levels were so low in general that we now refer to that time in baseball's history as the "dead ball" era; any hitter who reached double digits in home runs would likely lead his league for that season, so for a pitcher to complete a game was a less arduous task than it would be even ten years after that era ended. The ball wasn't really dead, but hitters were taught to put the ball in play and often were satisfied with hitting the ball on the ground, or, as Wee Willie Keeler supposedly said, to "hit it where they [the fielders] ain't." That means swinging early in the count and keeping the ball in the park, so the idea of a pitch count—a tally of how many pitches a starting pitcher has thrown to that point in the game—would have struck even coaches or executives of the time as meaningless. (There are still the occasional troglodyte comments from coaches and ex-pitchers about how today's starters are "babied" with pitch counts that, while the direct relationship is not precisely known, exist to try to keep pitchers healthy. Better we just run young arms right into the ground, I suppose.)

After 1920, offensive levels in baseball changed, spurred in part by the rise of Babe Ruth, who had seasons where he would out-homer entire opposing teams by himself before the league started to catch on and both acquire more power hitters and teach hitters to try to drive the ball. Yet the job of the starter remained essentially the same until the late 1940s and the 1950s, when we began to see the ancestors of today's modern relievers, pitchers who have been retroactively credited with saves and appear to the modern observer as "closers." (The save, a terrible statistic in its own right, gets its own two minutes' hate in a later chapter.) Baseball teams had also settled into the four-man rotation, which would last into the 1970s even though pitchers' careers frequently ended in that time period due to injuries that, from our modern perspective, appear to be related to overuse.

Today's pitching staff usage bears little resemblance to the patterns of a century ago. Starters are rarely asked to turn over a lineup—that is, to face opposing hitters—a fourth time and sometimes only have to turn it over twice in one start before the manager makes the call to the bullpen. We live now in an era of pitch counts, where 100 is seen as a magic number (because people have ten fingers, making 100 the pretty round number), and 120 is the top end of what a major-league starter might be asked to do. Pitchers work in five-man rotations, almost never throwing on short rest in the regular season, and skip starts or hit the disabled list at the first sign of trouble in their elbows or shoulders. It may be this new paradigm, rather than a recognition that the pitcher win is the homunculus of baseball stats, that finally kills this number once and for all.

In 1904, Giants pitcher Jack Chesbro started 51 games, completed 48 of them, threw 454 innings, and was credited with 41 wins on the season. Since the start of the modern, two-league era in 1901, no other starting pitcher has "won" more than 40 games in a season. Entering the 2017 season, there hasn't even been a pair of teammates anywhere in baseball who combined for 40 pitcher wins in a single season since 2002. These pitcher wins are still going somewhere—the accounting rules of baseball require someone to get a win, even if nobody pitched particularly well—but now they're going to relievers who might do a fraction of the work of the starter and sometimes are merely the pitcher of record at the time that his team happened to score. A reliever is said to have "vultured" a win if he entered the game with his team in the lead, gave up the tying run (or worse), and then was still the active pitcher when his team retook the lead that they kept till the end of the game. The game on the field hasn't changed at all, but the methods of accounting that were developed, arbitrarily, more than a century ago are no longer capable of describing what happened on the field in any meaningful way.

It is the nature of baseball culture to anchor on a number that's presented as if it has actual meaning—even more so if the number is nice and round: 100 RBI, for example, or 20 wins. For decades, a pitcher had to win at least 20 games to even get due consideration for the Cy Young Award, regardless of how else he pitched. Between 1969, the start of the four-division era in baseball, and 2010, the year Felix Hernandez won the award with a won-lost record of 13-12, there were 68 starting pitchers who won the Cy Young Award in full seasons. (This excludes 1981, 1994, and 1995, when MLB teams played fewer than 162 games apiece because the billionaire owners didn't want to pay the players more money.) Only 17 won fewer than 20 games in their award-winning seasons, even though the 20-game winners who did win those awards were frequently not the best pitchers in their leagues—just the guys who had the most help from their teammates.

The late Bob Welch's win in 1990 is one of the most glaring examples of writers who vote on postseason awards and the Hall of Fame (a system so bad it only remains because it's better than all the other possible systems), focusing so much on a win total that they ignored all the other evidence of how the pitchers actually pitched. Welch, playing for an Oakland A's team that went 103-59 and eventually won the American League pennant, was credited with a 27-6 record that season, but wasn't even the best pitcher in his own rotation:

	W	L	ERA	IP	Runs
Bob Welch	27	6	2.95	238.0	90
Dave Stewart	22	11	2.56	267.0	84

(There are more advanced stats that make the case for Stewart more strongly, but since we're just getting started, I'll save those for later in the book.)

Welch had five more pitcher wins and five fewer pitcher losses than Stewart did, but where's the evidence that he actually pitched better than his teammate—that is, that he produced more value for the team by preventing more runs? Stewart threw 29 more innings and yet allowed fewer runs than Welch did. If we just make the basic assumption, valid for our purposes here, that a pitcher's entire job is to prevent opposing teams from scoring, then Welch could not possibly have been better than Stewart in 1990, because to match his teammate Welch would have had to throw 29 more innings and "allow" negative six runs to un-score, or something like that. Welch had the season we remember, because of the award and because no pitcher has reached 25 wins in a season since then, but it should have been obvious, even to the phrenologists of the day, that Stewart was better.

If Welch wasn't even the best pitcher on his own team, where did he rank in the entire American League? Well, the writers of 1990 were apparently about as dim as a 10-watt incandescent bulb, because one of the best pitchers in history had one of the best seasons of any starter in the last fifty years in 1990, right under their noses . . . yet finished second in the voting. Roger Clemens—you might have heard of him at some point—threw 228 innings and allowed just 59 runs, 49 earned, for a 1.93 ERA. His won-lost record wasn't shabby at 21-6, but the gap in their ERAs means that for every nine innings Welch or Clemens pitched, Welch allowed one more run. That's close to a run per start, with both pitchers

averaging over seven innings an outing. I'm not relying on sabermetrics here, nor am I pointing to stats that weren't available in 1990.
I'm talking common sense: the pitcher who gave up way fewer runs
probably did his job better. As it turns out, more advanced metrics,
like Wins Above Replacement, mark Clemens's 1990 season as the
tenth-best pitching season in the last half century, yet it wasn't good
enough to beat Welch out because of those fancy, shiny pitcher wins.

Those A's teams of the late 1980s produced some statistical com-
edy because they were so good offensively, yet people inside and
outside the industry still didn't quite catch on to the folly of the
pitcher win. In 1989, Storm Davis had the season that first started
the break in my mind between the pitcher win and a pitcher's actual
value when he went 19-7, tying for the third-highest win total in
the league with teammate Mike Moore, despite a 4.36 ERA that
was the seventh worst among the 39 pitchers who qualified for the
ERA title by throwing at least 162 innings. The mere fact that a
pitcher can be that far below the median and still have one of the
league's best won-lost records should have tipped someone off that
the pitcher win was misleading. Instead, the opposite happened. We
continued to see pitchers lauded and paid primarily on the basis of
those records rather than their underlying performances, resulting in
egregious awards and contracts such as these:

- Willie Blair, a thoroughly mediocre starter who had a 4.73
  ERA through the first seven years of his career, went 16-8 with
  a 4.17 ERA in 1997 for the Tigers, signed a three-year, $11.5
  million deal with the Diamondbacks that winter. He was so
  bad for Arizona, posting a 5.34 ERA with a 4-15 (not a typo)
  record in four months, that the Snakes dumped him off in a
  trade to the Mets that July.

- Russ Ortiz went 21-9 for Atlanta in 2003 while leading the
  league in walks issued with 102, then went 15-9 for the club
  in 2004 while walking 112, before entering free agency that
  winter. He signed a four-year, $33 million contract with . . .
  oh, hey, it's the Diamondbacks again, having learned nothing

from running into the Blair ditch a few years earlier. Ortiz posted a 6.89 ERA in 2005, then was even worse in six starts for Arizona the next spring before they released him, which at the time marked an unofficial record for the largest salary still owed (about $22 million) to a player who'd been released.

- Bartolo Colon won 18 games in 2004 despite a 5.01 ERA that was well below the American League average; the next year, he went 21-8, winning the AL Cy Young Award even though he finished 8th in the league in earned run average. Minnesota's Johan Santana was actually the best pitcher in the league that year; he threw nine more innings than Colon and allowed 16 fewer runs, but with a 16-7 record he came in third in the Cy Young voting.

- Shawn Estes was on what appeared to be his final shot to remain a major-league starter when he signed a $600,000, one-year deal with Colorado during spring training of 2004. He went 15-8 for the Rockies that season, with a whopping 5.84 ERA, leading the NL in runs allowed with 133 . . . and the Diamondbacks signed him to a $2.5 million deal for 2005. Even accounting for the difficulty of pitching at Denver's altitude, there was no looking at that 5.84 ERA and seeing a million-dollar starter there, unless you were so blinded by the won-lost record that you couldn't accept how badly he'd actually pitched.

The market has shifted since these examples, as awareness of the worthlessness of won-lost records has permeated front offices and started to leak out into media coverage of baseball, but the mentality that a starting pitcher's job is to win the game still exists among fans, players, and even coaches. This belief, which requires a starting pitcher to record at least 15 outs (five innings) so that he'll qualify for the win as long as his team is ahead, is a major obstacle to the ongoing paradigm shift in pitcher usage that has starters working less in each start and relievers handling more of the work in later innings.

The flaws of the pitcher win stat run much deeper than its failure to reflect the modern game or to tell us how well the pitcher prevented runs.

The fundamental problem with the pitcher win is that it is an inherent failure of logic. It takes something—the team victory or loss—that is, by the definition of the rules of the sport, the result of the efforts of at least nine players on each team, and ascribes all of the credit or blame for each side to one man. If a company handled its cost accounting like this, the CFO would be drawn and quartered at dawn. The invention of the pitcher win was a sort of brain death of baseball statistics, and it took nearly a century for the industry to recover from this early misstep.

Think about what goes into a team winning a game, and what portion of that you might then assign to the starting pitcher. The team in question must outscore its opponent, and if you're wondering if you just paid good money to get that kind of insight, I'm sorry to report that yes, you did. But outscoring the opponent itself has multiple elements.

First, you've got to score—the job of the offense, and only the offense. That's half the game, by definition, and it belongs entirely to the hitters who appear in the game. That may include the starting pitcher if the game takes place in a National League park—but even if that's the case, the starter will get, at most, one-ninth of the plate appearances in the game, and is going to be the least effective hitter in the lineup, so his portion of the credit we give to the offense will be quite small. If we think of the entire game as a pie, cut into, say, ten slices, we just gave five of them to the offense, and the starting pitcher probably doesn't even merit a bite.

The other half of the game is run prevention, but that, as we know quite well today but didn't fully grasp thirty or forty years ago, is the result of the interaction of pitchers, hitters, and fielders, where apportioning credit is not as easy as it once seemed. I'll get into some of these effects—what we think we know now about fielding, and what we still don't know—in later chapters, but for now, I'm going to offer some conservative estimates on the subject. We know that fielding matters: if the hitter didn't walk, strike out, or homer, then one or more fielders were involved in the play, and may have had the chance to convert the ball the batter put into play into an out. How much fielding matters depends a bit on the pitcher, who may be a high-strikeout guy or a groundball guy or a guy who makes fans cringe when he's scheduled to pitch, but historical estimates of the effect of fielding on the outcome of a game have ranged from 10 percent upward. Even if we leave it there, that's another slice of the pie gone, with just four out of ten slices remaining.

What's left still can't all go to the starting pitcher. Today's starting pitcher rarely throws a complete game, with one or more relief pitchers—somewhat of a novel concept compared to baseball in the early twentieth century—finishing the game after he leaves. Not only does the starter therefore not fully control the pitching portion of the run prevention variable here, but he doesn't even control how many runs he gave up: in the Enronian accounting of baseball, if a runner scores, the pitcher who allowed him to reach base is said to have given up that run, even if the event that let him score occurred after that pitcher left the game. Say that David Price starts a game for Boston, begins the ninth inning on the mound, and walks the first hitter, after which he's pulled for closer Craig Kimbrel. Kimbrel immediately gives up a home run to the next batter, allowing the man Price walked to advance three more bases, from first to home. Kimbrel is assigned one run allowed, and Price is assigned one run. Whether that's fair or not—hint: it's kind of not—is a little beside the point here; the point is that Price didn't give up that run entirely by himself. So of those four pieces of the win-loss pie remaining, the relievers get to eat some; maybe it's one piece, maybe it's three, but suddenly we don't have very much left for the starting pitcher.

Even if the starting pitcher throws a perfect game—27 batters faced, 27 batters retired—he'd still have gotten some help from his defense. The most dominant pitching performances in history, such

as Kerry Wood's 20-strikeout one-hitter in 1998, still involved a little help from the fielders behind those pitchers. Giving those pitchers the full credit of a win or a loss is idiocy. Not only is it inaccurate,
giving us the impression that the pitcher had more to do with the
team result than he did, but it has the effect of reducing our understanding of the game.

"Win = pitcher pitched well" isn't even true; you can get a win
and still pitch poorly. Russ Ortiz (yep, him again) made a start on
May 21, 2000, against the Brewers where went 6⅔ innings, gave up
10 runs—that's one run for every two outs he recorded—and still got
the win because the Giants scored 16 runs that day. It was at least
the 34th time in MLB history that a pitcher gave up 10 or more runs
and was still handed a win. (The record, for the morbidly curious,
appears to be 12 runs, set by Gene Packard for the St. Louis Cardinals in 1918. The play-by-play data are only accurate from 1913
forward, and is available on Baseball-Reference.com's Play Index.)

On May 26, 1959, baseball saw one of the most egregious pitcher
losses in history, as Harvey Haddix threw nine perfect innings in Milwaukee for the Pittsburgh Pirates . . . then another perfect inning . . .
then another perfect inning, retiring the first 33 batters he faced,
only to have his offense unable to scratch a run across through their
first thirteen times at bat. In the bottom of the 13th inning, third
baseman Don Hoak (of *City Slickers* fame) made a throwing error
on what would have been the first out of the inning, allowing the
first Braves baserunner of the day. After a bunt and an intentional
walk (of Hank Aaron), Joe Adcock doubled to deep right-center,
ending Haddix's no-hitter, shutout, and the game itself. Haddix surrendered the only run of the game, and therefore was given the loss.
It's not the worst by line score—four years later, Milwaukee lefty
Warren Spahn went 15 innings and got the loss in a 1–0 defeat—but
it might be the most heartbreaking.

So why do we still do it? Why do we persist in handing out a
win to a pitcher in every game, and a loss to another pitcher, and
pat ourselves on the back for a job well done? Statistics in sport can
do one of two things for us: describe what happened, or interpret
what happened. Pitcher decisions (wins and losses) do neither. They

obscure the truth while adding no pertinent or useful information. The statement that such-and-such a pitcher "got the win" is the canonical tale told by an idiot, full of sound and fury, and signifying nothing. Yet they're still there on the stat sheet, on sortable pages of pitching stats, and in just about any news coverage of a baseball game, where the winning and losing pitchers' records will appear in parentheses after their names, or a trade or signing, where any pitcher involved is reduced to those two numbers, separated by the hyphen of ignorance.

One last note: You may hear the rationalization that pitcher wins are bad for evaluating a single start, or a season, but good for evaluating an entire career. It is somewhat true that a pitcher who sticks around long enough to win 250 or 300 games is probably a good pitcher, period. (Teams make dumb decisions, but letting a bad pitcher get that many decisions would be a whole new level of stupid.) However, using pitcher wins on the career level to evaluate performance merely compounds the errors of using them in single games or seasons. The factors that make pitcher wins useless in smaller samples do not just even out in larger samples because you want them to.

Take Bert Blyleven, who pitched most of his career for bad teams. Blyleven won 287 games, and for more than a decade he was denied entry to baseball's Hall of Fame by writers who pointed to his failure to earn 300 pitcher wins in his career. Yet Blyleven was a remarkably unlucky pitcher, spending most of his career pitching for bad— specifically, low-scoring—teams, and that lack of run support meant he "lost" a lot of games that starters for other teams would have won. Blyleven pitched 75 complete-game losses, the second-most in MLB since 1957, one behind Hall of Famer Gaylord "it's a hard slider" Perry. Blyleven made 40 starts in his career when he went at least seven innings, gave up two earned runs or fewer, and got the loss. In 35 of his losses, his team lost by just one run. In 41 of his losses, his team was shut out entirely. He didn't reach 300 pitcher wins because his teams stunk, not because he didn't pitch well, or because he lacked some sort of special pitcher woo that made his teams win when he pitched. And he nearly missed the Hall of Fame because of it, earning election in his fourteenth year on the ballot, one shy of the limit of fifteen years (since shortened to ten).

In a grand bit of irony, Blyleven, now a popular announcer for the Minnesota Twins, has been outspoken in his disdain for smarter baseball analysis. He said in 2010 that Hernandez didn't have enough wins to deserve the Cy Young Award and has dismissed the use of advanced statistics as "cybermetrics." Former ESPN color analyst Joe Morgan, one of the greatest players in MLB history, was an ardent critic of any attempts to use statistical analysis to value players, as well as the book *Moneyball,* in which author Michael Lewis chronicled Oakland's attempts to find undervalued players by using such methods, spearheaded by General Manager Billy Beane. (Morgan also claimed on television that Beane himself wrote the book, but refused to read it before criticizing it.) Morgan was a sabermetric darling of sorts as a player, because he did so many things well on the field, including posting high on-base percentages, leading the NL in walks drawn twice, and stealing bases at a high rate of success. So even beneficiaries of the new way of evaluating performance can't escape the tyranny of traditional stats, whether they're for pitchers or hitters, because batting average and pitcher wins and RBI are the way they've always looked at players.

3

RBI:

Baseball's Unreliable Narrator

Branch Rickey, the general manager of the St. Louis Cardinals and Los Angeles Dodgers who is best known for signing Jackie Robinson to his first MLB contract, called runs batted in "a misleading statistic" in a well-known piece he wrote for *Life* magazine in 1954:

> *As a statistic, RBIs were not only misleading but dishonest. They depended on managerial control, a hitter's position in the batting order, park dimensions and the success of his teammates in getting on base ahead of him.*

Sixty-two years later, the RBI remains a useful tool for measuring offense in the minds of fans, writers, MVP voters, and at least one major-league manager (since fired), Atlanta's Fredi Gonzalez, who told the *Atlanta Journal-Constitution* in March 2016:

> *I know in the stat-geek world RBI is not a big number, but it sure is. Because you can have all the on-base percentage you want, if you don't have somebody driving anybody in, you're not going to score runs.*

Unlike most of the other "basic" baseball stats like batting average or home runs, the run batted in, or RBI, statistic only entered
the baseball lexicon in 1920, the invention of *New York Press* writer
Ernie Lanigan, who began tracking the stat several years earlier,
along with the statistic we now know as "times caught stealing."
Lanigan and his editor, Jim Price, introduced the RBI into their paper's box scores and later convinced the National League to include
RBI totals in the league statistics. By 1920, it was an official stat for
MLB, and over the years many researchers have gone back to tally
and verify RBI totals prior to 1920. It was adopted as an accounting
of something that happened, but if Lanigan saw the RBI as holding
some greater meaning, it's been lost to time. Of course, when he created the RBI, the Most Valuable Player Award didn't exist, but RBI
totals have long been used by voters as one of the main criteria; if
you lead the league in RBI and your team makes the playoffs, you're
already a favorite to win the award.

How has more than a half century passed without this obviously
flawed statistic losing its place in basic evaluations of player performance?

It fails a simple logical test of its merits, and it has repeatedly produced the wrong conclusions in questions of player value. The RBI
stat is responsible for more bad postseason award decisions than any
other single factor in baseball history. And while I can't confirm this,
I believe strongly that it is responsible for more stupid comments by
game announcers than any other statistic, too.

Though the RBI was not an official MLB stat until 1920, it's now
enshrined in rule 10.04, which grants the batter a run batted in for
every run that scores as a result of a ball he safely hit into play, or as
a result of him drawing a walk or being hit by a pitch with the bases
loaded, or as a result of him making an out (except for a force double play) that allows that run to score. While most RBI are awarded
automatically, there are some situations, mostly involving fielding
errors, that allow the official scorer to have discretion over whether

to award the batter an RBI—and any stat that involves such human subjectivity is immediately reduced in value as a result. People are prone to so many cognitive biases and are so inconsistent in their judgments that allowing them to award or withhold an RBI seems like far too much responsibility.

Rickey nailed the most fundamental problem with RBI, however: it is an individual statistic that depends far too much on the performances of other players—in this case, whether the hitters ahead of the player get on base enough for him to drive them in. Barry Bonds, MLB's all-time career home run leader with 762, hit 450 solo home runs in his career, and had 412 baserunners on for his other home runs. Hank Aaron, whose record of 755 Bonds broke shortly before retiring, hit 399 solo home runs—and he had 482 baserunners on for his other home runs. So even though Bonds out-homered Aaron in about 300 fewer games (and got on base more often and hit for more power in total), Aaron ended up with about 300 more RBI in his career. Bonds was the better hitter, but Aaron gets the RBI glory.

Bonds holds the dubious distinction of being the only hitter in MLB history to qualify for the batting average title (503 plate appearances in 162 games) and drive himself in more than he drove in his teammates. The year he set the all-time single-season home run record of 73, in 2001, he had just 137 total RBI; since he drove himself in 73 times via home runs, that means he drove in his teammates only 64 times. As a result, the season that is number one on the home run list doesn't crack the all-time top 120 for RBI in a single year.

Bonds hit in the third spot in the Giants' lineup for nearly all of that historic season, 137 of his 148 games started (he batted fourth in the other eleven starts), yet came up to the plate with the bases empty in 54 percent of his plate appearances, and only had 393 baserunners aboard for him the entire year. He had seven other seasons in his career where he had more baserunners, and thus more opportunities, available to him than he did in that record-setting year. That's because Dusty Baker, then the Giants' manager—and, as this book goes to press, inexplicably now the Nationals' manager—chose to split the leadoff position between two hitters, Calvin Murray and Marvin Benard, who were not good at the most important role of the leadoff hitter, getting on base:

Hitter	OBP Overall (2001)	OBP as Leadoff Hitter (2001)
Calvin Murray	.319	.310
Marvin Benard	.320	.322
NL average	.331	.332

Neither player would play regularly in the majors again after 2001.

The Giants did have an excellent OBP guy in the second spot, Rich Aurilia, who posted what would be by far the best on-base percentage of his career, .369, in that 2001 season—thanks to a career-best .324 batting average, because, really, don't you want to throw him a strike with Superman standing in the on-deck circle? (More on that subject later in the book.) But Aurilia compromised Bonds's opportunities to drive in runs by hitting a career-best 37 homers of his own that season and a career-best 37 doubles. It wasn't all bad news; Bonds knocked Aurilia in 25 times in 2001, but the net result of two low-OBP guys splitting leadoff duties and a big power bat in the number-two spot ahead of Bonds meant that Bonds himself had unusually few RBI opportunities, and thus a relatively low RBI total for a guy with 73 home runs.

How do we judge Barry Bonds's 2001 season, then? Do we look at the all-time single-season home run record, what is now the ninth-best single-season on-base percentage of the modern era (Bonds himself had a higher OBP in each of the next three seasons), and the all-time single-season slugging percentage record, and say that this was the single greatest offensive season baseball has ever seen? What information does the RBI total impart to us that those other stats, ones that are independent of what his teammates did or any stupid manager tricks, could not?

The answer, of course, is: nothing of use.

*   *   *

The personal epiphany for me on the RBI's dishonesty was Joe Carter's season in 1990 for the San Diego Padres, his one season in California before he went to Toronto in one of the most star-laden trades in baseball history, a deal that sent him and future Hall of Famer Roberto Alomar to the Blue Jays in exchange for near Hall of Famer Fred McGriff and Tony Fernandez. Carter was very much a product of his time, a low-OBP slugger who would have a hard time holding an everyday job in the majors today but who spent twelve years as a full-time regular in the 1980s and 1990s, including playing every game from 1989 through 1991.

Carter's one year in San Diego was the worst of his career, as he hit for a career-low .232 batting average with a .290 OBP that was his career low until his last year as a regular at age thirty-seven. Yet Carter finished third in the National League in RBI that year with 115, even though he made more outs at the plate than any other hitter in the NL that season. How is a guy near the top of his league in RBI with all of those outs made?

Some of it is just power; Carter hit 24 home runs that season, good for 16th in the National League, and 27 doubles, although his slugging percentage, which is just total bases divided by at bats and thus incorporates batting average, was below the NL median. But Carter had 542 baserunners on board for his league-best 697 plate appearances—the most baserunners Carter had in any single season of his career—because he was behind a trio of on-base machines:

Lineup Spot	Player	OBP
2	Roberto Alomar	.340
3	Tony Gwynn	.357
4	Jack Clark	.441
5	Joe Carter	.290

The 542 baserunners on base for Carter's times at the plate were the most in the National League in 1990 by a huge margin; the next-highest mark was 496, so Carter had 46 more guys to drive in. In fact, that 542 figure for Carter would have led the National League in 1988 . . . and 1989 . . . and 1991 . . . and 1992 . . . and 1993. After Willie McGee had 544 baserunners on for him in the "rabbit ball" high-offense year of 1987, only two batters had more men on base for them than Carter did in 1990 through the 2002 season. Carter's RBI total might have been third in the NL, but it's a sad fraction of how many he might have driven in if he'd just been a better hitter to begin with.

There's zero sense in crediting Carter for having all of those extra opportunities. We can credit him for the hits he got with men on base, but we already do that in other statistics, like batting average and OBP and slugging, that don't include the noise of RBI. There is a strain of baseball thinking that we should think differently about hitters who perform especially well or poorly with men on base, a subject to which I'll devote some time in a later chapter, but for now I'll assert that this isn't actually a separate skill for batters. Hitters hit, as the late Tony Gwynn liked to say. It doesn't really matter who's where when they do.

One of the most common counterarguments to my "RBI are meaningless" philosophy is that the team with the most runs wins each game, so how can a stat that keeps track of who drives in those runs be a bad stat? Like many political statements, this argument confuses team stats and individual stats and relies on the listener to fall into the same trap.

Yes, the team that scores more runs wins the game—I can't argue with that—and tracking runs scored at the team level is an important measure of the quality of a team's overall offense. A lineup may look good on paper, but if it's not generating runs, then it's probably not as good as it originally looked. (There could be other explanations, too.) However, those runs are team events, generated at the team level, and other than home runs, they require more than one batter to happen.

Baseball essentially double-counts runs when working at the individual level: One player scores the run and gets a "run scored"; another player drives in the run and gets a "run batted in." That's two "runs" in individual stats for a single run on the field—maybe, since a player who knocks in a run by grounding into a double play doesn't get an RBI, and no RBI is awarded if the player scores on a fielder's error, a wild pitch, or other unusual event.

If a player did something in between to advance the runner, such as a single that advanced a runner from first to third, he gets a pat on the back (or somewhere else). So it might make more sense to think about the events that lead to a run scoring in fractional terms for the hitter, which is the philosophy behind "linear weights" methods of evaluating offense. With linear weighting, any event from a hitter is worth, on average, some fraction of a run, so if you assign the right fractional amount of a run to each of those events and add them all up, you'll get a number that measures in runs the value of all of that hitter's actual production for a given time period. When a hitter gets an RBI, it creates (or fosters) the impression that this hitter alone was responsible for the full creation of the run, and therefore the hitter with the most RBI on a team or in a league did the most to help his team win. This mistake thrives on the confusion I mentioned above, conflating a team activity with the attempt to measure individual performance. We are not trying to glean team performance from individual stats, so we shouldn't try to glean individual values from team stats.

When we look at the statistics of any single player, we are looking for one or both of two things:

1. What did the player actually do in his time on the field?
2. What might those statistics tell us about his likely performance going forward?

RBI give a partial answer to the first question; he did drive in those runs, so in the strict sense of counting the number of times that the hitter did something good that resulted in a run scoring, RBI more or less get the job done. But the way they're counted has contributed to the impression that the hitter who drives in a run created that whole run, which is wrong. (You could argue that it's not the RBI's fault, but I'll leave that to the philosophers.)

As for the second question, the answer is simple: nothing. A hitter who had a lot of RBI in a specific season played a lot and batted often with men on base, but that can't tell us that the same things will be true in the following year.

Runs Created is a simple measure of total offense that correlates pretty well with a team's total run-scoring, even though it lacks the precision of something like linear weights. Created by Bill James in the 1970s, Runs Created is most simply calculated as OBP * Total Bases, which is a simplified version of the formulas he initially presented in his *Baseball Abstracts*.

To return to Runs Created again as a very simple measure of total offense, RBI do a much worse job of predicting a player's offensive output the following year (as measured by RC) than his Runs Created total does. This correlation analysis measures how RBI per 100 plate appearances (PA) and RC per 100 plate appearances appear to "predict" RCs the following year:

Statistic	RBI/100 Plate Appearances	RC/100 Plate Appearances
Correlation with next year's RC/100 PA	0.521	0.623

(Data from all major-league hitters who reached 503 PA in consecutive seasons from 1961 to 2005. Total number of players in the sample = 4015.)

So, if you want to try to figure out what kind of offense a player might produce in the following season, his RBI rate tells you less than you would get from looking at his RC rate. In other words, the RBI column is just making us dumber. And that's by comparing it to a very simplistic stat like Runs Created.

But it has long made *everyone* dumber, because for much of the statistic's history, RBI was interpreted as meaning a player was a good hitter or had some sort of magic woo-woo that gave him a special ability to drive in runs. (Whether that same woo-woo also led to the hitters ahead of him getting on base more often was generally not acknowledged.) Hitters with high RBI totals would be placed in spots in the lineup that typically get more RBI opportunities, creating a sort of offensive death spiral when the hitter in question was someone like Joe Carter, more opportunist than actual run producer.

As we saw earlier in Carter's extreme case, a hitter can still rack up a lot of RBI even when he's not an especially good hitter. But when we put a good hitter behind one or more hitters who get on base often, we can get enormous RBI totals. That's how Rickey Henderson, the best player in the American League in 1985, helped fellow Yankee Don Mattingly win the AL MVP award that year.

Henderson reached base safely 274 times in 1985, good for fourth in the American League even though he missed 19 games that year, and led the league with 80 stolen bases. Mattingly, playing in all but three games that year, reached base 269 times—no slouch himself—but also drove in Henderson 56 times, helping him lead the AL with 145 RBI and win the award. When Hack Wilson set the major-league record for RBI in a single season in 1930 with 191—a record that still stands today—even he didn't drive in any single teammate more than 45 times.

In 2004, when Barry Bonds reached base an absurd 61 percent of the time, thanks in large part to 120 intentional walks (a record that I hope for all of our sakes is never broken or even approached), the cast of characters who had the good fortune to hit behind him all racked up RBI totals out of proportion to their actual performances. Edgardo Alfonzo batted directly behind Bonds more times than any other Giant that season, in 57 games, and knocked in 77 runs despite hitting just 11 homers and slugging only .407. A. J. Pierzynski had an almost identical line, with 11 homers, a .410 SLG, and 77 RBI, because he hit in the two spots behind Bonds more often than any other player.

But any readers age forty or over have probably been wondering when I'd bring up Tommy Herr, whose 1985 season earned notice even at the time for its outlier status. Herr was the slap-hitting second baseman for the St. Louis Cardinals, who won the NL pennant that year under manager Whitey Herzog, who encouraged a style of play called "Whiteyball," with lots of athletic, frequently African American players who could really run; the Cardinals had five players steal at least 30 bases in that season, led by Vince Coleman's

110, and they stole 130 more bases than any other team in the NL that year.

Herr wasn't as fast as Coleman or Willie McGee; he did steal a career-high 31 bags in 1985, but that's not why we're stopping at his house on memory lane right now. Herr hit only eight home runs that year, but knocked in 110 runs, becoming the first player since 1950 to knock in 100 or more runs while failing to hit ten homers. (Paul Molitor would later do it in 1996, but no one else has done it since.) Such high RBI/HR ratios were common prior to World War II, but the rise in home runs as baseball expanded and players became stronger had made them a thing of the past, until Herr and Whiteyball.

Runner	Times Knocked in by Herr	Stolen Bases
Coleman	35	110
McGee	35	56
Ozzie Smith	13	31

Herr's slugging percentage of .416 that year remains the lowest for any hitter who had 100 RBI in a season since 1938, and he owes nearly all of this to the three men listed above and their fleet feet.

Herr had another anomalous RBI season a few years later. The 1987 season was known as a "rabbit ball" year because home runs spiked across the game with no apparent explanation, although the widespread theory at the time was that MLB had changed the baseball. The power spike brought home runs to plenty of hitters who weren't normally long-ball guys—Wade Boggs hit 24 home runs in 1987, but only reached double digits in one other season, the strike-shortened 1994 year, when he hit 11—but not to Herr, who hit only two balls out of the park that year. Thanks to his speedy teammates, however, Herr became the first and still only player since 1943 to drive in more than 75 runs while hitting two or fewer homers; he ended up with 83, an RBI/HR ratio that would stand almost alone in modern baseball were it not for Ozzie Smith, still Herr's teammate that year, who had 75 RBI without a home run at all. That remains the highest RBI total for a homerless season since World War II.

The Cardinals' middle infielders were not great offensive players, although Smith was one of the best defensive shortstops the game has ever seen and made himself into a competent contact hitter. Their RBI totals were the products of their team's system, one that put guys on base and kept them moving into scoring position, so that it didn't take power, or even a hit, to drive them in.

RBI just don't tell us anything useful about a player's individual performance in a game, a season, or a career, but they remain prevalent in the minds of writers and fans. In November 2014, Rob Neyer wrote a piece on that year's MVP voting results for Fox Sports' *Just a Bit Outside* blog where he said that "the writers' obsession with RBI guys on first-place teams has long outlasted any excuses for it, and I'm tired of them." High RBI totals continue to pollute MVP ballots, albeit not to the extent they did twenty years ago, and to derail discussions of actual player value. Mike Trout lost two MVP awards to players with higher RBI totals on more successful teams, even though in both years (2015 and 2012) Trout had the better seasons. Ryan Howard won the NL MVP award in 2006 thanks to his 149 RBI and 58 home runs but wasn't even the most valuable player on the right side of the Phillies' infield that year.

There's really nothing RBI tells us about the player that we couldn't glean from other, less fuzzy statistics. The same is true about saves, perhaps the most ridiculous of all of the traditional stats because it has actually changed the way the game is played— unequivocally for the worse.

4

Holtzman's Folly:

How the Save Rule Has Ruined Baseball

In 2016, Baltimore Orioles reliever Zach Britton had one of the greatest seasons of any reliever in modern baseball history. Britton gave up just 4 earned runs in 67 innings pitched, for a 0.54 ERA on the season, the lowest ever by any reliever who threw at least 40 innings in a season. He gave up only one earned run after April 30. Throwing almost exclusively two-seam fastballs, Britton generated an 80 percent groundball rate, the highest we've seen since such data on batted balls first became available. And he was a perfect 47 for 47 in save opportunities.

On October 4, 2016, the Orioles played in the one-game wild-card playoff against the Blue Jays in Toronto, an elimination game for both clubs that determined who would advance to play the Texas Rangers in the next round. The game, somewhat contrary to expectations, was a pitchers' duel, still tied at 2–2 going into the bottom of the eighth inning, when Britton began warming up in the bullpen. He didn't enter the game in the eighth, however, as manager Buck Showalter chose to use his setup guy, Brad Brach, in that inning. Britton didn't appear in the ninth, when Brach started the inning, allowed a double, and later gave way to sidearmer Darren O'Day, who

threw one pitch and got an inning-ending double play. Britton—
again, who'd had one of the best seasons by a one-inning reliever
ever—didn't appear in the tenth, which belonged to O'Day and
Brian Duensing, or the eleventh, when Showalter went to erstwhile
starter Ubaldo Jimenez, on the roster as a long reliever. Jimenez allowed a single, a single, and a monstrous home run that ended the
game and the Orioles' season. Britton never threw a pitch.

After the game, Showalter defended his decision to use six relievers in the game but not his best one, saying Jimenez had been one
of the team's best pitchers down the stretch. (True, but still not as
good as Britton.) He also cited the concern that he'd use Britton,
the Orioles wouldn't score, and then he'd have to use someone else.
Afterward, ESPN's Dave Schoenfield said of the move, "This is simple: Showalter screwed up." *Yahoo!*'s Jeff Passan wrote, "Even the
smartest men are capable of ineffable stupidity." Even O's fan David
Simon, creator of TV series *The Wire* and *Show Me a Hero,* got in
on the act, quoting his own show with a tweet that read, "Where's
Britton, String? Where's Britton?"

The truth here is that Showalter was managing to a stat. Because
the Orioles were the visiting team, if they took the lead, there would
be a save opportunity for Britton, no matter the inning. (Once a
game reaches the bottom of the ninth, there can no longer be a save
opportunity for the home team.) Showalter mentioned hoping his
team would grab the lead so he could get Britton into the game,
but that entire line of thinking—don't use your best reliever to extend the game—is the result of the sport's obsession with the save
rule, which created a statistic that didn't even exist for the sport's
first hundred years, but a rule that ultimately may have cost the Orioles a playoff victory that night.

A common refrain of the modern dinosaur known as the "sports
columnist" is that sabermetrics or advanced statistics are somehow
ruining baseball. Jason Whitlock wrote a piece about it, calling analysts "stat geeks," for Fox Sports in 2011. Someone named Steve
Kettmann wrote it in the otherwise progressive *New York Times*

in 2015. What's even more embarrassing for the Grey Lady is that blogger Murray Chass wrote a piece with the same thesis in 2007 for them, too.

Here's the truth: no analyst and no sabermetric stat has done half as much to "ruin" baseball as the save, a statistic invented by—you guessed it—a sports columnist.

Jerome Holtzman spent most of his career writing for Chicago newspapers, earning the moniker "the dean of American baseball writers" from his editor at the *Chicago Sun-Times*, Lewis Grizzard. (Grizzard also remarked in the same essay that Holtzman "had the keys to Cooperstown. No major leaguer ever got into the Hall of Fame if Holtzman didn't want him there,"* an absolutely horrifying prospect of hubris and power concentrated in one individual.) In an era without any alternative voices—every baseball writer was a white man who wrote for a local newspaper or one of the very small number of national sports publications—Holtzman's views went un-challenged. This is how we ended up with Holtzman's Folly: the save rule.

If anyone tried to introduce a statistic like the save today, he'd be laughed all the way to a cornfield in Iowa. The stat is an unholy mess of arbitrary conditions, and doesn't actually measure anything, let alone what Holtzman seemed to think it measured. Yet the intro-duction of this statistic led to wholesale changes in how managers handle the final innings of close games and in how general managers build their rosters, all to the detriment of the sport on the field, and perhaps to pitcher health as well.

The idea behind the save was to create an analogue to the pitcher win, but to credit the reliever who recorded the final out or final few outs in his team's victory. It is true that relievers were undervalued relative to starters at the time, so the impulse to find another way to value their contributions may have been an honorable one if it hadn't had such a destructive result.

The save rule is the most convoluted of all of the "basic" stats,

---

* Lewis Grizzard, *If I Ever Get Back to Georgia, I'm Gonna Nail My Feet to the Ground* (New York: Ballantine Books, 1990), p. 362.

which only goes to emphasize its arbitrary nature. To be credited with a save under the current version of the rule (MLB Official Rule 10.20), which has been in place since 1975, a pitcher must record the final out in a game that his team won, but one where he didn't get the win, and the team can't win by too many runs because then he obviously contributed nothing at all. From the aforementioned rule:

Credit a pitcher with a save when he meets all three of the following conditions:

    I.   He is the finishing pitcher in a game won by his club; and
   II.   He is not the winning pitcher; and
  III.   He qualifies under one of the following conditions:
       A. He enters the game with a lead of no more than three runs and pitches for at least one inning; or
       B. He enters the game, regardless of the count, with the potential tying run either on base, or at bat, or on deck that is, the potential tying run is either already on base or is one of the first two batsmen he faces; or
       C. He pitches effectively for at least three innings. No more than one save may be credited in each game.

I don't think you could make a more context-dependent stat if you tried. It doesn't matter how well a pitcher performs in a game if he doesn't meet all three of these conditions, and he can still meet those conditions while pitching poorly. A pitcher can enter in a save situation, retire every batter he faces, and still fail to earn a save because he allowed an inherited runner—that is, a runner already on base when he entered the game—to score on an out.

The conditions of the save rule create all sorts of internal paradoxes. The pitcher who throws a scoreless seventh inning and a scoreless eighth inning gets nothing, while the pitcher who follows him, throws the ninth inning, and gives up a run but doesn't surrender the lead gets the SV in the box score. Which pitcher actually contributed more to his team winning the game? Yet which pitcher does Holtzman's Folly end up rewarding?

The tacked-on bit of rule (c) only adds to the rule's confusion. If the point of the save was to somehow reward clutch pitching—production in a high-leverage situation that, by definition, only matters if the team wins the game—then why are we throwing on this bit at the end about a pitcher who throws three or more "effective" innings even if his team was up by 15 runs at the time? How does that earn the pitcher the same SV as the pitcher who comes in with the bases loaded in the ninth and strikes out the final batter of the game to preserve a one-run lead? In other works, how does anyone look at baseball and say, "Those two things are equivalent—let's give them the same stat"?

In 2015, there were 114 relief appearances where the pitcher threw at least three innings and gave up zero runs, but only nine of those appearances earned saves for the pitchers. In eight of those 114 outings the pitcher threw at least 4⅓ innings—recording at least 13 outs—and none of those qualified as saves because they all came in losing efforts. Compare those to the thirteen saves recorded by pitchers in 2015 where the pitchers allowed two runs to score in one inning of work . . . but they protected a lead and finished the game, so they got the saves. Four scoreless innings in a loss: no save; two runs in the final inning in a win: save. This is all about the team's performance, not the pitcher's, so what exactly are we measuring?

What we think we're measuring with saves is sort of clear—some sort of intestinal fortitude that marks a man as a Proven Closer™, thus entitling him to millions of dollars in additional salary and to the full confidence of his manager as the Guy Who Pitches the Ninth Inning (Some Restrictions Apply, See Your Rulebook for Details). It's clear that that's not even quite true, given the example I just gave above of pitchers earning saves despite allowing two runs in one inning of work. But the save rule also creates a specious separation between closers and nonclosers that doesn't reflect the relative quality or value of their performances.

On July 7, 2016, Atlanta reliever Mauricio Cabrera did indeed save the day. Atlanta had taken a 4–3 lead over the Chicago Cubs in the top of the eleventh inning, and manager Brian Snitker chose to leave reliever Dario Alvarez, who had pitched a scoreless tenth inning, in the game to try to close it out. Alvarez allowed singles to the first two batters, so the Cubs had the tying and winning runs on base with nobody out. Snitker summoned Cabrera to replace Alvarez, and Cabrera got the first batter to ground into a double play and the second to fly out to preserve the lead. Cabrera was credited with the save and Alvarez with the win.

On August 20, 2016, Arizona reliever Daniel Hudson went one better. With the Diamondbacks leading the San Diego Padres 2–1 in the bottom of the eighth, two other Arizona relievers conspired to load the bases with nobody out, a mess Hudson was asked to come in and clean up without allowing a single run to score. Hudson recorded three pop-ups on seven pitches for a scoreless inning of work, but because he didn't record the final out of the game, he wasn't eligible for a save—even though he did what Cabrera did, recording three outs without allowing anyone to reach base or any inherited runners to score, and even had one more runner on base when he entered the game than Cabrera did. The save statistic creates an artificial distinction between these two outings, and the long-time emphasis on save totals has skewed the way we perceive certain relievers based solely on when they're used.

The most valuable reliever in baseball in 2015 wasn't a closer and only recorded nine saves on the season. The Yankees' Dellin Betances, a former top prospect who had trouble just throwing strikes as a starter and moved to the bullpen as a sort of last resort, has recorded some of the best strikeout rates in history since becoming a full-time reliever, and unlike the majority of closers, his usage isn't limited by the save rule. Betances threw 84 innings in 2015, more than any other MLB pitcher who didn't start a game, and posted the fourth-highest strikeout rate in baseball. His ERA of 1.50 was the second lowest among all relievers, behind only Kansas City closer Wade Davis, who threw 67 innings, 20 percent less than Betances did. By a statistic I'll discuss later called Win Probability Added, which measures the impact a player had on his team's chances of winning each game in which he appeared, Betances had more positive impact on his team's win total than all but three other relievers in MLB and all but three starters as well. Yet his save total didn't even reach double digits.

Betances's usage precluded him from getting saves, but that doesn't mean he wasn't used in key situations. Yankees manager Joe Girardi had a Proven Closer™ already in Andrew Miller—also a failed starter who found a second career as a high-strikeout reliever—which allowed him to deploy Betances earlier in games where the outcome was still uncertain. Betances made 74 appearances in 2015, and in 64 of them he entered the game in before the ninth inning began. Of those 74 total appearances, Betances entered the game 16 times with the score tied (thus making him ineligible for a save), and 18 times with the Yankees up by one but where he did not finish the game (also making him ineligible for a save). His low save total doesn't tell us anything about *how* Betances pitched, but just *when* he pitched.

Meanwhile, there were plenty of so-so pitchers who racked up big save totals, something that happens every year because if there's a close game, there will probably be a save to hand out, and managers today manage to the save rule rather than to win the game. The most egregious example in 2015 was Tampa Bay's Brad Boxberger, who had 41 saves, the fourth most in baseball, with a 3.79 ERA—right about league average for a reliever.

In fact, there have been seven seasons in MLB history where a pitcher racked up 30 or more saves despite posting an ERA over 5. Two pitched in Colorado and may be excused, since Coors Field is a hitter's paradise. Brad Lidge of the Phillies did it twice, including a 7.21 ERA in 2009 when he "earned" 31 saves. Joe Borowski led the NL with 45 saves in 2007 despite a 5.07 ERA. These guys did not pitch well, but they were used in a way that got them a lot of saves.

Mike Williams's 2003 season is one of my favorite examples of save-stat dopiness, where the save column drove the narrative around a player to the point that people forgot to look if the pitcher was otherwise any good. Williams was the token Pirate selected to the 2003 All-Star Game because the Pirates didn't have a lot of good candidates and Williams had 25 saves at the All-Star Break . . . and a 6.44 ERA, along with more batters walked (22) than strikeouts (19). He was having a terrible year, but the save total fooled someone into putting him on the All-Star Team. A week after the game, the Pirates traded him to the Phillies for a fringe prospect, and Williams didn't pitch in the majors again after that season.

W hat the save ends up doing more than anything else is glorifying certain one-inning relief appearances over others. A pitcher throwing a scoreless inning in a major-league game is not that rare; Baseball-Reference's play index shows more than 1,500 perfect (1-2-3) one-inning appearances by pitchers in the 2015 season alone. There were 469 such appearances that also earned saves for the pitchers in question, but why would we look at those innings any differently than, say, the perfect eighth inning Dellin Betances threw on July 17 of that year, preserving a one-run lead in a game the Yankees would win by that same margin?

(Some of you may see this and think, "Well, that's why we have the hold statistic for middle relievers." The hold has numerous problems, including no consistent definition and the possibility that a pitcher can receive credit for a hold without recording an out, but slapping yet another label-stat on a pitcher's outing merely adds to the confusion rather than resolving it. If saves are stupid, holds aren't even conscious.)

By giving saves to certain relief appearances based solely on their context in the score, the inning, and the end result, baseball has put a brand on these relievers that, as you've probably noticed above, I call the Proven Closer™ even though I'm not actually asserting any legal trademark protection for the term. Much as consumers will pay more for a brand, especially a national brand, than for store-branded products of equivalent quality and that might even be produced in the same facilities as the national brand, major-league teams will pay more for a reliever with saves than an equivalent reliever without saves—in fact, MLB's own arbitration process ensures that they do so by rewarding saves.

According to the MLBTradeRumors.com Arbitration Projection

Model, developed by Matt Swartz, a reliever entering arbitration with 20 saves in his most recent season—called the "platform year" in the vernacular of arbitration—would earn about $1.8 million extra through the arbitration process. Even worse, because subsequent arbitration salaries are based in large part on previous years' salaries, that onetime raise becomes cumulative, so, according to Swartz's work, the player would earn at least $4.5 million extra over three years just because of those 20 saves from his first platform season.

The cost wouldn't be so bad if teams were getting more work out of their closers, but that's not the case, because managers typically "save" their closers for save situations, declining to use them in other situations that may be important but aren't save situations according to Holtzman's arbitrary rule. (Buck Showalter's decision not to use Britton in the 2016 wild-card playoff typifies this kind of thinking.) In the last five MLB seasons, no reliever who has racked up 30 or more saves has even thrown 80 innings in that same year; only two relievers with 20 saves have done it, and one of those, Jenrry Mejia, only got to 80 innings because he made seven starts before he was moved to the bullpen. It's not that these relievers can't handle these workloads; twenty-seven full-time relievers reached 80 innings in a season in that same five-year span. It's that the save rule has led managers to use their best relievers less often, and that should immediately strike you as both perverse and counterproductive.

It's easy to just point to the save rule and say that managers are using their relievers to satisfy the rule, but there's most likely a third variable at work here. If a team gets into a save situation and the manager doesn't use his capital-C Closer, but then the chosen reliever gives up the lead, the manager will have to answer the postgame question of why he didn't go to his closer—from the media, from fans, perhaps from his boss. The easiest way to answer these questions is to avoid them entirely by using your closer in save situations and not using him in nonsave situations. It's suboptimal, but it takes more thought to recognize that burning your closer in a cheap save situation one day may make him unavailable for a tighter situation the next day, and managers don't face those questions nearly as often.

So here we sit, nearly fifty years after Jerome Holtzman fabri-
cated the save rule and no one thought to contest it or point out
that it was useless or as brain-dead a stat as the game-winning RBI
(RIP), with a game that has changed substantially because of one
writer's actions. The idea of the Proven Closer™ did not exist before Holtzman's Folly, but it has become a huge factor in how teams
build their bullpens as well as how managers deploy their relievers,
creating an assembly-line mentality of one-inning-and-done relievers
that wastes roster spots and probably hasn't improved any team's
chances of winning.

In the last five full seasons, 2011 to 2015, only four full-time
relievers have even reached 90 innings in a season, with 96 the highest. The last reliever to reach 100 innings in a single season was
Scott Proctor in 2006, but he did it in 83 games, and was thus still
mostly a one-inning guy. Even into the 1990s, the 100-inning reliever was still somewhat common. Mariano Rivera, who later became the greatest one-inning closer in the game's history, threw 107
innings in 1996 as a two-inning setup man to John Wetteland, and
then threw another 1,109 innings over the rest of his career without
ever suffering a major arm injury. Keith Foulke threw 105 innings in
67 games for the White Sox in 1999, then spent the next five years
working mostly as a closer for five teams before losing effectiveness. While I don't think we know if relievers throwing back-to-back
100-inning seasons are at risk of injury or decline, or if those 100
innings are less stressful to the arm if they come in 60 appearances
or 70, the current paradigm of reliever usage isn't doing anything to
keep pitchers healthy or to help teams manage their bullpens more
effectively.

Teams have believed for decades that they needed a Proven
Closer™ to be contenders, even though certain clubs—the Oakland A's in the late 1990s and early 2000s—would simply trade one
Proven Closer™, install a new reliever in the role the next year, and
trade him once he was similarly "proven" or just let him walk when
he became too expensive.

Oakland Closers with Save Totals as Oakland's Closer, After Trade

Year(s)	Name	Average Saves with Oakland	Saves First Year After Oakland
1997–99	Billy Taylor	27	0
2000–2001	Jason Isringhausen	33	32
2002	Billy Koch	44	11
2003	Keith Foulke	43	32

Taylor had one career save going into 1996, became the team's part-time closer at age thirty-four that year, and then was their full-time closer for the next three seasons. He was out of baseball twenty-four months after Oakland traded him to the Mets and never registered another save. Isringhausen was a failed prospect as a starter due to injuries; Oakland acquired him in the Taylor trade, made him a closer, and lost him to free agency after 2001. They traded for Koch from Toronto,* where he was already an established closer, and after he had a career year with the A's they traded him to the White Sox for Keith Foulke, who had lost his job as Chicago's closer the previous year. Koch pitched only two more years in the majors, with a 5.12 ERA for two teams. Oakland took Foulke—can you see the pattern here?—and let him reestablish himself as a closer for them, losing him to free agency after the season; he signed a four-year deal with Boston, helping them win the World Series in 2004, but started his decline the following season.

Few other teams caught on to the tactic at the time, or they simply didn't want to risk it themselves, even though the A's demonstrated that closers are made, not born. Most relievers capable of handling the eighth inning can handle the ninth, which means a team facing budget constraints can usually gamble on a cheap closer rather than overpaying for established production that may not even continue.

One reason teams don't wish to take the risk that Oakland took in that period is that they don't view the ninth inning as just another three outs. As we've seen many long-standing tenets of conventional

---

* Full disclosure: I was consulting to Toronto's general manager at the time of this trade, and joined the front office full-time a few weeks later.

baseball wisdom fall over the past ten years, one that we haven't entirely lost is the idea that the closer's job is harder than that of the pitchers who came before him. Yet consider this common situation: A team with a one-run lead enters the eighth inning, with the opponent's three best hitters due up. The team with the lead won't call on its closer, because that's not a save situation (described by the arbitrary rules listed above), so it will call on another reliever, known as a setup man, even though that pitcher probably isn't the best option. It also means the closer will pitch in the ninth, by which point he'll either face an easier slate of hitters with a one-run lead, or the lead will already be gone because the setup man gave up the tying run. So which reliever here had the tougher job, the setup man or the closer? And was using the team's second-best reliever for the hardest three outs really the right call, just because some long-dead sportswriter said the ninth inning was super-special?

Despite these less-rational, tradition-bound tendencies, we may have seen a turning point in reliever usage in the 2016 postseason, where several managers, notably Cleveland skipper Terry Francona, began using their ace relievers in nonsave situations, often much earlier in the game than they would have in the regular season, because such tactics maximized their chances of winning. It remains to be seen whether any team will adapt this usage to the regular season, where teams have fewer days off than they do in October, but I'm betting that some team or teams will try out a new bullpen paradigm in the wake of the 2016 playoffs.

Cleveland acquired Andrew Miller from the Yankees in a massive trade-deadline deal that cost them two of their top prospects. Miller had been the Yankees' full-time closer in 2015, racking up 36 saves, and then was a part-time closer for New York in 2016, with 12 saves before the trade, as Aroldis Chapman (who was himself traded to the Cubs) became the Yankees' primary option in save situations. Francona chose to use Miller earlier in games from the moment Miller came to Cleveland, retaining Cody Allen—a good pitcher but inferior to Miller in every way—in the ninth inning. Miller finished only one game out of the ten in which he appeared in October, in game three of the ALCS against Toronto, which was the only game in which he threw a pitch in the ninth inning all month.

But Miller also worked more within each game than a closer usually does or than Miller himself typically did: he recorded at least four outs in every playoff appearance, something he did just eleven times in the entire regular season. Miller came into his first playoff game in 2016 in the fifth inning, replacing the starter, Trevor Bauer, with a one-run lead, and entered game three of the World Series in the fifth inning with the score tied—both of these situations that, by the traditional, save-centric bullpen model, would be verboten for a team's closer.

The save just isn't necessary. It tells us nothing we couldn't already glean from the box score, and gives people the illusion of meaning by its mere existence, which has contributed to overspecialized relief usage and a perverse system where teams often reserve their best relievers for the ninth inning even if those aren't the toughest outs to get. It deserves its own plot in the stat graveyard, along with the pitcher win, the RBI, and one of the most useless stats baseball has ever seen, fielding percentage.

5

Stolen Bases:

Crime Only Pays If You Never Get Caught

Everybody loves the stolen base. It's the most exciting two seconds in baseball, because it's so visible and involves the actions of three or four different players at once. It's as if all of the surrounding play stops for a matter of two seconds while we wait to see if the throw gets to the base in time for the fielder to catch it cleanly and tag the runner out. If there's anything I miss about the way baseball was played when I was a kid, scouring box scores and waiting impatiently for the next Saturday afternoon Game of the Week on NBC, it's the prevalence of the stolen base in the 1980s, which disappeared when home runs surged the following decade.

When Hunter S. Thompson quoted the late Oakland Raiders owner Al Davis as saying, "Speed kills. You can't teach speed. Everything else in the game can be taught, but speed is a gift from God," it was meant to be in praise of the value of speed in football. In baseball, however, "speed kills" cuts both ways: You can run yourself out of a big inning even more easily than you can run yourself into one, because the cost of making an out on the bases is so much bigger than the benefit of moving a runner ninety feet closer to scoring. Even today, we still see managers fail to understand the very basic calculus of the stolen base.

This is not to say that the stolen base itself is bad, or that crediting hitters with adding value through base stealing is wrong; if anything, teams have spent resources trying to value speed on the bases more accurately during this ongoing analytics revolution. But stolen bases have a cost, and ignoring that cost means they're often overvalued. Baseball loves its fast players, and sometimes that means players like Joey Gathright or John Moses reach the big leagues because they can run, even if they can't do anything else. (Moses is the worst player, by total value, of all MLB players who stole 100 bases in the majors; in an eleven-year career, he managed just a .313 on-base percentage and .333 slugging percentage, and while he stole 101 bases, he was caught 57 times.)

Speed can help an offense, but it can short-circuit a rally, and a good manager must understand how to use steals judiciously. Making an out on the bases is costly. You have to know where the break-even point is to decide how often to steal and to determine whether a player actually helped your team score more runs with his base stealing.

The stolen base itself has long been part of baseball. The stolen base was first counted as a statistic in 1886; the next season, two players, including eventual Hall of Famer John Montgomery Ward, reached 100 stolen bases. (These totals have been adjusted for the 1898 rule change that gave us the stolen base as we count it today.)

Since 1901, the first year of the American League, stolen bases have fallen out of vogue and then come back in again, as you can see from the chart below:

Stolen bases peaked in 1911, with more than 210 steals per team in each league during the height of the "dead ball" era, be-

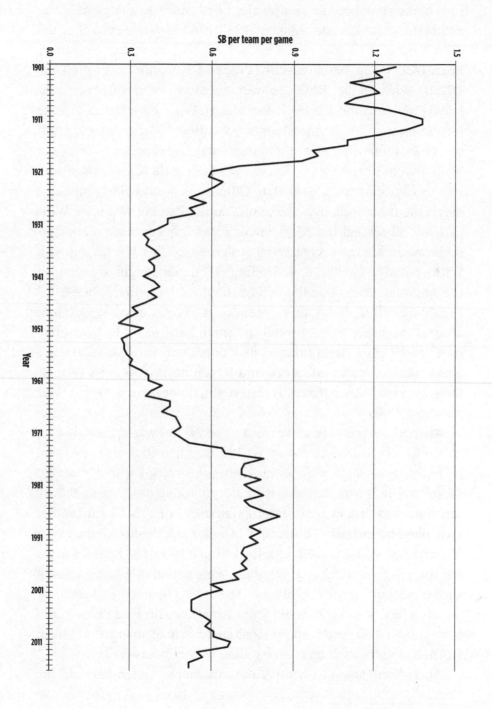

fore home runs became so prevalent or central to the game. (The eight American League teams of 1911 hit 198 home runs in total. Five American League teams hit at least that many by themselves in 2015.) Stolen bases steadily dropped from there through the 1920s, when Babe Ruth's power revolutionized offenses, and stayed low into the 1960s, when Maury Wills emerged as a force on the base paths for the Dodgers, stealing 104 bases by himself in 1962—more than any other single major-league team that year. Wills was followed by Lou Brock, who, after the Cubs traded him to the Cardinals in a deal that Cubs fans would likely rather I didn't mention, took over the annual stolen base crown from Wills in 1966. Brock led the NL in steals eight times in nine years, culminating in his then-record 118 stolen bases in 1974 (along with a less-noted yet still league-leading 33 times caught stealing, at the time the most since the end of the dead-ball era). When MLB decided to raise the pitcher's mound in 1968, destroying offense around the game, teams turned to "small ball" to try to "manufacture" more runs (today they'd just outsource it, arguing it's not where the real value-add lies), and stolen bases entered a twenty-five-year renaissance that only ended when home runs started their surge in 1993.

My personal coming-of-age as a baseball fan was during that renaissance's high period, the go-go 1980s, when Rickey Henderson, nicknamed the Man of Steal, broke Brock's record with 130 stolen bases in 1982, a record that still stands today along with the 42 times he was caught that season. (He even missed 13 games that year, so he attempted 172 steals in 149 games.) Vince Coleman later cracked 100 steals as well, topping out at 110 in 1985. In the eight full seasons from 1982 to 1989, there were a total of 49 seasons of at least 50 stolen bases by 26 players; 15 seasons of at least 75 steals by five different players, including one by my cousin Rudy Law*; and 5 of at least 100 steals, all by Henderson or Coleman. If you liked stolen bases, this was an amazing time to watch baseball.

There were some truly atrocious seasons of stolen bases in the

---

* Not actually my cousin.

1980s, too, though. Steve Sax stole 56 bases in 1983 but was caught 30 times; the latter was only surpassed by Henderson in the 1980s. Gerald Young stole 65 bases and was caught 27 times in 1988; Omar Moreno stole 60 bases and was caught 26 times in 1982. One of the worst base-stealing seasons in history came from current broadcaster Harold Reynolds, who, in 1988, stole 35 bases but was caught 29 times.

When offensive levels spiked suddenly in 1993, the value of the stolen base started to drop; even if managers didn't do the math, it was obvious that advancing a runner one base didn't matter as much if the batter at the plate was going to hit 40 home runs that year. Since Rickey stole 93 bases and Coleman 81 in 1988, no player has reached 80 steals in a season. Only one player has topped 75 steals in a season since the offensive surge—commonly, if somewhat spuriously, called the "steroid era"—started in 1993: Jose Reyes in 2007 with 78. Only five other players have even reached 70, with Kenny Lofton doing it twice. Even as offensive levels have dropped in the last few seasons, however, stolen base attempts haven't bounced back.

Much of this significant change in the way teams manage their baserunning has come from an increased understanding of the cost of losing a baserunner to an out. Take these two real-player seasons, with the names removed, both of which occurred in the American League since the year 2011:

	AVG	OBP	SLG	SB
Player D	.333	.359	.418	58
Player J	.298	.355	.426	52

The two players had roughly the same number of plate appearances on those seasons. Knowing no other information about them, which player would you say was the better offensive performer?

Player D has the higher batting average, but Player J makes up for that gap by drawing 22 more walks than Player D, so their OBPs are close to dead even. Their slugging percentages are extremely similar as well. If you see those stats and assume, fairly, that their performances with the bat are about on par, then shouldn't Player D get the edge for a few more steals?

Let's take this even one step further with another player who had similar rate stats:

	AVG	OBP	SLG	SB
Player D	.333	.359	.418	58
Player J	.298	.355	.426	52
Player R	.280	.354	.421	78

In reality, Player R had more than 100 more PA than the other two players did, but we're going to ignore that for the purposes of this exercise. If you assume that all three had about the same playing time, how would you rank their seasons at the plate?

The correct answer here is that you can't. Never mind getting it exactly right—you'd need a lot more information for that—but you can't even ballpark it, because that last column can't exist by itself. A successful stolen base is a net positive for the team, because it makes it easier for that player to score in a subsequent hitter's at bat; that is, it increases the probability that the runner will score. Nothing in baseball exists in a vacuum, but stolen bases are particularly guilty of telling half a good story:

	AVG	OBP	SLG	SB	CS	PA
Player D	.333	.359	.418	58	20	653
Player J	.298	.355	.426	52	4	636
Player R	.280	.354	.421	78	21	765

That next-to-last last column, times the runner was caught stealing, is far more important than the column to its left—as much as three times more important, depending on the year and how exactly you want to measure their relative values. (The range of estimates of their values isn't very wide.) So in this specific case, Player D, Dee Gordon in 2016, stole six more bases than Player J, Jacoby Ellsbury in 2013, but made 16 more outs on the bases to do so, a net negative for his team. Player R, Jose Reyes in 2007, stole 26 more bases than Ellsbury, but made 17 more outs on the bases to do so, which is also a net negative, although a somewhat less obvious one at first glance. So it turns out that even with the rate stats all fairly close, Ellsbury was the most valuable offensive performer of the three, even overcoming Gordon's advantage in hits and batting average, or Reyes's big playing-time lead.

Stealing bases is great fun, and can absolutely help an offense, but it has to be done well to work. If you're caught stealing more than about 25 percent of the time, as a player or as a team, you're putting a dent in your run-scoring capacity. It's better to try to steal less frequently but to be successful on a higher percentage of your attempts than to run wild without regard to the consequences of getting caught, as teams did in the 1980s. Most teams have caught on to this at some level, although we still see managers sending runners in a lot of situations where they'd be better off having the first base coach nail the runner's foot to the bag.

The hardest thing for any offense to do is to put a man on base; even the best hitters will still fail to reach base safely 60 percent of the time, and plenty of hitters will fail to do so about 70 percent of the time. Therefore, it stands to reason (and holds up statistically) that once you get a guy on base, the last thing you want is to lose him to an entirely preventable out like a failed stolen base attempt. What has only recently crept into mainstream baseball thinking is how to compare the cost of such a failure against the gain of a success.

Statisticians have long known how to look at this kind of question via something known as the Run Expectancy Matrix, a cumbersome name for a simple concept. Given a specific base-out state, referring to runners on specific bases with a specific number of outs, how many runs should the team at the plate "expect" to score in the remainder of the inning? Here's the matrix for 2015, provided by Baseball Prospectus in the Stats portion of their website:

Runners	0 Outs	1 Out	2 Out
000 (none on)	0.479	0.2572	0.0996
003 (man on third)	1.3045	0.8916	0.3606
020 (man on second)	1.0762	0.6487	0.3154
023 (men on second and third)	1.9017	1.2831	0.5764
100 (man on first)	0.8427	0.5004	0.2203
103 (men on first and third)	1.6682	1.1348	0.4813
120 (men on first and second)	1.4399	0.8919	0.4361
123 (bases loaded)	2.2654	1.5263	0.6971

These expected run numbers are just the average over all such base-out situations for the entire regular season of 2015.

So, from looking at this table, you can see that when a team has a man on first and zero outs, they should expect to score 0.84 runs for the remainder of that inning. If the next batter gets a hit, and the runner advances to third base, that expectation rises from 0.84 to 1.67, because they've added a baserunner and have pushed the first one up two bases.

In the case of a stolen base attempt, we are trying to compare two situations, the successful attempt and the failed one. The successful attempt with a man on first and zero outs takes us from 0.84 to 1.08, a gain of about a quarter of a run. To put it another way, every four successful steals of second with zero outs would be worth about an additional run to the offense.

A failed attempt, however, drops the team from 0.84 to the expectation for one out and nobody on, an expected value of 0.26 runs. You can see right away that the cost of a time caught stealing is more than twice the gain of a successful steal. Therefore, if you're Harold Reynolds in 1988, you're killing your team by running often but getting caught nearly half the time.

Using these numbers, which do vary slightly each year and would look very different if we were to consider a different baseball environment, like a high school game or the summer collegiate league on Cape Cod, we can estimate the break-even success rate for stolen base attempts that should be the starting point for any manager's decision on whether to attempt to steal.

Continuing with the example above, we'd look at the expected value of a success compared to the expected value of a failure, and in this somewhat simplified scenario*, a baserunner must succeed in at least 71 percent of his attempts to steal second base with zero outs for the move to have a positive expected value. If the baserunner starts at second base with zero outs, the breakeven rate for stealing third is even higher, 81 percent, because the runner was already in scoring position and could have scored from second with the right combination of two field outs.

These examples are a bit oversimplified because other things can happen on stolen base attempts, especially fielder errors such as errant throws, which can advance the runner an additional base. The expected value of a specific stolen base attempt also depends on factors like the speed of the runner and the batters at bat and on deck; you are more willing to risk the stolen base attempt if your eighth- and ninth-place hitters are coming up than you are with Bryce Harper at the plate. Indeed, if you're attempting a steal with Harper at the plate, you're an idiot, because it doesn't matter where the runner is standing when the batter puts the ball in the bleachers.

Compare this somewhat rigorous look at the expected value of a stolen base attempt with the traditional approach, which largely hinges on truisms like "don't make the first or third out at third base" or "a base stealer on first means more fastballs for the hitter." The book *Baseball Between the Numbers,* written by multiple Baseball Prospectus writers, including Nate Silver, found that the latter

---

* Here's the math:

a * EV (success)—(1—a) * EV (failure) = 0

a * (1.08—0.84)—(1—a) * (0.84—0.26) = 0

a * 0.24—(1—a) * 0.58 = 0

a * 0.24 = (1—a) * 0.58

a / (1—a) = 0.58/0.24 = 2.417

a = 2.417—2.417 * a

a = 2.417/3.417 = 0.707 ~= 71%.

wasn't true—a good base stealer on first actually reduced the performance of the hitter at the plate.

There's good anecdotal evidence that major-league teams are catching on to this idea of gauging stolen base opportunities by the runner's success rate and by the base-out situation. Since 2000, only one MLB player has stolen at least 20 bases with a success rate under 67 percent, Luis Castillo's comically bad 21-for-40 performance in 2003 for a rate of 52.5 percent. Matt Kemp was 19 for 34 in 2010; Ian Kinsler was 15 for 26 in 2013; but such seasons are becoming increasingly rare. In 2015, the worst base stealer by percentage was probably Jace Peterson, 12 for 22, the only player to fall under 67 percent in at least 20 attempts. Only D. J. LeMahieu did so in 2014, going 10 for 20 on the bases, an especially baffling statistic given that he played for the Colorado Rockies, whose hitter-friendly ballpark makes losing baserunners even more costly. Why send the runner when a routine flyball could end up a home run?

However, this calculation can change along with the game itself. The value of an additional base increases in a lower run-scoring environment; if home runs were to tumble again, then it would make more sense to try to grab an extra base that would allow the runner to score on a single or double. A major-league run expectancy table wouldn't apply to amateur games where tin bats lead to higher scoring and poorly struck balls can still fall in for hits, and the entire equation varies when you get further from the majors and fielders don't field as well.

While the stolen base as a statistic isn't bad, nor is it a bad tactic, judging players by their stolen base totals presents us with two problems. One is the imbalance between a stolen base and a time caught stealing I mentioned above: If I tell you a player stole 100 bases, is that good? Well, if he was caught ten times, yes, it's great. If he was caught 40 times, it's probably fine. If he was caught 90 times, what the hell is his manager doing?

Rickey Henderson and Tim Raines were two of the greatest players of the 1980s, and both were known for their prolific base stealing. Rickey is better remembered today, and was elected to the Hall of Fame in his first year of eligibility, specifically because of how often he stole. But Raines was the better percentage base stealer, which isn't as sexy as setting the single-season and career stolen base records but may mean Raines's legs were more valuable than Rickey's.

Before those two came on the scene, only two players in MLB history had stolen 800 or more bases: Ty Cobb, who stole 897 bases and held the career record until 1977, and Lou Brock, who broke it and ended up with 938 stolen bases. Henderson destroyed Brock's mark, finishing an amazing twenty-five-year career with 1,406 stolen bases, leaving Raines, whose total of 808 remains fourth on the all-time list, in his shadow.

But Raines has one advantage over Rickey and Brock: he was caught less frequently than either of those guys, less than half as many times as either player:

	SB	CS	Success Rate
Henderson	1406	335	80.8%
Brock	938	307	75.3%
Raines	808	146	84.7%

Since caught stealing became an official stat in 1920, only one player has stolen at least 200 bases with a higher success rate than Raines—Carlos Beltran, still active as of this writing, at 86.3 percent (311 steals, only 49 times CS).

In practical terms, all of those extra times caught stealing for Brock and Rickey negate many of the additional bases they stole when compared to Raines. Brock stole 130 more bases than Raines, but was caught 161 more times, an obvious loss of value even when comparing two different offensive eras. (Brock is also in the Hall of Fame, like Rickey; in January 2017, Raines was elected to the Hall of Fame in his final year on the ballot.)

Henderson stole 598 more bases but was caught 189 more times, a rate of 76 percent just on the excess. The most glaring difference in their base-stealing success rates comes on straight steals of third base; Rickey was much more likely to attempt to steal third base than Raines was, but was also caught there more frequently, with an 81 percent success rate in 244 attempts to steal third, compared to Raines's 42-for-43 career performance in steals of third.

	First/Second	Second Base	Third Base + Home
Raines	41/10	725/137	42/1 + 0/1
Henderson	137/24 + 0/1 2nd/3rd	1068/261	199/45 + 1/5

In addition to the idea that we've been viewing individual base-stealing accomplishments the wrong way, there is perhaps a more drastic, and substantial, flaw to the traditional view of base stealing than that.

The more math-inclined among you may also have noticed something about the stolen base from the charts in the previous sections: Stealing a base isn't as valuable as we—all of us, really—once thought it was. Its excitement exceeds its worth. Advancing a runner from first base to second base, into what is colloquially known as "scoring position," is worth just under a quarter of a run with zero outs, and only about .15 runs with one out or two outs. In other words, you need four successful steals of second base with zero outs to add up to one run of value, or one additional expected run scored for the offense. A stolen base is worth much less than a single or walk, for example—barely over half—and that's before we even consider the cost of a failed attempt. Stolen bases have their place, but they're no way to build an offense.

The tables above show only aggregate figures covering all situations for all teams over the course of the year. If Jon Lester, who has trouble throwing to first base and can't hold a runner on, is pitching, you'll be more inclined to send your runners. If Bryce Harper is at the plate, as I mentioned above, your first base coach should break out the epoxy. Think of "run expectancy" less as a mathematical concept and more as a baseball one: Do you think you've got a good chance to score here? Is the guy at the plate a good bet to hit a home run or a double, something that would make the stolen base totally unnecessary? Or are you at the bottom of the order, where getting two hits to score a runner from first is an unlikely outcome, so the value of a successful steal is probably higher? How scarce are runs in this ballpark? And, perhaps most important of all, who's running?

The data tell us that steals are good when successful and toxic to an offense when unsuccessful. The hardest thing for an offense to do in baseball, regardless of the era, is to put a man on base; deleting him with an ill-advised stolen base attempt is foolhardy. There is game-changing speed, of course, but it's rare, and players with speed aren't automatically good base stealers—nor is sending a runner the right move in every situation. Managers shouldn't drop the stolen base entirely, but they should be more judicious in its use. The value of a steal or of "team speed" has risen to mythical proportions, but myths, as we shall soon see, can still overshadow rational thinking in the way the game is played on the field.

6

Fielding Percentage:

The Absolute Worst Way to Measure Defense

Ozzie Smith was known as the Wizard of Oz for his incredible work on defense and his habit of doing a backflip whenever he ran out to his position at the start of a game. At the game's most challenging defensive position, Smith established a new standard for excellence. He was rewarded by fans with fifteen All-Star Game appearances and by coaches with thirteen Gold Glove Awards. (Gold Gloves don't always go to the best fielders, but Smith happens to have been worthy.) His unlikely NL Championship Series home run off Dodgers reliever Tom Niedenfuer helped the Cardinals win the National League pennant in 1985, one of three trips to the World Series they'd make with Smith at shortstop.

Smith played 21,785.2 innings at shortstop in the major leagues, over 19 seasons. He had 4,249 putouts, 8,375 assists, made 281 "errors," and was part of 1,590 double plays. Baseball-Reference values his defensive contributions at +239 runs, the most of any shortstop in MLB history.

Omar Vizquel played 22,960.2 innings at shortstop in the major leagues over 24 seasons; his 2,709 games at the position are the most in MLB history. He had 4,102 putouts at short, 7,676 assists, made 183 "errors," and was part of 1,734 double plays. Vizquel's Hall of Fame case—he'll appear on the ballot for the first time after the 2017 season—is a widely debated one, and his advocates often present him as a defender comparable to Smith.

So Smith played 130 fewer games' worth of innings at shortstop than Vizquel did, but recorded 147 more putouts and 699 more assists. To put it another way, Smith made 100 more plays *per season* than Vizquel did.

Omar Vizquel was a nice player, a good defender, but Omar Vizquel was no Ozzie Smith.

Advanced metrics agree with this. Baseball-Reference uses Total-Zone to measure defense from before the advent of good play-by-play data, which power today's advanced metrics like dRS and UZR; TotalZone values Vizquel's defensive contributions at +134 runs, but Smith's at +239 runs, the third best by any player at any position in MLB history.*

Yet if you looked only at the statistic that, until the last decade, was seen by nearly everybody as the most reliable measure of defensive prowess, fielding percentage, you'd have favored Vizquel, whose .9847 fielding percentage bests Smith's .9782 and ranks as the second best among shortstops with at least 500 games at the position (behind only the still-active Troy Tulowitzki). Indeed, Smith ranks just 15th among shortstops all-time in fielding percentage, behind such luminaries as Stephen Drew and Larry Bowa.

Measuring defense has long been the most difficult problem for anyone, from general managers to independent analysts, within baseball, because the numbers available to us for most of baseball history just weren't very good. As a result, fielding percentage, one of the only stats on defense we've had, rose to the top as a method of evaluating a player's abilities in the field. Fielding percentage is a simple stat; if you know the player's total chances in the field, mean-

---

* Brooks Robinson leads with +293 runs at third base; Andruw Jones is second with +243 runs in the outfield, primarily in center field.

ing putouts plus assists plus errors, and his error total by itself, you can calculate it: divide his errors by his total chances, and subtract that number from one. You'll get something in the range of .95 to 1.00 for most big leaguers, although occasionally an awful defender comes along and manages to come in below that.

The problem here is that you'd get an equally good measure of a player's fielding abilities if you rolled a pair of dice. Fielding percentage doesn't impart any useful information whatsoever. Pulling a number at random would be just as valuable to us. Hey, Andrelton Simmons is . . . (sound of dice rolling) . . . an 11! That's great, right? What's at the root of these problems and why has fielding percentage held such a prominent position in how people evaluate defenses? It all starts with an error.

One of the biggest problems with fielding percentage is that it's calculated based on a player's errors, and errors are highly subjective. So much so that the rules guiding these subjective calls have changed numerous times since they were first incorporated in 1878. In 1887, the National League adopted a rule from the American Association that stated, "[a]n error shall be given for each misplay which allows the striker or baserunner to make one or more bases, when perfect play would have insured his being put out," while also removing the earlier stipulation that a pitcher should be charged with an error when issuing a base on balls. (Yes, for four seasons, a walk was counted as an error for the pitcher.)

In 1888, the National League introduced the first rule specifying when a run should count as "earned," saying a run that scored "unaided by errors before chances have been offered to retire the side" would be earned, implying then that other runs would be unearned. This rule, however, was deleted in 1898, only to reappear in slightly different form in 1917.

In 1914, the guidelines for errors were expanded, introducing the first of many wrinkles that would reduce the statistic's usefulness for measuring defense or teasing out pitcher performance. If a catcher or infielder attempts to complete a double play but fails, he should not be charged with an error . . . unless the throw is so wild that one or more runners advance an extra base as a result. So a pitcher can induce what would be an inning-ending double play, only to have it muffed by a fielder and perhaps allowing one or more runs to score that would not have scored without the non-error error.

Similarly, an error committed during the course of turning a double play may have little to do with the fielder's range or even his defensive ability overall, especially prior to 2016, when MLB put into place a new rule that discouraged the "takeout" slides that runners would use to try to break up double play attempts. In October 2015, Dodgers second baseman Chase Utley slid at Mets shortstop Ruben Tejada to prevent Tejada from making an accurate throw to first; a potential double play turned into a fielder's choice with no outs recorded, with four runs eventually charged to pitcher Noah Syndergaard when that double play would have ended the inning with no runners crossing the plate. Oh, and Utley broke Tejada's leg in the process, which became the impetus for MLB's rule change.

Further refinements to the error rule followed in 1920, 1931, and 1950, followed by the rule change in 1951 that awarded an error to any fielder who commits interference or obstruction and thus allows a batter to reach base or a runner to advance one or more bases. Here again we see the use of the error bucket as a sort of trash can for miscellaneous events—if a fielder commits interference, it doesn't tell us anything about his defensive skills, specifically his ability to convert balls hit to him into outs. It's just noise.

Then we get to 1967, when the rulebook finally admits the flaw in the error stat that I think everyone knew was there: "Mental mistakes or misjudgments are not to be scored as errors unless specifically covered in the rules." The fielder who breaks the wrong way on a routine flyball and doesn't recover in time to make the play, allowing that ball to fall in for a hit, is not credited with an error; in fact, he's not credited (or debited) with anything at all, even though his mistake hurt the pitcher and the team. Official scorers aren't qualified to make this kind of judgment anyway, but the absence of such miscues from the error bucket destroys the stat's utility.

These changes and refinements have given us an error rule that, while long, still leaves the official scorer substantial discretion in the judgment of whether a play should be scored as a hit or an error.

9.12 Errors

An error is a statistic charged against a fielder whose action has assisted the team on offense, as set forth in this Rule 9.12 (Rule 10.12).

(a) The official scorer shall charge an error against any fielder:
(1) whose misplay (fumble, muff or wild throw) prolongs the time at bat of a batter, prolongs the presence on the bases of a runner or permits a runner to advance one or more bases, unless, in the judgment of the official scorer, such fielder deliberately permits a foul fly to fall safe with a runner on third base before two are out in order that the runner on third shall not score after the catch;
Rule 9.12(a)(1) Comment: Slow handling of the ball that does not involve mechanical misplay shall not be construed as an error. For example, the official scorer shall not charge a fielder with an error if such fielder fields a ground ball cleanly but does not throw to first base in time to retire the batter.

So, let's get into what this is really saying: a groundball hit directly to the shortstop, shortstop fields it cleanly but can't get the ball out of his glove to make a throw, runner reaches first base. How is this anything but an "error"? If we assume that the pitcher was partially responsible for inducing a groundball to shortstop that was playable, why would the pitcher be charged with a hit and, if the runner ends up scoring, an earned run?

It is not necessary that the fielder touch the ball to be charged with an error. If a ground ball goes through a fielder's legs or a fly ball falls untouched and, in the scorer's judgment, the fielder could have handled the ball with ordinary effort, the official scorer shall charge such fielder with an error.

Here's the key language: "in the scorer's judgment." The scorer isn't a trained scout or evaluator, and may face pressure from players or coaches who call the press box to complain about scoring decisions. With the error entirely subjective, lacking any consistency across games or ballparks, the scorer's contributions here tell us nothing of value about player defense.

For example, the official scorer shall charge an infielder with an error when a ground ball passes to either side of such infielder if, in the official scorer's judgment, a fielder at that position making ordinary effort would have fielded such ground ball and retired a runner.

Once again, we're relying on the scorer's judgment . . . and in practical terms, this just never happens. If the fielder doesn't touch the ball, he will almost certainly not be charged with an error, even when an average defender at that position would normally make that play. But the problem here again is that you are asking an untrained eye to discern what a typical fielder would do with that particular ball in play. Even experienced scouts may disagree on that question, so asking a single person to make that call is futile, and the sum of such judgment calls renders the statistic unreliable.

The comment here continues in the same vein, followed by five rather straightforward descriptions of errors, until we get to:

(7) whose throw takes an unnatural bounce, touches a base or the pitcher's plate, or touches a runner, a fielder or an umpire, thereby permitting any runner to advance; or

Rule 9.12(a)(7) Comment: The official scorer shall apply this rule even when it appears to be an injustice to a fielder whose throw was accurate. For example, the official scorer shall charge an error to an outfielder whose accurate throw to second base hits the base and caroms back into the outfield, thereby permitting a runner or runners to advance, because every base advanced by a runner must be accounted for.

What the hell is an "unnatural bounce"? Are we accusing the fielder of injecting the ball with steroids or horse tranquilizers? And if the fielder in question made an "accurate" throw, then why are we recording something that would count against him in defensive measures? By the way, if the outfielder's throw hits second base, it wasn't an accurate throw. That's just not how the game works.

The rule is riddled with references to "the scorer's judgment," but the scorer's judgment isn't worth squat—and the problem is exacerbated by the lack of any second opinion on these judgments. Since a typical infielder might only have 15–20 errors in a full season, adding or subtracting one due to a scorer's judgment can make a significant difference in how we perceive the player at the end of that season.

Furthermore, an error in the scorebook isn't always an error on the field, while errors on the field often show up as hits (but not errors) in the scorebook. If we think of errors as defensive mistakes, we get very different results from recorded errors, and can easily see how they mislead us as to fielding prowess.

Consider the case of poor Jose Valentin, the Puerto Rican shortstop who was frequently bounced to other positions because his employers thought his fielding at short was subpar. Valentin led the American League in errors committed twice, in 1996 while with the Milwaukee Brewers and in 2000 while with the Chicago White Sox, yet was among the best-fielding shortstops in the AL in both seasons. In 1996, he led AL shortstops with 37 errors, 15 more than the next-highest total (22 by Derek Jeter), but also fielded more balls in play than all but two shortstops in the AL, finishing fourth in the league in assists and third in double plays. Jeter played 80 more innings at short than Valentin but fielded 30 fewer chances, so TotalZone rated Valentin's defense as 26 runs better than Jeter's on the season—the opposite of the conclusion you might get from their error totals or fielding percentages.

In 2000, Valentin committed 36 errors—12 more than the second-highest total, again from Jeter—but fielded more balls than any shortstop in the AL but Miguel Tejada, even though Valentin only played in 141 games and had fewer innings at the position than the other shortstops who finished in the top five in total chances. Again, Valentin played less than Jeter, about 66 innings' worth, but handled 110 more chances in the field, more than making up for the handful of extra errors, so that the difference between their Total-Zone values was 33 runs in Valentin's favor.

There are two possible explanations for Valentin's particular brand of defense:

1. Valentin tended to make more errors than the normal short-stop on routine plays, but made up for it by fielding balls that the normal shortstop never touches.
2. Valentin tended to make more errors than the normal short-stop *because* he fielded balls that the normal shortstop never touches, earning "errors" when he personally would have been better served leaving the ball alone entirely.

This the perverse incentive of the error rule: the player concerned with his own statistics is better served by avoiding difficult plays where he might commit an "error" than by trying to make more plays for his team and risking harm to his basic fielding stats.

Flawed as errors are, they aren't even the worst thing about field-ing percentage.

The fundamental problem with fielding percentage is its omission of plays not made. Defense in baseball is not a question of avoiding mistakes, but a matter of converting balls hit in play into outs as often as possible. This is why teams now shift or reposition fielders to maximize their chances of recording outs, even though doing so would increase the chances of someone committing an error. (You can't mishandle a ball you never touch.)

Fielding percentage takes the wrong approach from the start: it only considers balls the fielders actually handle, without factoring in the vast number of balls put into play that might have been fielded but weren't. Scouts understand intuitively that defense includes range, and will grade a player with greater range—that is, the ability to field balls over a wider physical area on the field—higher than one with less. Yet fielding percentage doesn't even pretend to address that part of defense. If a fielder never touched a ball, in the eyes of fielding percentage that play *simply never happened*. It is the "see no evil" of baseball stats, and pretending that measures defense in any way, shape, or form is willful ignorance.

When I was a kid, collecting baseball cards and getting much of my baseball "insight" from *Baseball Digest,* I was impressed by the error-free ways of Angels outfielder Brian Downing, a converted catcher who didn't commit an error as a full-time outfielder in 1982 or 1984, resulting in fielding percentages of 1.000 for those seasons, and committed just one in 1983. He made only 7 errors in his tenure as an outfielder and retired with a fielding percentage of .995, which as of this writing is the third best in MLB history, after Darin Erstad (another Angel) and current Yankees outfielder Jacoby Ellsbury.

Yet by one very simple measure of range, called Range Factor, Downing ranks only 281st among MLB outfielders with a career mark of 2.174. Range Factor takes the fielder's total chances in the field, putouts plus assists, and normalizes it per 9 innings the way we calculate ERA:

Range Factor = (Putouts + Assists) * 9 / Innings Played

Range Factor is hardly a perfect measure of defense, but it does tell us one thing that fielding percentage can't: how many times per game the fielder actually, you know, fielded something cleanly. The top of the historical Range Factor leaderboards is stacked with center fielders, who by assignment have more ground to cover, and typically very fast ones who'd run down more balls in play with pure speed.

Even when we limit the range factor to left fielders, where Downing played most of his outfield innings, he drops from 3rd to 27th, again showing that Downing's low error totals were probably a reflection of his limited range: He made plays on balls hit right at him, but didn't cover much ground and thus didn't make many difficult plays that would have increased the chances of him committing errors.

Range Factor and similar statistics that are based on putouts and assists address one problem with fielding percentage—the emphasis on plays made cleanly without considering how many plays were made at all—but they don't do enough to get at the question of how many plays weren't made. Take the example of Willie Wilson, left fielder for the Kansas City Royals in the late 1970s and 1980s, and one of the fastest players of his era. Wilson made a lot of plays, so his Range Factor and similar stats are high, but that still gives us an incomplete picture of how good a fielder he was.

Wilson sits atop the all-time Range Factor leaderboards for left fielders, making about one more play per 27 innings than any other left fielder as far back as Baseball-Reference has data (roughly 1954). That's about 54 more outs recorded per season than the next-best left fielder, mostly putouts since left fielders don't record many assists. Wilson was one of the fastest players in major-league history and played quite a bit in center, so it's no surprise at all that he had tremendous range in left. But Wilson had some inverse help from his pitching staff, too.

The Royals won the American League pennant in 1980, the first pennant in the franchise's history, losing the World Series to the Philadelphia Phillies that fall. But one of their big weaknesses was the pitching staff's inability to miss many bats; they were 13th out of 14 AL teams in strikeouts recorded in 1980, and then finished dead last in the league in strikeouts the next three seasons. Fewer strikeouts means more balls put into play, so it's not a surprise that several members of those great Royals teams of the late 1970s and early 1980s have some of the highest career Range Factors/9 for their positions, including George Brett (6th among third basemen) and Frank White (11th among second basemen). Even Amos Otis, the center fielder who was probably more fast than he was a good fielder, ranks 28th for his position, which is by definition filled with good defenders and fast guys.

Indeed, the common flaw between fielding percentage and range factor is context. A fielder behind a high-strikeout pitching staff won't get as many opportunities as a fielder on the 1982 Royals did. An infielder behind a pitching staff full of sinkerballers like Kevin Brown or Brandon Webb will get disproportionately more opportunities than an infielder on another team, but an outfielder on that same squad will get fewer—and many of the balls he does handle will be groundballs that are already base hits by the time he gets to them. Fielders in ballparks with a lot of foul ground, such as the atrocity where the Oakland A's currently play their home games, will get more opportunities to field foul pop-ups, which are relatively easy to field and result in very few errors if misplayed.

Meanwhile, all plays made (or not made) aren't created equal, even though fielding percentage and Range Factor treat them that way. The most obvious example is the play where an outfielder reaches over the wall and catches a ball that would otherwise have been a home run. This play saves one run by definition, and possibly more if there were men on base; on average that play is going to be worth more than a run saved if we try to place a generic value on all catches that bring back home runs. That play is still recorded as one putout, the same as a routine pop fly to the second baseman, even though the savings in run prevention are obviously different. This idea, that each play made or not made has a different value, drives more advanced defensive metrics like dRS (defensive Runs Saved) and UZR (Ultimate Zone Rating), which I'll discuss in a later chapter, as they have strengths and weaknesses of their own, and have only become possible with the more detailed play-by-play data that have become available in the last twenty years.

In the meantime, forget fielding percentage. You'll certainly hear it less in 2017 than you would have five or ten years ago, but it still crops up as a weak measure of defense for people who aren't aware of the changes in how MLB teams think about fielding. Using fielding percentage to try to tell us who's a good fielder is like using the prices on a menu to tell us if the food's any good: if there's something useful in this information, it's going to be swamped by all the bullshit.

Which brings us back to where we began: despite anything else you've heard, Ozzie Smith is the greatest defensive shortstop at least of the modern era of baseball and likely in the sport's history, especially given how players today are much faster, stronger, and more athletic than their counterparts of the early twentieth century. Smith's defensive prowess plus his offensive contributions—in an era when shortstops didn't hit at all, Smith posted solid OBPs and was a high-percentage base stealer—made him a no-brainer for the Hall of Fame. Vizquel can't come close to Smith's value on defense, and was the inferior hitter as well, hitting .272/.336/.352* playing in a higher-offense era, while Smith hit .262/.337/.328 in the low-offense 1980s and was substantially more valuable on the bases.

Fielding percentage needs to die, and if it takes the error with it, I won't be sorry. Instead, we need to shift our minds around defense to thinking about plays made versus plays not made, while also considering whether those plays should be made at all.

	Play Should Have Been Made	Play Would Typically Not Be Made
Play was made	Okay, well, nice job	Bonus points
Play was not made	Epic fail	¯_(ツ)_/¯

The play made/not made distinction is clear and, in most cases, entirely objective. The other distinction, whether the play "should have" been made or would have been made by an average fielder at that position, is a more difficult one, especially today in an age where teams position their fielders differently for each opposing batter, but we can work with an objective basis by looking at all batted balls hit to the same spot on the field and seeing how frequently they were turned into outs. The same method can look at how much such plays were worth—an outfielder who catches a ball hit to the gap that would typically fall in for a double or a triple has helped his team more than the outfielder who comes in and robs a hitter of a

---

* The "triple-slash line" for batters of batting average, on-base percentage, and slugging percentage, which provides a far more complete picture of a hitter's performance than batting average alone ever could, but more on that later.

weakly hit single—and value defensive contributions not by number of plays, but in terms of bases or runs saved.

Fielding percentage and the underlying putout-assist-error framework can't do this. The "play should have been made, but wasn't" box is ignored unless the fielder committed an error; if he never touched the ball, it's as if it never happened. The fielder who makes a play that isn't typically made doesn't get any more credit than the fielder who fields a ball hit directly at him. We have plenty of data now to do better.

Fielding percentage may be awful, but there's some value in simply knowing how many plays a fielder made in total. In the end, though, that number only gives us a portion of the picture and doesn't tell us enough about what it's leaving out. It's comparable to stolen bases—unless it's accompanied by the number of times the player was caught stealing, a raw stolen base total isn't that meaningful.

The world of traditional stats is full of numbers like these, ambiguous totals and ratios that look like they tell us something, but in fact tell us almost nothing at all.

7

Bulfinch's Baseball Mythology:

Clutch Hitters, Lineup Protection, and Other Things That Don't Exist

Baseball's long history and onetime status as the national pastime have led to countless stories, legends, and myths about all aspects of the game. If you grew up any kind of baseball fan, you heard at some point about Babe Ruth calling his shot in the 1932 World Series (he didn't) or about Negro Leagues star Josh Gibson hitting a 580-foot homer at Yankee Stadium (physically impossible). Baseball just seems to attract this sort of malarkey, and it's not limited to stories like a kid begging of Shoeless Joe Jackson to "say it ain't so, Joe" after several White Sox players were tried for throwing the 1919 World Series.

Some baseball myths pertain to the playing of the game itself and affect the way broadcasters, writers, and fans discuss the game, and can still even play a role in team decisions on players. The rise of advanced statistics, and sometimes just the curiosity of people with some basic coding and math skills, allow us to examine these and determine whether the conventional wisdom holds any water.

As the great sabermetrician Carl Sagan said, extraordinary claims require extraordinary evidence, and it turns out many myths about baseball don't stand up to rational scrutiny.

There is no such thing as a "clutch hitter."

This is anathema to many baseball fans, and to narrative-starved sportswriters, but the truth of the matter is that good hitters are good hitters regardless of the situation. A good "clutch hitter" is just a good hitter. If you can hit, you can hit with men on base, with two strikes, with two outs, with runners in scoring position, with the score tied, whatever the case may be. The idea of the hitter who can elevate his game in these "clutch" situations, loosely defined as at bats taking place late in games with the score close, is a myth.

There are clutch hits, of course. The walk-off home run is, by definition, a clutch hit: it wins the game, perhaps breaking a tie or even bringing the home team from behind to win. We can discuss that hit itself as being clutch, perhaps even saying the whole at bat was clutch, although at some point it becomes unclear whether we're talking about baseball or a car with a manual transmission. But the idea that a certain hitter is somehow better in these close and late situations—or even that some hitters are demonstrably worse in said situations—is not based in fact, nor has it withstood dozens of attempts to verify it. There are clutch hits in clutch situations, but there are no "clutch hitters."

The mere idea of this player who can summon something extra from within himself like the hero of some ancient Greek epic certainly predates my fandom, and the first attempt to prove or disprove their existence of which I'm aware came in 1977, when I was just four years old. Dick Cramer wrote a seminal piece in SABR's *Baseball Research Journal* asking the simple question in its title: "Do Clutch Hitters Exist?" Cramer used a statistic called Player Win Average, a precursor to today's Win Probability Added, and which assigned points to hitters based on each event in their seasons and whether those events (hits, outs, walks, etc.) increased or decreased their teams' chances to win each of those games. He looked at data from 1969 and 1970—bear in mind, this was essentially the era of the abacus when it came to data analysis—and found the hitters who were supposedly "clutch" in one year were no more likely to be so in the other year than players who weren't "clutch." Cramer concluded that the supposed clutch ability was merely random variation, and that "[g]ood hitters are good hitters and weak hitters are weak hitters regardless of the game situation."

Subsequent studies have fared no better, although some analysts, including Bill James (who initially supported Cramer's work), have gone from nonbelievers in the clutch hitter to agnostic in the interim. Tom Ruane ran an extensive study using play-by-play data from Retrosheet from 1960 to 2004 and found no confirmation that the clutch hitter is real, with his results looking very much like a random distribution of player results would. Absence of evidence is not necessarily evidence of absence—that is, just because you didn't find it doesn't prove it's not there—but, as Ruane says in his conclusion, "One could argue that the forces at work here, if they exist, must be awfully weak to so closely mimic random noise, and if they are really that inconsequential perhaps we could assume they don't exist without much loss of accuracy."

In *The Book,* a 2007 tome from Tom Tango, Mitchel Lichtman, and Andrew Dolphin, the authors took a different approach to the question, figuring an "expected" clutch performance from hitters by adjusting for certain variables that might otherwise obscure a clutch effect in the statistics. They also found no evidence for the skill, and concluded that, "for all practical purposes, a player can be expected to hit equally well in the clutch as he would be expected to do in an ordinary situation." (They also conducted the most extensive study I've seen on whether pitchers exhibited the "clutch" skill, specifically relief pitchers, and again found no evidence of such an effect.)

In fact, the only serious analytical work in the last forty years to claim that the clutch hitter was a real thing, a skill distinct from the basic hitting skill, was done by the Elias Sports Bureau as part of their annual Baseball Analyst books in the 1980s. These books didn't just argue that the clutch hitting skill was real, but attacked those who argued otherwise. Unfortunately for Elias, their own lists of the best clutch hitters (using their own homegrown definition of "clutch") varied so much from year to year that an analysis published in 1989 in the *Baseball Research Journal* by Harold Brooks, now a meteorologist for the National Oceanic and Atmospheric Administration, found that "the conclusion that the Elias definition of clutch hitting is irrelevant is inescapable. Clutch hitting, as presently defined, is a mirage at best."

Indeed, many of the hitters most often labeled as "clutch" today actually aren't. Miguel Cabrera, for example, has hit .321/.399/.562 in his career (through the end of the 2016 season); he's actually been slightly worse than that in "late and close" situations, .298/.393/.514. He's probably faced more tough relievers in those situations than inferior hitters would, so I would not argue that he's somehow unclutch; I think we're looking at a great hitter who's still a great hitter in those situations we'd ordinarily define* as clutch.

David Ortiz, who in 2016 had one of the great swan-song seasons in baseball history, is called "clutch" so often he might as well make that his middle name. But Ortiz, a great hitter in all situations, isn't anything more than that in situations we'd typically call "clutch:"

Situation	Avg.	OBP.	SLG.
Overall	.286	.380	.552
2 outs, RISP	.256	.417	.534
Late and close	.256	.371	.499

Even in the postseason, where Ortiz's reputation became something of a caricature in 2013 (even as he went 2-for-22 in the ALCS

---

* Definitions pose a big problem with the myths I discuss in this section; when you've got a falsehood you're trying to defend against the assault of facts and/or data, one popular trick is to move the goalposts, changing the definition to try to revitalize your dead belief after it's been proven false. Clutch hitters and lineup protection often fall into the line of thinking of the "god of the gaps" belief found in philosophy, where the existence of one or more deities is presumed to fill in the cracks not presently answered by science.

win over Detroit), he's still just the same hitter he always is, hitting .289/.404/.543 in 369 career playoff plate appearances, or a little more than half a season's worth of playing time, getting pitched around a bit more in October than in the regular season.

And how about Derek Jeter, the player whose very nickname, "Captain Clutch," invokes the term?

Situation	Avg.	OBP.	SLG.
Overall	.310	.377	.440
2 outs, RISP	.298	.399	.418
Late and close	.283	.376	.400
Postseason	.308	.374	.465

Nope. Even the Captain can't transcend the basic limits of human ability: if you're a good hitter, you're a good clutch hitter, and if you're a good clutch hitter, you were just a good hitter to begin with.

For many readers, this is a hard conclusion to accept. We all think we know about performing under pressure and then impute the same travails to big-league ballplayers. In my opinion, however, any player who can't maintain his skill set when playing in a high-pressure or "clutch" situation won't get very far in baseball. To reach the majors, a player has to succeed at the multiple lower levels of baseball, whether it's high school, college, the minors, or foreign leagues. A talented player who can't handle a high-pressure situation would be flushed out of pro ball early, which is one possible explanation for the fact that we don't see such players in the majors. (Another is that this type of player doesn't exist, period.) Many of the myths that fans and writers hold so dear, like the clutch hitter who can elevate his game when it counts—speaking of which, what the hell was he doing the rest of the time? Damn slacker—might actually hold true when we're dealing with lower levels of baseball. But when it comes to the majors, the Clutch Hitter isn't just dead; he was never alive in the first place.

*   *   *

The myth of lineup protection has some intuitive appeal, even though it doesn't fully hold up under further analysis. A good hitter is "protected" in the lineup by having another good hitter batting right behind him so that a pitcher can't simply pitch around the first hitter (or in some cases walk him intentionally) to get to the weaker hitter in the on-deck circle. Since setting the lineup is one of the most tangible things that a manager does to affect the team's offense, understanding where lineup protection breaks down is key to figuring out who should bat where in the order.

Lineup protection does exist, at least in those lesser environments I mentioned above. The high school superstar who's going to be a first-round pick might find himself intentionally walked four times in a game, because whoever's hitting behind him is a tiny fraction of the hitter he is. The team is worse off for the free baserunners, because that superstar might be a .500 or .600 hitter with a slugging percentage near 1.000—that is, he had a better-than-even chance of reaching first base anyway, and was probably going to hit the ball hard enough to advance runners on base by a couple of spots. Walking him intentionally, while rather unsportsmanlike, could be the right move for the opposing coach. (It is, however, grossly unfair to the scouts who may have flown or driven for hours just to see that hitter swing the bat.)

In the major leagues, however, lineup protection does not exist. Again, people have looked for it, and found no evidence of its existence. Now, it's possible that the shape of a hitter's production will change if there's a huge drop-off to whoever's hitting behind him, but the overall value of his production will remain about the same.

Lineup protection has stuck around as a prevalent belief because it's founded on a bit of common sense. If a great hitter has a not-so-great hitter behind him, opposing pitchers may try to pitch around him or walk him to get to the inferior guy on deck.

Tom Tango wrote a passage in the aforementioned *The Book* about lineup protection, finding, as you might expect, no tangible evidence that it exists, when he looked at thousands of MLB plate appearances where it might have manifested itself. Hitters who were less "protected" were moderately more likely to walk, but their performance in nonwalk plate appearances was unaffected by the lack of protection behind them. Since walking a major-league hitter is, in most cases, not a positive move for the team in the field, the lack of protection wasn't hurting the offensive clubs in those situations—they got some free baserunners out of it. The lack of protection would become an issue if the next hitter (or sequence of hitters) was so bad that the probability of that free baserunner scoring was close to zero—for example, walking the eighth-place hitter on a National League team to get the pitcher up to the plate. That effect exists, as you can often see with mediocre eighth-place hitters who post surprising walk rates amid terrible offensive stat lines but can't maintain the "patience" when hitting elsewhere in the lineup. Seeing the protection issue crop up when the pitcher is on deck may contribute to the endurance of the myth that protection exists elsewhere in the lineup, too.

Thus, lineup protection might change the shape of a hitter's production, but there's no evidence that protection (compared to a lack of protection) helps a hitter's overall production. The shape of it might matter to fantasy baseball players who don't care about walks, and it might matter to a manager trying to construct a lineup that will maximize the team's run-scoring potential. These results, which confirmed previous, smaller studies on the question of lineup protection, also should serve as a deterrent to opposing managers considering the strategy of "pitching around" a hitter: you're more likely to walk him, but aren't any more likely to get him out just by trying to avoid giving him something to hit.

Speaking of intentional walks—let's talk about the supposed benefit of those, which is also another myth. While the intentional walk isn't a mythical creature like the clutch hitter or woo-woo like lineup protection, it is a wildly overused strategy in baseball that feeds off the belief in lineup protection and a general misunderstanding of run expectancy. The good news, at least, is that intentional walks have come down over the last forty years; the AL level is about half of its late-1960s peak, while the NL is down about 80 percent. Intentional walks are boring; you might argue they're cowardly; but most of all they're just bad strategy.

Let's look, once again, at the run expectancy table:

Runners	0 Outs	1 Out	2 Out
000 (none on)	0.479	0.2572	0.0996
003 (man on third)	1.3045	0.8916	0.3606
020 (man on second)	1.0762	0.6487	0.3154
023 (men on second and third)	1.9017	1.2831	0.5764
100 (man on first)	0.8427	0.5004	0.2203
103 (men on first and third)	1.6682	1.1348	0.4813
120 (men on first and second)	1.4399	0.8919	0.4361
123 (bases loaded)	2.2654	1.5263	0.6971

Now, bear in mind that these stats cover all batters in all situations, so we're looking at an average over tens of thousands of at bats here. Barry Bonds's career is in there somewhere, and so is Doug Flynn's. (Flynn hit .238/.266/.294 over a ten-year, 4,000-PA major league career. You can find a worse hitter, but I wouldn't recommend it.) And the table will change depending on who's at the plate. I'll circle back to this in just a moment.

Major-league teams issued 951 intentional walks in 2015, and 95 percent of them came in one of three situations: man on second (47 percent), men on second and third (30 percent), and man on third (18 percent).* So we can examine the boost that adding a trailing runner on first gives in each of those situations, which turns out to be 0.3637 with no outs, 0.2432 with one out, and 0.1207 with two outs. That's the probability of any runner on first scoring depending on the number of outs, regardless of who else is on base.

---

* There was one intentional walk of a hitter with no one on base in 2015. On July 11, the Cardinals walked Andrew McCutchen intentionally in the bottom of the eleventh inning with two outs and nobody on. If that sounds weird—putting the winning run on base is a bad idea just about any time you might even think about it—there's a good reason: The hitter on deck was pitcher Deolis Guerra, who was swapped into that spot in an earlier double switch. He grounded out. As of this writing, that remains Guerra's only major-league plate appearance.

Putting a runner on via the intentional walk with no outs is like handing the opponent a card that says he gets to roll one six-sided die, and if the roll comes up 5 or 6, he gets an extra run.

There are some valid reasons for an intentional walk, however.

A manager may also choose to intentionally walk one hitter to get a more favorable platoon matchup with the next hitter. If the pitcher is a left-handed reliever with a large platoon split—meaning that he's much more effective against lefties than against righties—then walking the right-handed hitter to get to the left-handed one could be sensible. MLB teams now have mountains of data on hitter tendencies as well, so a manager could try to match up his sinkerballer against a hitter who puts a lot of batted balls on the ground, hoping for a double play. These decisions, however, should no longer be a question of a manager's "gut," but informed choices that consider whether the team is better off putting an additional runner on base to gain some sort of advantage, preferably a substantial one, against the next hitter. You're always worse off in the average case if you allow an additional baserunner, so the default argument should be not to intentionally walk a hitter; to argue in favor, you must have some solid evidence that doing so still reduces the probability that you'll allow one or more runs in the inning.

But many intentional walks are nothing more than handing the opposition that aforementioned free shot at a bonus run. If the intentional walk does not give you a more favorable platoon matchup, or doesn't at least bring a substantially worse hitter up to the plate, it's probably a terrible idea. When you hear about walking a guy to set up a double play, it's probably a terrible idea. When you hear about walking a guy intentionally because he's "hot," that's almost certainly a terrible idea. And when you hear about how you can't "let that guy beat you," well, I'm pretty sure the goal is to not let anyone beat you, so that's a terrible idea, too. Terrible ideas abound in baseball. It would be good to have fewer of them.

While we're on the subject of intentional walks and lineup protection, let's talk about the actual lineup itself. If you've spent any time watching or playing baseball, you know you're supposed to bat your best hitter third, so that the first two guys can get on base for him and he can drive them in. This is also wrong, for reasons that should have been obvious from the start. Your best hitter should hit second, and we're starting to see a few teams figure that out—although unlike some of the other changes I've described so far in this book, this particular adjustment is taking a while to trickle through.

Here's the crux of the argument: Every spot in the lineup gets about 2.5 percent more plate appearances over the course of a full season than the spot after it, which amounts to another trip to the plate every eight or nine games. That means moving your third-place hitter up to the two hole in the lineup will get him something like 18 more PA over the course of a season. It's a marginal gain, but it's essentially all upside: why wouldn't you want your best hitter to come to the plate 18 more times over the course of the season?

Lineup construction itself has been heavily studied and found to not make that much of a difference; if you compared an optimal lineup to an average one for a major-league team, the gain in runs over the course of a single season will likely be only about 10–15. (That figure, like many in this section, also comes from *The Book,* by Lichtman, Tango, and Dolphin.) The impact all around is small, but any advantage you can capture with a move that is essentially costless is worth capturing.

There is a bit of randomness involved in how often and when the hitter you've moved up in the lineup gets those extra plate appearances, but one potential benefit, albeit an unpredictable one, is decreasing the probability that your best hitter ends up standing in the on-deck circle to end the game. Baseball-Reference's Play Index found 363 games in 2015 where one team ended the game with 38 plate appearances—four times through the order plus the first two batters getting a fifth turn each, so the number-three hitter was left in the on-deck circle; those teams were 177-186 in those games. There were 1,492 games that went beyond the 38th plate appearance, and as you might expect the teams' records improve with each additional PA:

PA	W/L Record
37	207-246
38	177-186
39	194-142
40	178-117
41	144-81
...	...
47	47-12
48	31-10

That's 363 games where the number-three hitter was left in the on-deck circle, and 453 where he was left "in the hole," all games in which the teams on aggregate had losing records. If your best hitter is indeed hitting third in the lineup, bumping him up a spot at least gets him to the plate in more of these situations, about 23 times per team in 2016 (363 PA/30 teams), and allows him to at least extend the game. It's an easy, obvious switch to make.

You may well ask why I wouldn't go further and simply suggest that the best hitter lead off, with the team's remaining hitters sorted in reverse order of offensive ability. The answer is that the leadoff spot in the lineup comes up far too often with the bases empty, and thus moving the best hitter to that spot gains you another 20 or so PA but at the cost of a lot of run-scoring opportunities from other baserunners. *The Book* showed that the leadoff spot has 64 percent of its PA come with the bases empty, far more than any other spot in the lineup, none of which comes in above 56 percent. So your leadoff hitter should be someone who gets on base at a high clip but doesn't have much power—speed is nice, but entirely optional—while your number-two hitter should be the best overall bat on the club, preferably someone who gets on base and also hits for power.

While this particular myth isn't really dying, just fading in fits and starts, we are seeing one change in lineup construction around the National League, and this one is based in some actual evidence. Pitchers nearly always hit ninth in NL lineups (and in the AL prior to the 1973 introduction of the designated hitter) until the last few seasons, when some NL managers have shifted the pitcher to the eighth spot and used the final place in the lineup as a sort of "second lead-off" position, placing a batter there with solid on-base skills so that the leadoff and number-two hitters are more likely to have someone else on base for them. I'd rather just see pitchers batting eliminated entirely—in 2015, MLB pitchers hit .132/.160/.170, dropped 488 sacrifice bunts, and struck out 42 percent of the time they didn't bunt—but if you've got to have one in your lineup, considering batting him eighth instead.

The productive out is a new yet horribly misguided statistic that briefly came into vogue as a way to reward hitters for making outs that advanced runners, a bit of baseball pseudoscience that sounds good because it has a veneer of validity covering an empty core. Born of a longtime bias against hitter strikeouts—the truth is a strikeout is only very slightly worse than most field outs, and of course it's better than hitting into a double play—the productive out ascribes far too much value to a field out, because all field outs reduce the team's "run expectancy," how many runs, on average, the team could expect to score in that inning based on the number of outs and the men on base.

The fundamental problem with the productive-out stat is that there is never a situation where you would prefer an out to a hit or a walk. That is, the expected run production of the inning always goes up when you put more men on base, and goes down when any hitter makes an out. Making outs is bad, and getting on base is good. Even if the hitter walks and that man on third base doesn't score right away, the probability of him scoring hasn't gone down—the next hitter gets a crack at it—and the expected total runs scored for the inning goes up.

Part of the appeal of the productive out is the explanation that there are outs that are clearly "productive"—namely a walk-off out, one that pushes across the winning run in the bottom of the ninth or in extra innings. But in those situations, the out is only as valuable as a hit, not more valuable; the upside of the hit is capped because of the game state, not because the out is suddenly worth more. You can't win the game twice, and there are no extra points for technical merit or artistic impression if you win on a hit rather than a sacrifice fly. A win is a win, so an out that scores the go-ahead run is worth as much as a hit that does the same thing—but it's not worth more, because it can't be.

Think about the dice game craps. Most bets at the craps table, like most bets in any casino, have an expected negative return on investment (ROI)—if you play the same bet repeatedly over a long enough sample, you can expect to lose money. There is one exception, however: the bet behind the pass line, which is one of the only bets you can place anywhere in a casino that has an ROI of zero, meaning you can expect to neither gain or lose any money on it. If you want to gamble, but don't want to do something that almost guarantees you'll walk out with less money than you had when you started, that's your best bet, pun intended.

The out-versus-hit comparison is similar: The walk-off situations where an out is as valuable as a hit are the equivalent of that pass-line bet. They are the outliers, and can mislead you into thinking that there's something to the "productive outs" concept. In reality, you would never strictly prefer an out to a runner reaching base safely, even if the latter doesn't score a run immediately, because you've still increased the probability that you will score the run in the inning and/or increased the total number of runs you can expect to score in the inning. Hits and walks are good, and outs are bad. The fact that some outs are marginally less bad than others doesn't outweigh the fact that making an out cuts your expected output for the inning, no matter the type of out in question.

A specific kind of "protective out" is, of course, the sacrifice bunt.

If you've spent any time on Twitter, you've probably come across baseball fans and analysts criticizing manager decisions to bunt, from the band Puig Destroyer's crude but effective song "Stop Fucking Bunting" to my own term #smrtbaseball, an allusion to a *Simpsons* episode where Homer calls himself smart, spells it S-M-R-T, and then sets the house on fire. Here's the main reason for all of this vitriol: in the majority of situations when it's used, the sacrifice bunt is a terribly stupid play.

Defenders of the bunt, often generally advocates of the type of offensive strategy called "small ball" (so called, I think, because it produces smaller numbers on the scoreboard), claim that it helps "manufacture" runs by moving one or two baserunners up on the bases, making it easier for them to score later in the inning. This sounds somewhat logical, but doesn't hold up to the most cursory scrutiny, as you can see from the run-expectancy table that shows the probability of scoring at least one run from each base-out state from the 2015 season:

Runners	0 Outs	1 Out	2 Outs
000	0.265	0.156	0.069
003	0.833	0.666	0.271
020	0.656	0.447	0.255
023	0.847	0.666	0.264
100	0.499	0.362	0.263
103	0.919	0.695	0.365
120	0.649	0.447	0.268
123	0.889	0.670	0.331

The first column shows the runners on base; 0 means a base is empty, while 1, 2, and 3 refer to those specific bases, so "120" means runners on first and second but not third.

Let's highlight some specific scenarios where you might see the bunt applied. The most common such scenario is a man on first and zero outs, which is a particular favorite of college coaches who find it easier to teach kids to bunt than it is to teach kids to hit. With a man on first base and no outs, a major-league team's probability of scoring at least one run in the inning in 2015 was 0.499, or roughly 50-50. Pushing that runner up to second base in exchange for an out reduced those odds to 0.447, or just under 45 percent. So not only does the bunt reduce the number of runs the team could expect to score in that inning (from 0.84 to 0.65, as we saw in the earlier run expectancy table), but it reduces the team's odds of scoring any runs at all. Remind me again what the point of the bunt was?

There are six common situations where you might see a manager call for a sacrifice bunt, so I've pulled those out and put them into another table that's a little easier to read. Each row here describes the starting situation, the probability of scoring at least one run in the starting state, the same probability after a successful sacrifice bunt, and a cell saying whether the team was better or worse off as a result of the bunt. It's not pretty.

Situation	Pre-bunt P (1 Run or More)	Post-bunt P (1 Run or More)	Better/Worse Off?
100, 0 outs	0.499	0.447	Worse
100, 1 out	0.362	0.255	Worse
020, 0 outs	0.656	0.666	Push
020, 1 out	0.447	0.271	Worse
120, 0 outs	0.649	0.695	Better
120, 1 out	0.447	0.264	Worse

In four of the six situations, a successful bunt makes the team worse off just in terms of pushing one run across in that inning. (Every successful sacrifice bunt reduces the team's total run expectancy for the inning.) The only situation that is a net positive for the team is men on first and second base, zero outs, where the successful bunt slightly increases the team's chances of scoring at least one run, albeit not by very much.

These tables are aggregate figures covering all situations for all teams, all hitters, all ballparks, and so on. A manager's decision at a specific moment to call for a bunt should include those other factors, especially the biggest one of all: who's at the plate. If we're playing in a National League park and the pitcher is batting, his odds of getting a hit or drawing a walk are not that high, so a sacrifice bunt attempt is mathematically sound. (It's also a damn good argument for putting the DH in the National League, because I have yet to meet the fan who bought a ticket to a major-league game because she really wanted to see guys drop some sac bunts.) If we're in a high-offense environment, like Coors Field or minor-league parks like those in Albuquerque or Lancaster, California, the bunt makes almost no sense for nonpitchers because home runs are easier to come by and merely putting the ball in play is usually favorable for the hitter.

Bunting with your number-two hitter, as college teams are so fond of doing, ahead of your number-three hitter, who is usually the best bat in the lineup the way managers and coaches typically construct them, is incredibly counterproductive, especially when the number-three hitter has power. In the 2001 postseason, Arizona manager Bob Brenly repeatedly had number-two hitter Craig Counsell lay down bunts in front of number-three hitter Luis Gonzalez, who hit 57 home runs that season. In the third inning of game one of that year's World Series, against the Yankees, Counsell bunted Tony Womack over from first to second; four pitches later, Gonzalez homered, scoring Womack from second base as easily as it would have scored him from first. Brenly gave away an out for no gain whatsoever, and surrendered the chance to put Counsell on base ahead of the home run. In game four, Counsell bunted Womack over three times for Gonzalez, with one of those leading to a semi-intentional walk of Gonzalez; those three bunts led to zero runs and Arizona lost that particular game by one run. If Counsell wasn't a good enough hitter to try to reach base in front of Gonzalez, why was he hitting ahead of Gonzalez at all?

Aside from the pitcher batting, there are two other major exceptions to the whole "stop bunting" thing. One is the bunt for a hit, which is entirely separate from a sacrifice bunt—that is, a bunt for an out. If the batter is quick and/or a good bunter, and has a reasonable chance (somewhere above one-third) at a hit from a bunt attempt, then the attempt itself is often a smart move, especially since a good attempt can yield a wild throw or other misplay that might result in further advancement. The other exception is when a hitter attempts to take advantage of a poor fielder, such as when Miguel Cabrera played third base for the Detroit Tigers to accommodate Prince Fielder at first. Bunting on a third baseman who's slow or who has an erratic arm has a higher rate of success for the team—reaching on an error won't reflect positively in the hitter's individual statistics, but it would help the team improve its outlook for the rest of the inning, since an errant throw would advance the runner(s) farther and perhaps allow a run to score.

These probabilities and expected outcomes make some manager and player tendencies particularly maddening because they are just so stupid. Cleveland shortstop Francisco Lindor, the runner-up in the AL Rookie of the Year voting in 2015, led the American League with 13 "successful" sacrifice bunts despite appearing in only 99 games. His OBP, which excludes those sac bunts entirely, was .353, so in 35 percent of his other plate appearances he reached base safely, as opposed to none of those 13 times he bunted a runner over. He did this while typically batting second in the order, one spot ahead of the team's best hitter, Michael Brantley. And those bunts, on the whole, did not help the team score more runs.

6/22, 3rd inning, 0 outs, Jason Kipnis on 2nd, runner scored on single, no further runs scored, team lost by 3

7/5, 3rd inning, 0 outs, Kipnis on 2nd, runner scored on single, no further runs scored, team lost by 2

8/3, 1st inning, 0 outs, Jose Ramirez on 1st, runner scored on single, HR later in inning, team lost by 1

8/5, 8th inning, 0 outs, Ramirez on 1st, runner did not score, team lost by 1

8/7, 1st inning, 0 outs, Ramirez on 1st, runner did not score, team lost by 1

8/8, 1st inning, 0 outs, Ramirez on 1st, runner scored on single, team won by 13

8/12, 1st inning, 0 outs, Ramirez on 1st, runner did not score, team won by 1

8/13, 1st inning, 0 outs, men on 1st and 2nd, runners both scored (SF, single, single), team lost by 2

8/17, 1st inning, 0 outs, Ramirez on 2nd, Lindor reaches on error, no runners score, team won by 6

8/25, 1st inning, 0 outs, Ramirez on 2nd, runner scored on double, team won by 5

8/30, 1st inning, 0 outs, Ramirez on 2nd, runner scored on double, team won by 7

9/10, 3rd inning, 0 outs, men on 1st and 2nd, runners did not score, team won by 2

9/19, 1st inning, 0 outs, Ramirez on 2nd, runner did not score, team lost by 1

In six of the thirteen instances here, the runner advanced on the bunt never scored, and in three of those six instances Cleveland lost the game in question by just one run. In five of the remaining seven instances, the runner advanced by the bunt would have scored any-way if subsequent events were unchanged:

- Kipnis is a fast enough runner to score from second base on most singles (6/22 and 7/5).

- On 8/3, Ramirez would have scored anyway on the home run later in the inning.

- On 8/25 and on 8/30, Ramirez would have scored anyway on the next hitter's double.

That's 11 of 13 so-called successful bunts that went for naught, and in all 13 situations, Lindor didn't give himself a chance to get on base safely and create another run-scoring opportunity. He reached once on a fielding error, instead of the four times in 13 we'd expect to see him reach base, perhaps even driving in a run or two him-self. Lindor apparently liked to do this on his own, which is some-what appalling for a player who's otherwise praised for his baseball acumen—he may really think he's doing something positive. Some-one needs to show Francisco the numbers and ask him the question every GM should ask his bunt-happy manager: "If what you're doing makes us worse off, why are you doing it?"

The hardest myth for fans and even baseball folks to give up, in my own experience, is the myth of the "hot hand." The term itself derives from basketball, but there are many equivalents you'll hear in baseball, from "in the zone" to "locked in" (an unfortunate term given its second meaning in medicine) to "feeling it." The story goes that a player, nearly always a hitter, has somehow captured some extra magic and is on a run at the plate in which his results are consistently better; he's hitting the ball harder, or balls are falling into play. You'll hear announcers say a pitch must have looked like a beach ball to him, or that his confidence is through the roof. The problem with this myth, as with the others, is that the evidence from reality shows that this effect either barely exists or doesn't exist at all. It's merely our brains' attempts to find patterns in data that are pretty close to random.

Hitter performances throughout a season include a lot of randomness; there certainly isn't any predictability in when a hitter will be more or less productive—like, say, Joey Bagodonuts is a really great July hitter, or Twerpy McSlapperson is much better on Tuesday afternoons. You expect that a hitter's line at the end of a full season will probably look a lot like his lines from the season or two before that; the more at bats a guy has, the more we expect his production to look like whatever his underlying true talent level might be. A hitter whose "true" on-base percentage, meaning his natural ability to get on base, is around .400 could easily have a month where he only gets on base at a .300 clip. You might think he's slumping, but in reality it's just a normal turn of the baseball screw: every hitter has periods of highs and lows, but barring some other explanation like an injury, players will eventually return to form—the baseball version of what statisticians refer to as "regression to the mean."

However, our brains are not well wired to handle randomness; we tend to think random distributions look more like uniform distributions, when random series tend to be clumpy and uneven, giving the impression of pattern where there's none. Alex Bellos, who's written several wonderful books on mathematics for the popular audience, wrote in London's *Daily Mail* in December 2010, "As humans, when we come across random clusters we naturally superimpose a pattern. We instinctively project an order on the chaos." He brought up the example of the random song shuffle feature on the original iPods, which produced random results like clusters of songs by the same artist, which, of course, confused listeners who thought the system was therefore not random. Apple had to make its randomizer less random to convince people it was random enough.

This is what happens in baseball—and other sports, as far as I can tell, although it's heretical for me to even admit the existence of other sports—when a hitter has some sort of "hot streak," "slump," or anything that doesn't seem random to our pattern-seeking minds. (In fact, you hear a lot that a certain hitter is "streaky"; all hitters are streaky, because random distributions are not uniform. If a hitter never had a streak, I'd suggest we all bow to our new robot player overlords.)

A landmark 1985 study of streakiness in basketball by Cornell psychology professor Thomas Gilovich and Stanford professors Robert Vallone and Amos Tversky looked at data from several players and teams in the NBA and found no evidence of the so-called hot hand effect: a player who has made several recent shots is, in fact, no more likely to make his next shot. If you like semantic games, you would say that he has been "hot," but he is not "hot." That is, he's made a few shots in a row, but he is still the same shooter he was before that streak of success.

Indeed, many researchers continue to try to find evidence of the hot hand effect in various endeavors, as if we just don't want to accept that our sports narratives are untrue. (Cf. "On the possibilities of self-propelled aerial locomotion," by Kelly, R., 1996, Atlantic/Jive Records.) Many attempts to identify and quantify the hot hand effect have appeared, with a recent paper from two economists, Jeffrey Zwiebel and Brett Green, claiming to have found evidence of this streakiness in baseball at a magnitude previously unheard of in the field. It didn't hold up under scrutiny: they used small samples to establish the players' base ability levels and thus tended to confuse changes in true talent levels with streakiness. The resulting consensus among sabermetricians who examined this study was that there might be some "hot hand" effect in baseball, maybe, but if it's there, it's minuscule, to the point where managers could safely ignore it.

There are real changes in player performance that teams need to monitor. Players get hurt and see temporary changes in skill levels. Hitters who suffer hand or wrist injuries lose some of their grip strength and thus may see a decline in power or in the quality of contact, while pitchers fighting just about any kind of malady can see a change in their mechanics and lose velocity, the ability to locate pitches, or both. Mechanics can change for the better, typically between seasons but sometimes during the year. Pitchers can add new pitches or change grips. Hitting and pitching coaches work with players on all of these things as part of their jobs, often reviewing video after each game and sometimes between at bats or innings to identify tiny yet tangible differences that might prevent the player from performing at his optimal level. (I was in the clubhouse occasionally for some of these conversations while I was working for the Blue Jays. Some were beneficial, but others involved a lot of complaining about the umpires, too.) This is why teams long employed advance scouts, watching the next series' opponent to see who might be healthy, who didn't seem to have a good grip on his breaking ball, who wasn't running as well as he normally did, and so on. Today, some teams have dispensed with advanced scouts in favor of sophisticated video and computer systems that can track plays and players more thoroughly, often with young front office employees reviewing the results to provide detailed notes for the major-league coaching staff.

But none of this is "hot hand" nonsense—it's looking for physical, verifiable changes, not arguing that some player has been temporarily possessed by the spirit of Honus Wagner at the plate. So the next time you hear that a hitter is locked in or that a starting pitcher is cruising, just remember, it's probably a narrative sitting awkwardly on a pile of random data.

This appeal of the narrative says a lot about why all of the myths here are able to persist in the absence of data. We want baseball to be the sepia-toned sport of our constructed memories. In a game that goes back at least 150 years, there is no shortage of stories for the sharpshooter to pick to try to support his preconceived notions about the game or his desire to find a narrative in the noise. We romanticize the past, we canonize the players we like (while demonizing those we don't), and we pick and choose what stories to remember or to believe. This irrationality drives so much of baseball coverage and discussion because of what we want baseball to be, when the game provides plenty of real, fact-based stories that are rooted in truth, not mythos.

For a long time, we lacked the information or the tools to adequately dispel these ideas about baseball—and other sports as well—to the point where we might see behavior change, but the last fifteen years have seen a revolution in baseball thinking. This upheaval in baseball thinking, from using better metrics based on the traditional stats to the incoming wave of new data that's changing the way front offices build their teams, won't get rid of great stories. We'll get new great stories now, stories about underdogs who were overlooked by traditional methods of evaluation but whose hidden talents came out because of the new data.

Most important, though, our stories about the stars will be driven by fact, not wishful thinking, which makes the stories more compelling, and the greatness of the game's best players that much easier to appreciate.

PART TWO

Smart Baseball

8

OBP Is Life:

Why On-Base Percentage Is the Measure of a Hitter

If on-base percentage is so important, then why don't they put it up on the scoreboard?

—Jeff Francoeur, 2009, failing to realize that OBP did indeed
appear on the Turner Field scoreboard for each batter

If you knew nothing about baseball statistics, traditional or modern, how would you try to measure the value of a baseball player's performance? In other words, what if you had to start from zero and build a new vocabulary of baseball stats?

This is the sort of question that the earliest baseball analysts, from Branch Rickey and Earnshaw Cook to Bill James and Pete Palmer, tried to answer, sometimes deconstructing older statistics and sometimes just building their own new ones from scratch. So much of what I'll discuss in this section of the book builds on their work and the work of others, writers and thinkers who realized things that today seem obvious—for example, that outs are bad and form the "cost" of offense, or that pitchers control some outcomes more than others. In the world in which most of us grew up, prior to radar and computer systems that could identify each pitch and its velocity and spin, we had to take the most basic accounting information about each game and try to figure out what data really mattered.

I'll start here, with the most useful of all basic offensive statistics, on-base percentage, which tells us the simplest and yet most important thing of all about a hitter: How often does he make an out? If you asked the average baseball fan what a hitter's job is at the plate, he or she would likely answer with something along the lines of "to get a hit." Maybe something more nuanced, like "to drive in runs." This is what we've been told since we could first sit up on our own in front of the TV set. Hitters hit.

It sounds good, like Baseball Populism, but it's not right. A hitter's job is to not make an out. If you'd prefer to phrase it in a positive way, then his job is to get on base. The result of every at bat is that the hitter reaches base or he makes an out. If we're just talking performance, there is no particle smaller than this one. Getting on base, or not making outs, is a definable, repeatable skill for hitters. And nothing measures that skill better than on-base percentage.

Sabermetrics started to creep into mainstream baseball writing in the early 2000s, after the publication of *Moneyball,* the Red Sox's hiring of Bill James as a consultant, and other smaller changes alerted the less retrograde journalists covering the sport that they needed to adapt to keep up with the teams and front offices they covered. (The sport's media were and still are infected by a strong Luddite streak that won't go away until that generation of writers has died off.) We didn't get rid of the bad stats, but we started to see new ones appear in print.

The most obvious change was the inclusion of what is commonly called the "triple-slash line"—batting average, on-base percentage, and slugging percentage, in that order. The triple-slash format is common enough that you will frequently see those three stats (separated, actually, by just two slashes, but let's not be pedantic here . . . there are better targets for our pedantry to come) without labels.

Bryce Harper, the unanimous National League MVP in 2015, hit .330/.460/.649 in that season, leading the National League in the final two categories. But regardless of how we present these stats, my belief here is simple: you can't tell the story of a hitter's season without knowing at least his on-base percentage, and while slugging percentage isn't as essential, it tells a lot of the story as well.

The proverb "OBP is life. Life is OBP" has been going around sabermetric circles for a while now; writer Joe Sheehan used it as the title of a 2006 piece on Baseball Prospectus's site, and in that article he credits BP cofounder Gary Huckabay with coining the phrase. There is simply nothing more important to powering a baseball offense than putting men on base—and, conversely, not making outs.

On-base percentage is the most complete of all basic hitting stats, because it includes almost everything the hitter does, and the excluded events are justifiably thrown out. The common formula for OBP is:

OBP = (Hits + Walks + times HBP) / (At bats + Walks + times HBP + Sacrifice Flies)

While that's a lot of terms, the underlying logic is simple: take the number of times the hitter got on base, and divide it by the number of times he came up to the plate in total. In fact, you could also express OBP as:

OBP = (Times on base) / (Plate appearances − Sacrifice Bunts − Catcher's interference)

Those last two items are excluded from OBP for good reason: as discussed, the sacrifice bunt is a deliberate (and stupid) waste of a plate appearance, and reaching on catcher's interference has nothing to do with the hitter. (It's also quite rare. I go to a lot of games, and if I see it twice a year, that's a lot.)

That makes OBP the measure of the player's frequency in reaching base. We express OBP as a three-digit decimal, as we do batting average, but it would make just as much sense to express it as a percentage, so Harper's .460 OBP in 2015 becomes 46.0 percent—that is, he reached base in 46 percent of his plate appearances, which led all of Major League Baseball.

The converse of OBP is never seen, but its importance might be more apparent to readers who haven't spent much time reading or thinking about OBP. If you subtract a hitter's OBP from 1, you get his out percentage: How often did his plate appearances result in an out. If I tell you that Wilson Ramos had a .258 OBP in 2015, the worst among qualifying hitters, that probably sounds bad. If I tell you that Ramos made an out in 74.2 percent of his plate appearances, you'll wonder how the heck he wasn't demoted to triple-A.

At a team level, on-base percentage is the best predictor of a team's run production, which should be obvious with a moment's thought: put more runners on base and make fewer outs and you will score more runs. With just 27 outs at your disposal each game, hitters who reach base more frequently (and thus make outs less frequently) will improve your offense.

In MLB history, the correlation between team OBP and team runs scored per game is huge—stronger than the correlation between team batting average and team runs scored. Using the common statistical measure of the correlation between two variables we discussed earlier, in chapter 1, where 1 is perfect positive correlation and 0 is no correlation, we find the following results:

All MLB teams, 1901–2015	
Batting average to team R/G	0.827
OBP to team R/G	0.894
All MLB teams, 1960–2015	
Batting average to team R/G	0.828
OBP to team R/G	0.897

In fact, in the 232 seasons of the major leagues from 1901 to 2015 (that's 115 each for the AL and NL plus the two seasons of the Federal League), the team with the best OBP in its league also led its league in runs scored in 135, or 58 percent of the time, versus 53 percent for teams that led in batting average.

Useful as OBP is on the team level, it's when you move it to individual players that you begin to see just how powerful it is at showcasing players' actual ability to avoid getting out. One of the worst MVP votes in history came in the "rabbit ball" year of 1987, when home runs spiked without warning throughout the game, only to drop back to contemporary levels the following year, fueling rumors that MLB had altered the ball to try to boost offense and thus increase fan interest. (The league has never admitted to doing so, although it's commonly accepted that the ball was different that year.)

That year also came in the midst of MLB's collusion scandal, where a bunch of dim-witted owners, egged on by Commissioner Peter Ueberroth, decided to ignore American labor law and the existence of the league's collective bargaining agreement with the players' union by coordinating their interests in free agents, driving down prices, and in some cases eliminating the markets for certain players entirely. One of the players hit by this cartel-like behavior—for which owners eventually paid $280 million in fines and lost salaries—was Andre Dawson, who had hit a respectable .284/.338/.478 with 20 home runs in 1986 for the Montreal Expos (#RIP). Dawson was a three-time All-Star, six-time Gold Glove winner, former Rookie of the Year, and two-time runner-up for MVP, so he was certainly well regarded as a player, and at thirty-two appeared to have plenty of production ahead of him. He found no takers whatsoever in free agency in the winter of 1986–87, and finally told the Cubs he would play for them for any amount of money—the "blank check" offer of legend—because he felt that the artificial turf in Montreal's home ballpark was destroying his knees. The Cubs signed him to a one-year, $500,000 deal, maybe a third or a quarter of what he would likely have gotten in a clean free-agent market.

Dawson provided the Cubs with a career-high 49 home runs,

leading the National League in that category and in RBI, winning a Gold Glove (primarily on reputation at that point), a Silver Slugger, and the NL MVP award, the last one by a significant margin over St. Louis defensive wizard Ozzie Smith and Smith's teammate Jack Clark. The vote was silly at the time but has since become a standard example for the sheer idiocy of past awards voting, where the MVP usually just went to the league leader in RBI and the Cy Young to the league leader in pitching wins, because not only was Dawson *not* the National League's most valuable player, he wasn't even in its top ten.

To hit all those home runs and drive all those other runners in, Dawson had to get to the plate a ton of times, and in the process he made a lot of outs—the fifth-most outs at the plate by any hitter in the National League that year. Think of those outs as the cost of the production: To "buy" the 49 homers and the 24 doubles and the hits and the walks and so on, the Cubs had to "pay" with 445 outs. Dawson's OBP of .328 was the 42nd best in the NL that year out of 56 hitters who had enough plate appearances to qualify for the batting average title; that OBP means that he made an out in 67.2 percent of his trips to the plate. The beat writers who voted on the MVP award focused on what Dawson did in the one-third of his plate appearances where he did something good and ignored the two-thirds where he didn't.

The voting results are even harder to fathom today because the NL player who actually was the most valuable in 1987 was a household name at the time and remains one today, so it's not a case of voters overlooking an unknown or disliked player in favor of a more popular one. The real MVP of the NL in 1987 was future Hall of Famer Tony Gwynn.

Gwynn and Dawson had nearly identical totals of plate appearances in 1987, with Gwynn getting 680 to Dawson's 662, yet Gwynn did much, much more with his trips to the plate than Dawson did. Other than home runs, where Dawson's total of 49 dwarfed Gwynn's total of 7, Gwynn led Dawson in commanding fashion in every other category that mattered, especially the one that most explicitly addressed a hitter's fundamental job: don't make an out.

Dawson made 70 more outs at the plate than Gwynn did in 1987, even though Gwynn had a few more plate appearances. Gwynn had more singles, more doubles, more triples, and more walks than Dawson did, reaching base in 44.7 percent of his trips the plate, compared to Dawson's 32.8 percent. The cost of Dawson's production relative to Gwynn's was all of those extra outs. Gwynn made fewer outs and provided those singles, doubles, triples, or walks, each of which increased rather than decreased the Padres' chances of scoring runs.*

Gwynn was also a better baserunner and defender than Dawson in 1987, which should have made the voters' choice easier—and he was a beloved figure, witty and popular and good with the press, so even some of the usual nonsense that might have hurt a candidate (like Clark) didn't apply here. Instead, 11 of the 24 ballots listed Dawson first overall, while none had Gwynn at the top, and Dawson garnered 269 voting points[†] to win the award, while Gwynn only earned 75 points and finished eighth. It probably didn't help Gwynn's cause that the Padres finished with the worst record in the league that year, but the Cubs didn't fare much better, going 76-85 to finish last in the National League East.

Egregious as this vote was, there are plenty more like it, often between players even more beloved and revered in Cooperstown. Another botched MVP vote came in 1941, pitting a popular Yankee

---

* Mathy stuff: Using the run estimation values from Pete Palmer, who created the sabermetric stat Batting Runs by calculating an estimated run-production value for each offensive event, Gwynn's offense alone, ignoring defense and baserunning, was worth about 6 runs more than Dawson's:

Batting Runs = .47H + .38D + .55T + .93HR + .33(W + HB) −.28 Outs

Gwynn's BR = .47 * 218 H + .38 * 36 D + .55 * 13 T + .93 * 7 HR + .33 (82 W + 3 HB) −.28 * 375 outs = 54

Dawson's BR = .47 * 178 H + .38 * 24 D + .55 * 2 T + .93 * 49 HR + .33 (32 W + 7 HB) −.28 * 445 outs = 29

So, despite Dawson's enormous advantage in home runs, Gwynn was actually the more valuable hitter by 25 runs because he did more of everything else and did it while making fewer outs.

† A player earns 14 points for a first-place vote, 9 for a second-place vote, 8 for third, and so on down to 1 point for a tenth-place vote.

who set a record that still stands as of this writing by collecting a hit
in 56 straight games against a less-popular member of the Red Sox
who set a record for the highest OBP in a single season that stood
until 2002.

Both Joe DiMaggio (Joltin' Joe, the Yankee Clipper) and Ted Williams (the Kid, Teddy Ballgame, the Splendid Splinter) stand in the
inner circle of all-time greats in the history of baseball. Both are
obvious Hall of Famers, on merit and on the whole "fame" thing.
DiMaggio inspired his own song while still playing, and then appeared in an iconic line from Simon & Garfunkel's "Mrs. Robinson."
Williams became a highly decorated pilot, serving in World War II
and the Korean War, and his retirement inspired one of the most fa-
mous pieces of literary baseball writing ever, novelist John Updike's
New Yorker essay "Hub Fans Bid Kid Adieu," which itself opens
with an iconic line: "Fenway Park, in Boston, is a lyric little bandbox
of a ballpark."

But in 1941, the twenty-six-year-old DiMaggio and the twenty-
two-year-old Williams were the two best position players in the
American League, rising stars in a country not yet at war, playing
for bitter rivals who would eventually finish 1-2 in the standings,
with the Yankees taking the pennant by 17 games. DiMaggio's hitting streak made him front-page news for much of the summer and
enhanced his stature as a celebrity beyond the field, but even those
56 games couldn't get him close to Williams's level of production.

Stats from 1941 look like typos today given how strikeouts are
now at record levels in the majors, but Williams and DiMaggio were
especially adept at putting the ball in play. Williams punched out
only 27 times in 1941, the lowest total in any of the 13 seasons
where he qualified for the batting average title. DiMaggio struck out
just 13 times in 1941, the lowest figure of any of his 13 seasons; in
April and May 2016, Colorado shortstop Trevor Story struck out at
least once in 24 consecutive games, 41 strikeouts in total, more than
DiMaggio ever struck out in any single season of his career.

DiMaggio's hitting streak helped him to a fine season,
.357/.440/.643, 43 doubles, 11 triples, 30 homers, and, if you care

about such things, 125 RBI. In many years that might have made him the (lowercase) most valuable player, but in 1941 he couldn't touch Williams's line: .406/.553/.735, 33 doubles, 3 triples, 37 homers, and 120 RBI. The two players' power outputs were similar, especially when you consider that Fenway Park was an easier place to hit for power than Yankee Stadium was in 1941, but DiMaggio made 78 more outs that season than Williams did in just 16 more plate appearances. That gap is how Williams led DiMaggio by more than 100 points of OBP, and no player other than Barry Bonds has ever posted a higher on-base percentage than Williams did that year.

The hitting streak and the players' relative popularity with the press—Williams's antagonistic relationship with writers was well documented during and after his career, including in his own memoir—trumped Williams's commanding advantage in, you know, actual value. DiMaggio took 15 first-place votes to Williams's 8 (one writer, likely from Chicago, put White Sox pitcher Thornton Lee first) and won the award 291 points to 254. And that is how the player who put up one of the 30 most valuable seasons by any hitter in MLB history ended up without an MVP award to show for it.

One reason why fans don't seem to consider the "cost" of production in terms of outs is that we don't really count outs as an individual stat. We count hits, and walks, and specific types of hits, and we count certain outs like strikeouts and sacrifice flies and double plays (which aren't even an individual stat, really), but there's no column even on most online sortable stat pages that says "Outs." Some sites, like Baseball-Reference, provide "Outs" but calculate it in peculiar fashion, double-counting those times the hitter grounded into a double play, adding in times caught stealing (that's not his at bat), even adding in sacrifice hits (often a manager's call, which is why we exclude them from plate appearances entirely).

In fact, just looking at the all-time leaders in outs casts a bit of a new light on some of the all-time leaders in certain offensive categories:

Player	Outs*
Pete Rose	9876
Hank Aaron	8714
Carl Yastrzemski	8674
Cal Ripken Jr	8494
Eddie Murray	8209
Robin Yount	7989
Dave Winfield	7988
Rickey Henderson	7973
Brooks Robinson	7920
Craig Biggio	7897
Omar Vizquel	7803
Derek Jeter	7788
Willie Mays	7689
Luis Aparicio	7629
Paul Molitor	7625
Rafael Palmeiro	7571
Rabbit Maranville	7473
Alex Rodriguez	7452
Lou Brock	7355
Ty Cobb	7245

*"Outs" here just refers to outs made specifically by the player in his at bats, and is equal to AB + SF− H.

Pete Rose is the Hit King, with more hits (4,256) than any other player in MLB history, having passed Ty Cobb's previous record of 4,192 in September 1985. But to get there, Rose had to make more outs than any other hitter in MLB history, 2,600 more than Cobb did. (Granted, Cobb played a very different game, with his entire career in the dead-ball era—and prior to integration as well.) This doesn't change the fact that Rose is MLB's all-time leader in hits, but the magnitude of that accomplishment is diminished by how many extra outs he made to get there.

The next nine players on the list are all in the Hall of Fame, followed by Omar Vizquel—whose poor case for the Hall of Fame I discussed in the chapter on fielding percentage—and certain Hall of

Famer Derek Jeter. Rabbit Maranville is the only name that might be unfamiliar to some readers, and if you know him at all, it's probably because so many folks have called him the worst player (or simply one of the worst players) in the Hall of Fame.

Then there's Finger-Pointin' Raffy, Rafael Palmeiro, who testified before Congress that he'd never taken performance-enhancing drugs (PEDs), then tested positive for an anabolic steroid, stanozolol, a few days after recording his 3,000th hit. The Baseball Writers' Association of America, a subset of whose members vote for the Hall of Fame, would likely have given Palmeiro the honor had he not failed this test, but instead he failed to reach the 5 percent threshold to remain on the ballot in his fourth year and did not appear on the ballot again.

On merit, Palmeiro probably had a Hall of Fame–caliber career; *Sports Illustrated* writer and author Jay Jaffe's work on Hall of Famers pegs Palmeiro's production as about average for a Hall of Fame first baseman. He's among the top 100 players of all time as measured by the total-value metric Wins Above Replacement, and his career total of 569 home runs would, in and of itself, have meant automatic enshrinement in an earlier era. I'm not going to argue that Palmeiro was not a Hall of Famer as a player, or that he wasn't good, but you can see why his case was soft enough that the failed test was the death knell for his candidacy rather than just a point against him.

Palmeiro produced, but at some cost. His career OBP of .371 ranks just 248th all-time, and he only finished in the top ten in his league in OBP twice, finishing 9th in the AL in 1999 and 2002. Palmeiro did damage when he didn't make an out, but he made more outs than any other member of the 500 home run club except for Hank Aaron (755 homers), Alex Rodriguez (696), Willie Mays (660), and Eddie Murray (504).

"Steady Eddie" might be—or have been—Palmeiro's most favorable comparison, another first baseman who was never a star but was an above-average big leaguer for a very long time, and, like Palmeiro, wasn't particularly well liked by teammates. In fact, in the somewhat frivolous stat called a Similarity Score, developed by Bill James as a rough way to measure how similar the career stats of two players are, Murray is the second-most-similar player to Palmeiro, and Palmeiro is the most similar player to Murray. Murray played a bit longer, and if you adjust for the different offensive eras in which they played, with Palmeiro's production worth a bit less because he played in a much higher run-scoring period, their offensive production comes out nearly even. If you believe that Hall of Fame credentials adhere to the transitive property, then if Murray's in, Palmeiro belongs in, too. But since Palmeiro's candidacy revolved heavily around the two big milestones—3,000 hits and 500 homers—it's fair to look at the cost of that production, which in his case was higher than that of his peers.

In the end, it's not that making outs makes you a bad hitter or entirely negates the value you bring to your team. Looking at the names on that list, it would be hard to argue that any of them weren't assets to their teams. But hits alone aren't enough to judge the full scope of a hitter's contribution.

If you tell me I can only know one thing about a hitter, I want to know how often he gets on base—that is, how often he doesn't make an out. It's a simple number that encapsulates a couple of core skills, from the ability to make contact to plate discipline and pitch recognition, and has more predictive value going forward than batting average does. It also covers every time the batter came to the plate and did something related to hitting; the only things excluded are freak events like reaching on catcher's interference or managerial mistakes like sacrifice bunts.

Of course, it's not a complete measure of what a hitter did at the plate. It treats a single and a home run as equivalent events, because in the eyes of on-base percentage, they are equivalent: The hitter reached base safely. OBP is essentially a binary stat—you did or you didn't, period. To get more detail on the value a hitter produced, we need to look at other statistics, and eventually we'll have to find a way to put these different pieces together into a measurement of the whole player.

9

The Power and the Glory:

Slugging Percentage and OPS

In 1975, Mike Schmidt, the twenty-five-year-old third baseman for the Philadelphia Phillies, posted a .249 batting average, which ranked him 50th out of 62 qualifying hitters in the National League that year. Schmidt could work a walk even at that young age, so his OBP was much better at .367, but still not even top 20 in the league. So how did he end up the second-most-valuable player, by modern metrics, in the NL that year?

Schmidt didn't hit for much average, but when he did hit, he hit it hard. He led the National League with 38 home runs, and finished in the top ten in doubles with 34. Add in three triples and he led the league in extra-base hits and was fourth in total bases. That gave him a slugging percentage, a crude but effective rate stat that rewards power, of .523, good for third in the NL, night and day compared to his standing in the other common rate stats.

Schmidt is one of the greatest players in the game's history and 1975 wasn't even one of his best seasons, but he hit for so much power even in what was, for him, a "down" year that he was still among the league's best position players. Of the stats you might find on the back of Schmidt's baseball card, slugging percentage gives you the best explanation of why.

Slugging percentage gets to the stuff on-base percentage doesn't: power. It's a brute-force approach to the question, just taking a player's total bases and dividing that into his at bats.*

Slugging percentage correlates with run-scoring better than straight batting average, albeit not quite as well as on-base percentage. This makes intuitive sense, as slugging percentage incorporates more information than just plain batting average does, but less than on-base percentage. Of course, combining the two in some form will give us even more information about a team's underlying offensive performance . . . but that will have to wait for the moment.

Slugging percentage is, in many ways, just smarter batting average. Whereas batting average treats all hits as having equal value, slugging percentage assigns each hit a whole-number value—the number of bases the hitter reached safely as a result of the hit. A single is worth one base, a double two, a triple three, and a home run four. Those numbers are not precise measures of those hits' actual in-game values, but they are more accurate than simply assuming every hit is the same. We know that an infield single and a home run into the gloaming are not equal. To take one extreme, if absurd, example:

Player, Year	Singles	2B	3B	HR	AVG	SLG
Luis Castillo, 2000	158	17	3	2	.334	.388
Barry Bonds, 2001	49	32	2	73	.328	.863

I assume it is fairly obvious which of these players was more valuable based on the information above, but batting average alone would argue in favor of Louis Castillo, or that the two were roughly equal in value, because of how much information it omits—in this case, 71 homers and 15 doubles of omission.

---

* The specific formula is (1*singles + 2*doubles + 3*triples + 4*home runs)/at bats, which is equal to (hits + doubles + 2*triples + 3*home runs)/at bats. Total bases is the shorthand for the numerator in the first equation.

Even in recent history, the tendency within and outside of the game has been to speak of hitters' power by their home runs and RBI. I've discussed the RBI in a previous chapter, but to reiterate, the use of even a rough stat like slugging beats home runs and RBI for a few reasons.

- RBI are context-dependent—the guys in front of you in the lineup have to get on base—while slugging has no such dependence on who else is in the lineup or how they perform.

- Slugging percentage also includes doubles and triples, which are measures of power and to some extent speed, while home runs and RBI exclude those entirely. (Triples are an oddball occurrence; in the modern game, they're relatively infrequent, and hitters who get a lot of them tend to have one or both of two factors working in their favor: they're fast, or they play in ballparks that have deep outfields that favor triples.)

- Slugging percentage is a rate statistic, whereas home runs and RBI are bulk or counting statistics. The more you play, the better those two stats get, while slugging percentage measures total bases per at bat, so it increases only with more production rather than more playing time.

Team slugging percentage's correlation to team run-scoring (again using the coefficient of correlation tool) is 0.846, or about 84.6 percent, from 1901 to the present. If we start in 1921, the beginning of the live-ball era, the correlation creeps up slightly to 86.5 percent. Measuring home runs alone, either in the aggregate or on a per-game basis, against runs scored produces correlations in the 49–58 percent range depending on time period. If you hit for more power, you score more runs, whether we're talking doubles or triples or homers or even folding singles back into the equation. (Deleting singles and looking just at extra-base hits, a statistic known as isolated power and which is equal to slugging percentage minus batting average, drops the correlation to runs/game to 65 percent.)

How telling are on-base percentage and slugging percentage? Looking at the top 100 offensive seasons in history according to Baseball-Reference,* all one hundred hitters posted at least a .410 OBP (Frank Robinson, 1966), and only one hitter posted a slugging percentage under .550 (Nap Lajoie, 1910, the middle of the dead-ball era). Willie Mays had the best season ever by a player with an OBP below .400, when he hit 52 homers with a .398 OBP in 1965 for the San Francisco Giants. Several dead-ball era hitters had all-time great seasons with slugging percentages below .500, but the best of those since 1920 came in 1988, when Wade Boggs hit .366/.476/.490, leading the league in batting average, OBP, and in doubles with 45.

Boggs is an interesting case study in producing value via OBP without home-run power. Boggs slugged .500 just once in his eighteen-year Hall of Fame career, during the rabbit ball season of 1987, his only season with more than 11 home runs. He led the American League in OBP six times, had over 3,000 hits and 1,400 walks, and retired with the 14th-best career OBP of the modern era. Baseball-Reference ranks him 30th all-time among position players in offensive value produced, even with just 118 career homers and a .443 career slugging percentage.

A big part of why slugging percentage has become so valuable to the modern game, and largely replaced batting average in its usefulness in the process, is that it's a stat that actually reflects the evolution of modern baseball. In earlier eras of baseball, batting average was sufficient because there weren't as many people hitting for power, but because the game itself has changed, the metrics we use to examine it have to change as well.

Today's game would be unrecognizable for a time traveler from 1890 or 1915, not just because of technology or the presence of nonwhite players (although those are rather significant upgrades),

---

* Using the Batting Runs stat, which adds up the values of all offensive events into a single total, adjusted for park and year.

but because the way the game itself is played is so different from how it was played a century or more ago. The original spirit of the game was that hitters were there to put the ball in play; striking out was disdained, and home runs didn't come into vogue until Babe Ruth became a full-time hitter at the end of the 1910s and started out-homering entire teams, beginning the first New York Yankee dynasty.

On average, in the dead-ball era, which ended around 1920, each team would hit about a homer every five games, which seems hard to fathom if you're under the age of about forty and have never seen anything but the current high-offense era of the sport. Home run totals gradually crept up into the early 1960s, with a brief dip during World War II, then experienced a drought in the late 1960s around some rule changes (including the disastrous decision to raise the mound in 1968) and a wave of higher-velocity starters like Bob Gibson and Nolan Ryan. MLB crossed the one homer per team per game margin first in 1987's rabbit ball year, crossed it again in the strike year of 1994, and has been at one or more in sixteen of the twenty full seasons since then, peaking at 1.17—seven homers per six team-games—in 2000. While the shape of offensive performance has changed many times in the game's history, the home run is not going anywhere; predictions, for example, that home run rates would drop with improved testing for PEDs have not borne out in reality, as we're below the 2000 peak but still well above any point in MLB history from prior to 1994.

As home runs have increased, however, so have strikeouts, which stands to reason as swinging harder to try to maximize power (making harder contact, which we now measure via the ball's "exit velocity" off the bat) also means swinging and missing more frequently. Strikeouts per team per game didn't even reach four until 1952— that is, four strikeouts per side in a game, so eight total given that it's hard to play a game without two teams—but crossed five before the decade was out. In 1994, when MLB crossed the one homer per team-game barrier and stayed there for fifteen years, strikeouts also spiked, crossing the six per team-game mark that same season, then hitting seven in 2010. As I write this in mid-2016, MLB is on pace for an all-time high of more than eight strikeouts per team-game—sixteen per game total, more than double where the rate was in the dead-ball era.

The rise in power has come with more strikeouts, which again makes intuitive sense, but the more subtle effect is that more strikeouts make hitting for power much more important, too. If you're putting fewer balls in play overall, you need to accomplish more when you do put the ball in play. Batting averages and on-base percentages haven't changed much over the last 115 years, but slugging percentage has. Home runs are at historical highs, and doubles have returned to their 1930ish peak level. (The 1930 season itself was an early rabbit ball year, as run-scoring jumped across the game; three of the seven cases in history of a batter knocking in 170 or more runs occurred that year, and Hack Wilson's 56 home runs in 1930 stood as the NL record until 1997.) Hitters are bigger and stronger than ever, and pitchers are throwing harder than ever, which has resulted in harder contact and more swings and misses. It's still our game, but it's not the game our great-grandparents knew, and that makes evaluating hitters strictly on batting average even more foolish than it was back then. If you aren't hitting for power as a team in 2016 and beyond, you're not going to score enough runs to compete: in the 232 complete league-seasons from 1901 through 2015, 139 of the teams that led their respective leagues in slugging percentage also led their leagues in runs scored.

Slugging percentage, by itself, only tells a portion of the story; it's leaving out lots of information, including a hitter's ability to draw a walk, and it doesn't value events perfectly. But as a quick look at a hitter's power output, it's useful. The top ten players in MLB history by career slugging percentage include seven inner-circle Hall of Famers, along with Barry Bonds, Mark McGwire, and Manny Ramirez. The next ten include four more Hall of Famers, eventual members Albert Pujols and Miguel Cabrera, and Mike Trout, who is threatening to rewrite the record books by the time he's done. Hank Aaron ranks 22nd, right behind Frank Thomas. If you hit for power, you'll have a high slugging percentage, and if you do that you're probably among the all-time greats.

So, if OBP is good, and slugging percentage is good, and each stat includes important information the other one doesn't, why don't we just add them together and get one glorious stat that covers everything! This stat exists, and has entered the mainstream in the last decade, under the name of OPS, for on-base plus slugging. It's an ugly mess underneath the hood, and I do not use it in my writing or any kind of evaluation of individual players . . . but at a team level it actually works rather well at the one thing that matters: predicting runs scored.

OPS itself is just bad math. If you think back to fourth grade, you'll remember that you can't add two fractions with unlike denominators, yet that's exactly what OPS does. On-base percentage is just the number of times a hitter reached base safely divided by most of his plate appearances. Slugging percentage is a hitter's total bases divided by his at bats, a denominator that in nearly all cases will be smaller than the denominator of OBP because it doesn't include walks, sacrifice flies, or times hit by pitch. If you do this in elementary school, you get back a paper covered with red ink, and maybe a dunce cap. If you do it in baseball writing, you get a gold star.

The problem with OPS's formula—if it even rises to the level of a formula, rather than a mash-up the way a toddler smushes two lumps of Play-Doh together and calls it a present for Mommy—is more than just an academic one. The two components have vastly different scales, so adding them together underweights one component, OBP, and overweights the other, slugging.

Imagine two players, each with an .800 OPS in the same total number of plate appearances. Player A has a .300 OBP and a .500 slugging percentage. Player B has a .400 OBP and .400 slugging percentage. Which player was more valuable at the plate?

Before I answer that—and it may be obvious already—consider why the scaling issue of the two components of OPS is a problem. The range of on-base percentages for full-time hitters in MLB in 2016 ran from .256 (Wilson Ramos, Washington Nationals) to .460 (Bryce Harper, also Washington Nationals). Of 141 qualifying hitters, meaning hitters who had 3.1 plate appearances per game their teams played, 115 fell between .300 and .400, about 82 percent of the total.

The range of slugging percentages, however, ran from .320 (Alcides Escobar, Kansas City Royals) to .649 (young Mr. Harper, again). That's a span of 329 "points" of slugging from high to low, compared to 204 points for OBP. A similar span covering 82 percent of hitters around the middle of the slugging distribution would run from .358 to .540, about a 142-point swing compared to the 100-point swing I chose when looking at OBP. These two ratios operate on different scales, because they're measuring different counting events on top and dividing them by different units on the bottom, with OBP's units by definition equal to or larger than the quantity in slugging. I love pesto, and I love hot fudge, but I can't just mix the two together and pretend I've only kept the best of both sauces.

If your memory is particularly astute, or you're about half my age, you may have thought of the way you can in fact add two fractions with differing denominators: finding the lowest common denominator of the two fractions. You do this by multiplying each figure by some fraction equivalent to one, and then adding the numerators with the new denominator staying in place. If you were to do that with on-base percentage and slugging percentage, you'd probably get a more telling number, but it would lose the ease of calculation of OPS, and the final number wouldn't accurately weight a hitter's ability to get on base.

All this talk of fractions and denominators only speaks to part of the problem with OPS. The larger, more looming issue with OPS is that all bases achieved are not created equal. The hardest thing to do in baseball is to get to first base, and on-base percentage measures only that: how often the hitter, or the team's hitters, got to first base safely—that is, did not make an out at the plate. Doing so is difficult, of course; the aggregate on-base percentage of all MLB hitters in 2015 was .317, meaning that 69.3 percent of the time all hitters came to the plate (excluding sac bunts and a few other rarities), they either made an out or did something that should have resulted in one or more outs but was mishandled by a fielder. Once that hitter is out, it's over. He's dead, Jim. He's not coming back.

Compare that to the question of the extra base once a runner has already reached first. Almost exactly one in three hits results in extra bases, but even a batter who singles can still be advanced by subsequent events, whether they're more hits, walks, or even certain field outs. It's much harder to get to first base than it is to advance to bases beyond that.

If you recall the run expectancy table from chapter 5, you can see the specific boost from getting to first base dwarfs the gain from each additional base after that. Here's the same table, reorganized to highlight what each additional base is worth:

Expected Runs for the Remainder of an Inning from a Specific Base-Out State.

Runners	0 Out	1 Out	2 Outs
000 (none on)	0.479	0.2572	0.0996
100 (man on first)	0.8427	0.5004	0.2203
020 (man on second)	1.0762	0.6487	0.3154
003 (man on third)	1.3045	0.8916	0.3606
Gain from previous state			
Reaching first base from batter's box	0.3637	0.2432	0.1207
Reaching second base from first	0.2335	0.1483	0.0951
Reaching third base from second	0.2283	0.2429	0.0452

Aside: You'll notice that little blip in the bottom middle, where reaching third base from second with one out is the most valuable thing a hitter can do other than reaching first base to begin with. With one out (or zero), that runner can still score on many kinds of outs in play, which isn't true with two outs. This is why the attempt to steal third base with one out is more valuable than doing so with zero outs, when any number of subsequent events might score that same runner from second, or with two outs, when you're ending the inning for only a tiny potential gain.

For any specific number of outs, getting to first base is the most valuable thing a batter can do. Stretching a single into a double or a double into a triple is still valuable, but the best thing the batter will do once he leaves the batter's box is step on first base safely.

Extra-base hits have additional value, which I'll explore more when
I discuss how teams think about and measure offensive performance
in the chapter that explains linear weights, because they can score
more runners that are already on base than a single can. The value of
extra bases is not enough to make slugging percentage as important
as OBP.

Because not all bases achieved are worth the same thing, these
little tangents add up to one key point about looking at on-base percentage and slugging percentage independently, and that you can't
forget when looking at OPS: one more point of OBP is worth more
than one more point of slugging percentage. (A point here refers to
.001, or one-thousandth, equal to reaching base one more time in
1,000 PA or accumulating one more total base in 1,000 at bats.) In
Moneyball, still an essential read for anyone looking to understand
more about how front offices are thinking about the game even
today, author Michael Lewis quotes Paul DePodesta, at the time an
executive for the Oakland A's, as saying that a point of OBP was
worth three times as much as a point of slugging, if not more. The
precise value is lower than that, but he was directionally correct. If
the baseball gods told you, the GM of a major-league team, that you
could give one player in your system a potion that would grant that
player the ability to raise his OBP by 10 points or his slugging by 10
points—or even 15 points—you'd take the OBP potion every single
time.

That should make the answer to the question at the start of the section obvious: you take the guy with the .400 OBP and .400 SLG over
the guy with the .300 OBP and the .500 SLG. The first guy, Johnny
Walksalot, will reach base 60 more times in a typical 600 at bat season, meaning he'll make 60 fewer outs, than the second guy, Tommy
Hackenstein. Hackenstein compensates with 60 extra bases—say, 30
more doubles and 10 more homers, or no more doubles and 20 more
homers than Walksalot. But the cost of those extra bases is those
60 outs, and you would not trade 60 outs to get 60 more bases,
just as you would not accept a 50 percent caught-stealing rate from
a baserunner. It can seem counterintuitive if you've never thought

about hits or bases having a cost before, but the cost in outs is real—the great Baltimore Orioles manager Earl Weaver always preached that outs were precious, since your supply of them is limited—and understanding that cost allows you to see when a player who seems to produce more stuff is actually less valuable.

Yet OPS would tell you that Walksalot and Hackenstein are equally valuable, or equally productive, because each has an OPS of .800. The stat obscures useful information. So why do so many people use it?

One obvious reason is that it's easy. Everyone wants a single number that sums up a player. It's much easier to say that Joey Bagodonuts is a .900 OPS guy than to start breaking him down in two or three different numbers, even though the latter approach gives you a more complete picture of the player's abilities. And I can tell you that when discussing players on live radio or TV, you don't often have a lot of time to make your points, so a shorthand like OPS is appealing (even though I don't use it) because in two seconds you've slapped a number on that player to say he's good or he's bad.

But, in spite of all the objections I raised above, the truth about OPS at the team level is that the damn thing works: it correlates better with team runs scored than OBP or SLG do alone. Where OBP's coefficient of correlation to runs per game is .893, and slugging's is .846, OPS's is 0.914. It's a modest improvement, but it is indeed better. We can fine-tune that to crank up the correlation even more, and we will do that in a later chapter to get a more precise way of valuing hitter performance, but for a quick and dirty measure of team offense, OPS does the job—in ugly fashion, yes, but it does it.

Where OPS fails us is at the player level, yet that's where you're most likely to see it used—by fans, writers, even occasionally by a team executive discussing a player in the media. A player can post an .800 OPS and be a below-average hitter; he can post a .750 OPS and be an above-average one. Now, if a player has an 1.100 OPS or a .500 OPS, that's probably all you need to know about him—the first is a star and the second one had better be a pitcher—

but most of the players you're going to want to know about fall somewhere in the great middle.

The allure of a single number that sums up a player's performance is tough to ignore, something I'll return to in the discussion of WAR (Wins Above Replacement), but in this particular case you're better off with two numbers, OBP and slugging, separately than you are with one.

10

wOBA/WRC:

The Ultimate Measure of the Hitter (Until the Next One)

People want a number. They don't want lots of numbers, because that's too many numbers. They want one number that answers the question. That's a mixed bag, because one number destroys all nuance. It doesn't show your work; it just gives the answer, without context. You could apply this to many spheres of life, and it's no less true in baseball than anywhere else. Fans and writers want to point to a single number that sums the whole player up. He's a 20-game winner. He's a .300 hitter. Incomplete picture be damned, let's just slap a number on that fella and call it a day!

A single number does actually help us, because it gives us a quicker means of comparing multiple players, and eventually a team has to decide what a player's production is worth in one dollar figure. The key is to work with numbers that capture everything a player does and weights each of those things accordingly. I've mentioned linear weights and Batting Runs as the way to total up the values of all a hitter's contributions over the course of some period of time—

including deducting value for the outs he makes—to give us a bulk total figure. This hitter produced 55 runs of value in 2015; this other hitter produced 46 runs of value; therefore, if you didn't catch it already, the first hitter was a more productive hitter.

Bulk totals, also called counting or cumulative stats, are not scaled for playing time; if Joey Bagodonuts played 162 games and Jimmy Ballplayer only played 110 games, but each produced 50 runs of value by his hits, walks, extra bases, and so on, then Jimmy was the better player on a per-game basis. Looking strictly at the bulk number doesn't give us that information, so our desire for the One True Number leads us astray again.

While the flaws in OPS on a player level are clear, you can at least understand the intention: to take two common numbers and combine them to get the best of both stats. There are many numbers floating around that attempt to provide a "one number" answer for hitters on a rate basis, something like batting average, maybe even that looks like batting average, but that includes everything we'd want to know about a hitter's performance. For some time, we had runs created per 27 outs, which was wildly imprecise, followed by Equivalent (now True) Average from Clay Davenport and Baseball Prospectus, and VORP (Value Over Replacement Level) and VORPr from Keith Woolner . . . and so on. There was even Total Average, developed by *Washington Post* writer Thomas Boswell, a rather stunning bit of innumeracy that just added a bunch of stuff together without regard for whether these things actually *should* be added together, then divided it by some other stuff without regard for common decency. It had the veneer of legitimacy but, as any computer programmer will tell you, garbage in yields garbage out. None of these ever really caught on, and even the stats I like to use for this purpose have failed to make much of a dent in the public discourse.

The best of these new rate stats is called wOBA, or weighted on-base average, and was created by sabermetrician Tom Tango to provide a rate on the same scale as OBP that considered all batter events: hits, extra bases, walks, times hit by pitch, and outs. The specific coefficients—that is, the weights assigned to each event—vary slightly by year, depending on the specific offensive environment, but the overall scale that measures wOBA is always the same.* If you look at a hitter's wOBA and see a number that would make a good OBP, then the hitter has a good wOBA and thus is having a very productive season at the plate. A hitter with a .400 wOBA is extremely productive; a hitter with a wOBA under .300 had better be a great fielder—or a pitcher.

To give you a sense of how wOBA works in the real world, here are the leaders in wOBA for 2015 for hitters with enough plate appearances to qualify for the batting title:

Hitter	wOBA	AVG	OBP	SLG
Bryce Harper	.461	.330	.460	.649
Joey Votto	.427	.314	.459	.541
Paul Goldschmidt	.418	.321	.435	.570
Mike Trout	.415	.299	.402	.590
Miguel Cabrera	.413	.338	.440	.534

Harper was the unanimous MVP in the National League and posted one of the best offensive seasons in major-league history; the American League MVP, Josh Donaldson, was only sixth in the majors in wOBA—behind both Mike Trout and Miguel Cabrera in wOBA—but he boosted his value with strong defense and getting help from the tired old misbelief that an MVP should come from a playoff team.

And now, the worst hitters in 2015, also by wOBA:

---

* The coefficients change to reflect the changing run environments of the game. When run-scoring is down, runs are scarce, meaning the value of a run is higher, so the value of anything that leads to a run is higher. When run-scoring is up, as it was from 1993 till around 2010, runs are plentiful, so the value of a run is lower. Those 50-homer seasons that became commonplace were less valuable than 40-homer seasons in previous eras. You do not need to know the coefficients to use or even understand wOBA, or similar weighted stats; pay no attention to the statistician behind the curtain and everything will be fine.

Hitter	wOBA	AVG	OBP	SLG
Chris Owings	.255	.227	.264	.322
Wilson Ramos	.265	.229	.258	.358
Jean Segura	.268	.259	.281	.336
Alcides Escobar	.271	.259	.293	.320
Michael Taylor	.274	.227	.282	.358

Owings, Segura, and Escobar are all shortstops, with Owings and Escobar considered above-average defenders. Ramos is a catcher, and Taylor, who lost his job after the season, is a center fielder. It's not a coincidence that hitters this bad all play in the middle of the diamond, where it's harder to find players capable of playing those positions; a corner player with a sub-.300 wOBA shouldn't last very long, because it's easier to find players who can handle those positions and can hit a little more capably. In 2015, nineteen players qualified for the batting title and posted wOBAs below .300; only three played corner positions, and two of the three lost their jobs before the following season.

The main deficiency in wOBA is that it is not park-adjusted—that is, it does not make any adjustment for the ballparks in which the hitter played. A wOBA of .350 in Coors Field in Denver, a tremendous hitter's park at an elevation of 5,200 feet, is not the same as a wOBA of .350 in Petco Park in San Diego, the majors' best pitcher's park, located a mile below sea level (latter figure may be approximate). This matters because in a park where offense is harder to come by, a positive offensive event is worth more, since it takes fewer runs to win a game.

Fangraphs offers a park-adjusted analogue to wOBA called wRC+, weighted Runs Created, which takes a hitter's offensive contributions, adjusts them for park, compares them to the league average, and produces a number around 100: if a hitter's offensive value is greater than league average, his wRC+ will be higher than 100, and if it's lower than the league average, it'll be lower than 100. (The league averages in this case exclude those of pitchers hitting.) The two rate stats are similar, both using the same linear weights model underneath, but wRC+ adds park adjustments while creating a less intuitive, nonlinear scale.

Although comparing any player's production to the league average is useful in an industry where "average" is extremely valuable and the language of evaluation has always included references to above- or below-average tools or players, I think wRC+'s scale can be misleading. Some is simple arithmetic—a player who is twice as productive as the league average will have a wRC+ of 200, 100 points above the average, while a player who is half of league average will have a wRC+ of 50, 50 points below the league average. But the bigger problem is that value in baseball is *nonlinear*—that is, a player who produces twice as much as another player is not simply "worth" twice as much, because roster spots are limited.

Mike Trout's production at the plate alone has been worth about 53 runs a year above average in his career through 2016. If you could trade Trout for two players who have been worth 26.5 runs per year apiece—assuming for the moment that other stuff, like salary and age, are equal—would you do it? Looking just at the baseball rationale, you shouldn't. Getting those 53 runs of production out of one spot on your twenty-five-man roster is better than getting 53 runs out of two spots, because Trout's production frees up another roster spot for you to go find another productive player. If roster spots were unlimited, then player value might be linear—that is, the player who produces twice as much would probably be worth twice as much, in baseball terms or in financial terms. But with roster spots a scarce resource, getting more production out of a single roster spot is particularly valuable because it gives you more ways to improve in other roster spots. This, incidentally, is why fan- and writer-proposed trades for superstars are nearly always terrible: they assume that throwing five or six names at the Angels (for Trout) or Nationals (for Bryce Harper) would simply overwhelm the team with the superstar into acquiescing. It's almost impossible to get fair value back in a trade for the best player in baseball, and if you could, the other team probably shouldn't do it.

To return to my issue with wRC+, it's the best publicly available, park-adjusted rate stat for hitters . . . which makes it sound terrifying, but in fact, that's the number we want if we're trying to get a sense of how good a hitter was over a season or the year to date. Add up the values of what he did, compared to the outs he generated, and adjust it for the environment(s) in which he played.

Either of these stats would suffice as the One True Number for hitters, assuming you're just looking for a rate statistic that would fill the role since vacated by batting average. "He's a .300 wOBA hitter" doesn't have the same ring to it—I'm still not really comfortable with saying "wobba" instead of just spelling it out, because it's a good way to sound like an idiot—but it answers the question of how good a hitter the player is. I happen to prefer wOBA, even without the park adjustments, because the scale is more intuitive to me and to my regular readers, although I rarely present it without also providing the triple-slash line of average/OBP/slugging. You could also use wRC+ if the scaling doesn't bother you and you prefer a park-adjusted number. If you want that one number to sum up a hitter's offensive rate of productivity, either of these would fit the bill.

11

ERA and the Riddle of Pitching Versus Defense

Let's get back to the pitcher, evaluating whom has been at the heart of many statistical advances and sabermetric debates, inside and outside of front offices, over the last twenty years.

We've dispensed with the anachronism of pitcher wins and the two-steps-back "progress" of the save rule, but we have to judge pitchers by something. Why not earned run average (ERA), that old standby of baseball cards and on-screen graphics that complements won-lost record to try to give us a more complete picture of the pitcher's performance? His job is to avoid giving up runs, so a stat that reflects how many runs he gave up per game should be good, right?

The answer is yes . . . and no. While it's by no means a "new" stat, ERA has clear value in helping us understand what happened while the pitcher was on the mound, but it's very noisy, meaning that there are a lot of other confounding factors that can cloud the "signal," the indication of just how well that pitcher actually pitched. You'll know a lot more about how well a pitcher performed if you look at ERA rather than won-lost record, but you'll still only have a vague idea because of how ERA is calculated and because it assumes that the pitcher was solely responsible for those runs that he allowed (or didn't allow).

There are single metrics that encapsulate the total production of a hitter, whether as a rate (wOBA, wRC+) or as a total (Batting Runs or any other linear-weights stat). Offense, as the sabermetricians in the Bluth family might say, is a freebie: other than park effects there isn't a ton of noise to clean up in a typical hitter's line. We can talk about whether a hitter did something that he's unlikely to repeat, but calculating the value of what he did is pretty straightforward.

Pitching, on the other hand, is much harder to evaluate the same way, because pitching isn't simply the converse of hitting. A hitter's performance is an independent phenomenon, but the same can't be said of a pitcher's performance, which includes all kinds of outside influences that can't be easily disentangled from the pitcher's own contributions. The pitcher is part of a team's run prevention, and so is the team's defense, a relationship that has been at the heart of sabermetric advances and debates for the last fifteen years and that helped drive MLB to adopt new technology so teams can make more progress in this area. Very little of what a pitcher does is "clean" data; if he strikes a batter out or walks a batter, that's just his responsibility, but when the ball is put into play the credit or blame is shared across many players.

This itself is a break from past thinking. Before the year 2000, everyone assumed a pitcher was totally responsible for whether he gave up more or fewer hits. A groundbreaking study around that time showed that this was not the case, and parsing the responsibility for a hit has been a grail of sorts for analysts since then. It turns out that the defense behind a pitcher matters—the quality of the fielders and where they're positioned affects whether a ball hit into play becomes a hit.

Traditional pitcher stats also assign full blame for a run scoring on the pitcher who first put the runner on base. Smith walks a batter, is pulled for reliever Jones, who gives up a home run. Smith is charged with the first run, but didn't Jones play some part in that?

Exonerating the reliever who allows inherited runners to score is like accepting "the runner was already scoring when I got here" as an excuse. But splitting that up isn't as easy as dividing the run in half or into quarters, either.

The good news is that there are myriad ways to attack the question of how much a pitcher's performance was worth. There are multiple new metrics that get at this question, most of which try to adjust the credit or blame to account for the influence of defense or other pitchers. And there are some old stats that, while imperfect, still contain useful information that we shouldn't discard just because the stats are old. One stat in particular tells us less than we thought but still tells us something we want to know: earned run average, commonly known as ERA.

First, let's look just at what ERA is and what it purports to measure. ERA's formula is fairly simple and, for the young me at least, a good way to make a baseball-obsessed kid practice things like multiplying by 9 and dividing double-digit numbers:

*ERA = Earned runs allowed * 9 / Innings pitched*

The idea is to produce a rate stat that shows how many earned runs the pitcher allowed per nine innings pitched, a concept that made perfect sense in an era where pitchers routinely threw complete games, but that still works today because we are very used to thinking in chunks of nine innings. It also creates an easy baseline to compare a pitcher to the league average for runs scored or allowed (same thing) per game. In a league where the average team scores 4 runs a game, a pitcher with a 4.50 RA (run average, slightly different from ERA for reasons I'll get to a bit later) is worse than average; and a pitcher with a 3.50 RA is better.

Earned runs allowed form a subset of total runs allowed; a pitcher can allow a run that is "unearned," in the discretion of the official scorer, if the run scored as a result of a fielder's misplay, either a fielding error or a passed ball. It is incredibly subjective, and can lead to absurd consequences in the case of runs allowed with two outs after an error that would have ended the inning.

For example, on June 5, 1989, Yankees pitcher Andy Hawkins allowed 10 runs in 2+ innings of work against the Orioles, but his ERA went down because none of those runs was earned. In the first inning, Hawkins retired the first two batters, then allowed a double and two walks to load the bases. The next batter, Jim Traber, hit a flyball that center fielder Jesse Barfield misplayed, allowing all three runs to score. Even though Hawkins put all three runners on base himself, the runs were unearned because they scored on an error.

In the third inning, things got ridiculous. The first three batters reached on fielding errors—one by Hawkins himself—allowing the first batter to score. I think we can all agree that dinging Hawkins for that run would be misleading, since he did his job as a pitcher, getting three groundballs that were not fielded cleanly. Hawkins didn't retire another batter at the plate, allowing the next five batters to reach via a single, a double, an intentional walk, and two more singles, with three more runs crossing the plate. Reliever Chuck Cary came in, got a groundout, and then gave up a grand slam, which scored three more of Hawkins's runners, for a total of ten runs charged to Hawkins . . . all of them unearned, because by the time Steve Finley hit that slam, there were two outs.

Once there are two outs and the third out should have been made but wasn't due to an error, every run that scores thereafter is unearned. Hawkins had some bad luck, but he also gave up four clean hits and a walk, which you cannot do without either allowing a run or getting two outs on the bases somewhere. For him to walk out of this with zero earned runs despite allowing eight baserunners in 2⅓ innings pitched is both bizarre and unhelpful if we're trying to use ERA to gauge his performance on that day or on the season as a whole. (As if that weren't enough, Hawkins tied for the American League lead with 111 earned runs allowed that year, and led the league with 127 total runs allowed, finishing with the fourth-worst ERA in the American League.)

Hawkins's 10 unearned runs allowed is tied with Tim Wakefield's performance for the Red Sox on May 5, 1996, for the unofficial record for the second-most UER allowed in one game.* Wakefield's case was more straightforward. In the fourth inning against Toronto, Wakefield allowed a single, a line drive misplayed by the third baseman, and a strikeout, so there was one out and a man on base who'd reached via an error. The first run scored on a passed ball, which is automatically unearned, although Wakefield, a knuckleballer, was especially prone to wild pitches (earned) and passed balls (not). The batter then singled home the runner who'd reached on an error, so that was unearned. After a walk and a flyout, there were men on first and third with two outs, but the hypothetical third out should have been recorded, making everything that came after "unearned" even though there were no more errors or passed balls in the inning.

From there? Single, single, double, two-run home run. Six more runs scored, all unearned even though the runners who scored reached base safely via walk or hit and scored via walk or hit. Wakefield gave up one earned run in the sixth and left the game with two outs and men on first and second. The first batter faced by reliever Mike Maddux (yes, Greg's brother) hit a flyball to right that was misplayed for a two-base error that scored both of the runners Wakefield allowed to reach base safely. That's 11 runs allowed but just one earned run despite Wakefield allowing ten hits and five walks.

This bit of selectivity, identifying some runs that count against a pitcher's ERA and some that don't, is also incredibly subjective because the decision on what constitutes an error belongs to one person, the official scorer, not an analyst, scout, or anyone who might at least bring a better background to the job. A fielder who fails to make a routine play but never touches the ball will almost never be charged with an error, even though the spirit of the earned run rule is to charge the pitcher only with runs he was responsible for allowing; if he got that groundball but the third baseman never touched it, it's not an error, but we might say the pitcher did his job.

---

* The highest unearned-run total for any single game in Baseball-Reference's Play Index, which goes back to 1913, is 13, allowed by Lefty O'Doul on July 7, 1923, when he allowed 16 runs total in 3 innings, in a game his team eventually lost 27–3.

*   *   *

ERA is of limited use when looking at starting pitchers, but it can really miss the mark for relievers, who each year throw about one-third the innings that starters do and frequently come into the game with men on base or leave the game with runners on base for the next guy to try to strand. The problem of inherited runners is one that baseball people have understood for a long time; stats such as Inherited Runners and Inherited Runners Scored have been available for twenty years, showing how many runners were on base when a reliever entered games and how many of them he allowed to cross the plate. Stranding runners is a good thing, but it isn't quite a separate skill from just getting batters out in the first place; if a pitcher can pitch well from the stretch rather than the windup, he'll strand lots of runners, and if he's not very good from the stretch, well, he's probably not going to last long enough in the big leagues for us to get very worked up about his strand rate.

But inherited runners and their analogue, the bequeathed runner—one can imagine a Victorian-era baseball game in which a pitcher departing the game presented his successor with a document laying out exactly which runners were the property of the latter and limiting the ways in which he might dispose of them—pose the problem described earlier in the chapter of assignment of blame. A reliever who comes into a game with the bases loaded and promptly gives up a home run is charged with only one run allowed, even though four scored as a direct result of his actions. And just imagine how that pitcher who walked off the mound having put a runner on every base felt as he watched the home run leave the yard; he'd probably think a somewhat less family-friendly version of "Ye gods, there goes my ERA!"

Distilling the reliever's performance is not fundamentally different from distilling a starter's performance; any pitcher's job is to get outs, preferably via strikeouts (because they can't advance any runners or be misplayed), while avoiding walks and home runs. If all you do is strike guys out, you're not going to let any inherited runners score, in case that wasn't already blindingly obvious to you. A reliever who does these things will be a Good Reliever, and may even grow up to be a Proven Closer™, which is worth a Lot of Money. Current relievers Aroldis Chapman, Craig Kimbrel, Kenley Jansen, and Dellin Betances have posted some of the best strikeout rates in baseball history, and, not coincidentally, they are Good Relievers, with the first three also becoming Proven Closers™ in recent years.

The problem of inherited and bequeathed runners makes ERA especially dicey when looking at a single season for a reliever. A full year of pitching for a reliever might only include 60 innings, so a swing of three runs allowed—say, one day when the reliever left a game with the bases loaded and two outs, only to have the next reliever give up a grand slam—will raise his ERA for the entire year by 0.45. A difference of seven runners bequeathed, scoring or not scoring, would mean over a run in the pitcher's ERA for the year, even though the pitcher himself would not have pitched any differently. (A pitcher who allows 15 runs in 60 innings pitched would have an ERA for the season of 15 * 9/60 = 2.25. That same pitcher, with seven more runs allowed on the year due to other relievers allowing them to score, would see his ERA rise to 22 * 9/60 = 3.30.)

We want our relievers to hold leads, which often means preventing inherited runners from scoring, but then we judge them on superficial statistics that don't reflect whether they did so. Of course, getting outs is any pitcher's primary job, and that will be reflected to some extent in ERA and to a greater extent in other statistics like his opponents' OBP, but it's too easy for a pitcher to come in, fail to clean up someone else's mess, and leave with his ERA intact.

The other major problem with using ERA to measure relievers is the result of the small workloads of the modern reliever: one really bad outing can torch a reliever's season ERA, even if he pitches well in all of his remaining appearances.

Hall of Famer John Smoltz came back as a reliever after missing the 2000 season due to Tommy John surgery, working a mostly full season in 2001 and becoming Atlanta's full-time closer after spending his pre-knife career in the rotation. In 2002, he started the year by throwing a scoreless inning on April 1, and then had the worst outing of his entire career five days later, recording two outs while allowing eight runs (all earned) in an 11–2 loss to the Mets. His season ERA after that outing stood at a comical 43.50, and it never dipped below 3 for the rest of the season. But for the rest of the 2002 season, Smoltz pitched just like the old John Smoltz: 78.2 innings, 22 runs allowed (21 earned), 81 strikeouts, and a 2.40 ERA from April 7 onward, bringing his ERA down from 43.50 to 3.25 after the end of the year. He didn't allow more than three runs in any other appearance in 2002, and in 69 of his 75 appearances on the year, he allowed one run or fewer. That one torching he received on April 6 added nearly nine-tenths of a run to his season ERA and meant the difference between finishing in the top 20 among major-league relievers in ERA that year and finishing 44th overall, just below the MLB median for full-time relievers with at least 60 innings pitched in 2002.

Those eight runs he surrendered still counted—throwing out an outlier just because we don't like it is not good science—but their effect on Atlanta's season didn't extend beyond that one game. Had he had two four-run outings, that would have been worse for the team. Four more two-run outings might have been worse as well, given the way he was typically used, with about two-thirds of his appearances coming with Atlanta tied or winning by one or two runs. For relievers, ERA or even RA is accurate, but it doesn't tell us what we particularly want to know about the pitcher. For any pitcher, ERA includes all kinds of noise that obscures the part of run prevention for which the pitcher was truly responsible, at least to the best of our current understanding.

Though these issues with ERA for starters and relievers are a part of the problem with ERA, the whole concept of the defensive play behind the pitcher is a more looming issue. For much of baseball history, what we long believed about pitchers and allowing runs was simple: if the pitcher allowed the runners to reach and score safely, those runs were on him. It's his job to get outs, any way he can, whether it's via strikeout or groundout or flyout. Every hit was his fault, so to speak, so he'd be charged with any runs resulting from that hit, whether it's that hitter scoring or knocking in another run.

Today teams look at the question differently, because we've increased our understanding of how defenses, from fielding prowess to fielder positioning, affect pitchers' stat lines. The same pitcher might have two different results pitching the same way with the same balls put into play but two different defensive units behind him: the line drive Adrian Beltre fields at third base might get by Nick Castellanos, turning an out into a hit through no fault of the pitcher's own.

There is some pitcher effect on this phenomenon, because pitchers have some control over the types of balls in play they allow. Some pitchers generate lots of groundballs; some are more flyball-prone. Pitchers who give up lots of line drives tend not to last very long because a line drive is about three times as likely to become a hit as a groundball or a flyball. Infield popups are almost never hits, and sometimes are outs by statute (the infield fly rule, which applies with at least two men on base and fewer than two outs). So a pitcher can help his cause in this way, but he can't direct a groundball right to a fielder and he can't make that fielder any better than he actually is.

So ERA is a noisy statistic, but that doesn't mean it's devoid of value. Stripping all context out of ERA to use a component-based alternative also means we're removing some factors the pitcher really could control. I mentioned above that some pitchers exhibit a little control over the results of balls they put into play. It's also true that some pitchers pitch noticeably worse with runners on base (that is, from the stretch, as opposed to pitching from the windup), which can contribute to a gap between their ERAs and what their components might indicate. A pitcher who's terrible with men on base will allow more runs than a pitcher who allows the same rates of hits and walks but doesn't lose effectiveness with men on. Analysts refer to this aspect of run prevention as "sequencing." The order in which things happen matters, even when those things are independent of each other.

The philosophical discrepancy between ERA and alternative measures draws from whether you want a number that is descriptive or one that is more prescriptive. The pitcher with the 4.50 ERA but whose peripherals say he should have had a 3.50 ERA may have just been unlucky, or he may have made poor pitches in high-leverage spots, or some of both. Using component-based stats absolves him of all sins. Using ERA and value-based stats that build off it reflects what actually happened—the pitcher let these batters reach base and they scored. I find this a little unsatisfying because it still hurts the pitcher working in front of a bad defense or whose bullpen comprised seven guys with gas cans and matches, but even in this somewhat theoretical world of what "should have happened" it's important that we don't lose sight of the runs on the scoreboard.

In 2001, an analyst named Voros McCracken discovered that pitchers' hit rates, or batting averages allowed, had little correlation year over year once you factored out the strikeouts, after he noticed that the pitchers who led the league in hits allowed tended to vary wildly from year to year and often included names you wouldn't expect to see on the wrong end of the leaderboards. He showed that pitchers whose batting averages allowed on balls hit into play, now known as BABIP, deviated from the league average tended to regress toward the league average the following year, to the point where we would do better at predicting a pitcher's ERA the next year if we assumed he'd have a league-average BABIP than if we used his actual BABIP. McCracken called the new system DIPS, for Defense-Independent Pitching Statistics, and his discovery underlies all advanced pitching metrics still in use.

BABIP may be new to many of you, but it has become increasingly useful in the sieve major-league teams use to try to separate a pitcher's performance from the effects of defense and luck. It's equal to the number of hits a pitcher allowed divided by the total number of balls he allowed batters to put into play, or BABIP = (H −HR) / (AB −K −HR + SF).* If the variation in a pitcher's BABIP from one

---

* Home runs are typically excluded because they are not balls in play, but hit out of play, so they can't be defended. This isn't an easy or obvious choice, because if you're trying to look at how much quality contact a pitcher gave up when he allowed any contact at all, home runs probably should count. (It also excludes inside-the-park home runs, which absolutely are fielded, but fortunately they're not that common and we can just sort of hand-wave them away because they're rare and bothersome.)

year to the next is largely out of his control, it stands to reason that we'll have better results predicting his future ERA (or RA) using a neutral number instead of his current BABIP.

New data streams have helped us refine such predictions, but for a quick back-of-the-envelope look at a pitcher's performance, FIP, or Fielding Independent Pitching, is useful because it's on the same scale as ERA but does what I just described—swaps in a league-average BABIP for the pitcher's actual BABIP. It's like saying, "Hey, this guy had great help from his defense turning lots of balls in play into outs, so what would he have pitched like had he pitched in front of an average defense?"

The concept is to strip the noise away from the signal in the pitcher's ERA; DIPS's introduction was, and to some extent still is, controversial, because many people, including pitchers, did not like the idea that they lacked control over the results of balls in play. (One popular trend of the early 2000s was for mischievous sports-writers to present pitchers with low BABIPs with the conclusions of McCracken's studies. Hilarity ensued.) It flies in the face of what we always heard growing up—a pitcher induced that groundball, he got that weak contact, the hitter didn't pop up but the pitcher "popped him up" (as if the hitter was merely a kernel of corn)—and that kind of shift in how we perceive the game is uncomfortable. A pitcher has the most control over three things: striking hitters out, avoiding walks, and avoiding home runs. He has some control over the type of contact he allows, such as a groundball or a flyball, but once the ball's in play, whether it's fielded cleanly or not has nothing to do with what the pitcher did before contact. It's the baseball equivalent of learning that all life on earth evolved from a single common an-cestor: whether it's what we want to hear doesn't matter because the evidence says it's true.

Defense-Independent Pitching Statistics first emerged on the old Usenet discussion board rec.sport.baseball and came to wider atten-tion when Voros McCracken consolidated his findings into an article on Baseball Prospectus titled "Pitching and Defense: How Much Con-

trol Do Hurlers Have?" The shocking answer was "not that much."
Whether a ball put into play became a hit or was converted into an out
appeared to be out of the pitcher's control almost completely:

> *The pitchers who are the best at preventing hits on balls in*
> *play one year are often the worst at it the next. In 1998, Greg*
> *Maddux had one of the best rates in baseball, then in 1999*
> *he had one of the worst. In 2000, he had one of the better*
> *ones again. In 1999, Pedro Martinez had one of the worst;*
> *in 2000, he had the best. This happens a lot. There is little*
> *correlation between what a pitcher does one year in the stat*
> *and what he will do the next. . . . This is not true in the other*
> *significant stats (walks, strikeouts, home runs).*

This shouldn't happen at all if the then-conventional wisdom that
pitchers could prevent hits on balls in play were true. (This conventional wisdom hasn't died entirely in the fifteen-plus years since
Voros's piece appeared; you will often see references to a pitcher's
batting average against or hits allowed per nine innings, both of
which are almost entirely functions of his BABIP.)

McCracken argued that great pitchers were great not because
they had some sort of special woo-woo to prevent hits on balls in
play, but because they allowed fewer balls in play to begin with.
You'd be better at predicting a pitcher's performance in the following season by assuming his BABIP allowed would regress to the
league average than by using his actual BABIP allowed in the previous season. He was positing that BABIP made us dumber when it
came to predicting pitcher stats, and by and large he was correct.
(As an aside, it turns out that the converse is not true for hitters:
There are absolutely hitters who can make better or worse quality
contact on a consistent basis and thus regularly post BABIPs that
vary from the league average. Mike Trout, the best player in baseball
as of this writing, has a career .356 BABIP; Bryce Harper, the other
best player in baseball as of this writing, has a career .331 BABIP.
The league averages for their careers are just under .300.)

The issue of untangling a pitcher's own contributions to run prevention from his teammates' efforts, especially on defense, isn't going away anytime soon. As the 2016 season drew to a close, the Cubs were posting the lowest BABIP allowed by any team in a full season in forty years, and one of the best relative to the league BABIP in MLB history. The 2016 Cubs were a very good defensive unit, with plus defenders at multiple positions, including Jason Heyward, one of the best right fielders in recent years, playing right and occasionally center. They were also one of the most analytically driven teams, including how they used data to position their fielders for each batter. So how much do we want to credit their pitchers for work that might have been the result of great defense?

All five of the Cubs' starters made at least 29 starts in 2016, and every one had an ERA at least 0.40 runs lower than his FIP. Kyle Hendricks led the Cubs and the NL with a 2.13 ERA but his FIP was 3.20—the largest gap between ERA and FIP of any of the Cubs' starters. He allowed a .300 BABIP in a full season in 2015, but allowed just a .250 BABIP in 2016. It's almost certain that the drop in his rate of hits allowed on balls in play was the result of the Cubs' best-in-class defense and some good fortune, with little if any of the improvement the work of anything Hendricks specifically did, especially since his other key rates—strikeout rate, walk rate, home runs allowed—have barely changed year over year. Hendricks's season is an extreme example, but it shows that several things can be true at the same time:

- Hendricks had a very good season. He was an above-average starter for the Cubs.

- Opposing teams barely scored when Hendricks was on the mound for the Cubs.

- Some portion of the credit for the second point goes to the Cubs as a team rather than Hendricks specifically.

- Going forward, Hendricks is likely to allow more hits and more runs, especially if the Cubs' defense should change for the worse or Hendricks should end up pitching for another team.

These two challenges—separating the descriptive (what happened) from the prescriptive (what will happen), and splitting credit for something among different players—are at the heart of many sabermetric debates and define what team analysts do with the piles of data coming their way each day. You can't discuss the future without understanding what happened in the past, and understanding what happened includes figuring out which parts of the past really tell us something about each player's true ability or skill. That's why looking at a pitcher's ERA or, better, his RA, tells us something, but not everything. We can see from his RA how many runs opposing teams scored while he was responsible for the runners on base—but the picture RA or ERA gives us about the pitcher's true skill, and thus about how he's likely to pitch in the future, is too blurry to be all that useful. That's why, when we're talking about value produced or making projections for the future, we want to use something that's a little more precise at carving out what the pitcher did himself from what his teammates did to help or hurt him.

FIP, originally developed by the sabermetrician Tom Tango, predicts next-year ERA better than ERA does, but while it tells us quite a bit about a pitcher's performance in a specific year, FIP too is imperfect. It replaces a noisy number (the pitcher's BABIP) with a dead-neutral one, and that may indeed throw out the baby with the bathwater. (My wife and I always sent the bathwater down the drain, but that's just us.) Over long enough samples, slight abilities by certain pitchers to suppress hits on balls in play can emerge, although the quantity of innings required to confirm this is so large that it's not terribly useful for baseball decisions. Clayton Kershaw is one such pitcher, with a career BABIP allowed of .271, coming in below the league average in every full season of his career through 2015; Mariano Rivera, who lived by throwing one pitch, a cut fastball, that hitters found very difficult to hit squarely, is another, finishing his illustrious career with a BABIP of .263. Such pitchers will be underrated by FIP, because this skill they have at limiting hits is deleted from the equation entirely.

On the other hand, FIP can also fake us out on pitchers who truly *can't* limit hits on balls in play. If you took someone from your local beer league who could throw 80 mph and sent him to pitch in the majors, he'd allow a lot of balls in play, and most of them would be hit hard enough to send fielders running for cover. DIPS theory does not apply to him, and it doesn't take examples quite that extreme to break with this idea of BABIP regressing to the mean. Glendon Rusch had a short career as a durable fifth starter who threw a ton of strikes but always seemed to give up too many hits, finishing with a career ERA (5.04) well above his FIP (4.29) because his career BABIP, .326, was about 30 points above the league average for the years in which he pitched. In both of these cases, ERA might actually tell us more about the pitcher than FIP or other such stats, called ERA estimators or component ERA metrics, could.

What ERA, or RA, or FIP gives us—and to be honest, I look at all of them when trying to evaluate a pitcher's performance or consider what his future performance might be—is a rate stat: how much damage did a pitcher allow per nine innings pitched. It was a sensible framework in the days when pitchers finished most of their games, but now nine innings is more of an accepted standard of measurement than a meaningful unit on its own. Perhaps someone should introduce a "metric ERA" that shows runs allowed every ten innings rather than every nine. (Don't do that. Please.) But regardless of which runs-allowed average you use, it's still just a rate stat. It's more useful than simply looking at the bulk total of runs allowed, but ERA or FIP can't tell us how valuable the pitcher's performance was because neither includes his innings pitched. To figure out a pitcher's total value, we'll have to bring those two variables together to figure out how many runs the pitcher prevented compared to a set standard of performance.

More refined data on balls put into play are now making their way to teams from MLB via their Statcast product, which I'll discuss in a later chapter; these data should help improve our understanding of how much control pitchers might have on affecting the way a ball is put into play, and thus the likelihood that the ball is fielded for an out.

*   *   *

This discrepancy between a pitcher's ERA and how he might have pitched given neutral support from his defense or his bullpen became particularly clear in the debate over who should win the 2015 NL Cy Young Award, which came down to three candidates having historically great seasons: Jake Arrieta of the Chicago Cubs and Zack Greinke and Clayton Kershaw of the Los Angeles Dodgers. Arrieta won the award, but who you think deserved it depends a lot on how you view ERA and the idea of judging a pitcher on his peripherals rather than his more traditional stats.

Pitcher	ERA	Opp OBP	K%	IP	BABIP	FIP
Zack Greinke	**1.66**	.231	23.7%	222.2	.232	2.76
Jake Arrieta	1.77	.236	27.1%	229.0	.247	2.35
Clayton Kershaw	2.13	.237	**33.8%**	**232.2**	.283	**1.99**

Bold text indicates that the pitcher led the National League.

There's a lot going on here, so let me start from the left. You know what the pitcher's name means, and what ERA is. The opponents' OBP is just what it implies: the aggregate on-base percentage of all batters that pitcher faced. Expressed as a percentage (.231 = 23.1 percent), it says what percent of opposing batters reached base safely against that pitcher.

K% is strikeout rate, just strikeouts divided by total batters faced. This is better than strikeouts per inning or strikeouts per nine innings because strikeouts are measured in batters, while innings can contain any number of batters from three up.

IP is innings pitched, included here just to show that all three pitchers had about the same workload and thus the same opportunities to add value to their teams.

Which of the three pitchers pitched the best—contributed the most value by preventing runs—to his team in that year? The old answer would likely have been Greinke, whose ERA of 1.66 was the lowest in MLB in twenty years, the lowest in a nonstrike season in thirty years. And Greinke undoubtedly pitched well, as even his defense-independent statistics tell us, thanks to his stinginess with walks and his especially low BABIP.

Arrieta pitched almost as well by ERA standards, thanks to a second-half run where he pitched about as well as any pitcher has thrown in any half season in history, posting a 0.75 ERA in 107.1 innings while allowing 55 hits, 23 walks, and 2 home runs against 113 strikeouts.

But when it comes down to the things we *know* a pitcher is responsible for, Kershaw wasn't just the best in the National League in 2015, but one of the best in history. His FIP—again, a rough look at how well a pitcher fared when focusing on strikeouts, walks, and homers—was the ninth-best FIP by any pitcher who qualified for the ERA title since baseball's live-ball era began in 1921. The fourth-best FIP on that list was also Clayton Kershaw, just the year before. Kershaw led the NL by a huge margin in strikeout rate, allowed fewer walks (on a rate basis) than Arrieta while almost dead even with Greinke, and allowed five more homers than Arrieta and one more than Greinke in a few more innings pitched. Kershaw had a very good case to win this award; Greinke had a solid case; and Arrieta ended up winning the award, with Greinke finishing second and Kershaw finishing third. Arrieta wasn't a bad choice, but he wasn't clearly the best one . . . and one has to wonder if his MLB-leading 22 wins played a part in the voting.

That particular Cy Young debate is a convenient example of the complexities of evaluating pitcher performance once you've moved beyond pitcher wins and have recognized that ERA doesn't give us the perfect, single answer. Working with what we know about BABIP, about defense, about luck and randomness, we end up with a story around the pitcher's performance that's more nuanced than any single number can express. Teams continue to develop new metrics to try to isolate pitching performance and project pitchers' values going forward, meaning this is a topic we'll continue to hear about for quite a few more years to come.

12

WPA:

Measuring Clutch, If You Must

I want to detour for a moment from the various stats I've presented that help us isolate a player's production by stripping out context, or stats that help us better project a player's performance going forward, to look at one stat that is all-descriptive—it tells us more about what happened, and actively considers the context of the player's performance. The stat, Win Probability Added, is all about context—was the player's team better or worse off in that particular game based on what the player did?

There's no existing stat that WPA tries to replace; it grew out of a desire to identify "clutch" performers by looking at which players did the most to swing outcomes of specific games. Such players don't exist—if you can hit, you can hit in the clutch and the unclutch and everything in between—but the effort gave us a new set of stats, led by WPA, that at least allows us to determine the impact of a specific hit or out on each team's chances of winning that specific game, and to add up such opportunities for each player over the course of a season.

The good thing about WPA, as opposed to the typical codswallop claims of players who are clutch or who "smell an RBI" or "know when to bear down," is that WPA is deaf to your excuses. WPA accepts no rationalizations like luck or bad defense or anything of the sort. WPA does not care for your explanations of context or your what-ifs. If a reliever comes in with men on base and gets a couple of hard-hit outs without letting any of those runners score, then his WPA for the game is going to be positive—the closer the game, the more positive it will be. His team had a certain chance of winning the game before he entered, and had a better chance after he was done. You might argue that his defense bailed him out, or that he was lucky those screaming line drives were hit right at the fielders, but WPA just looks at whether his team's odds of winning the game increased or decreased.

The earliest public recording of a stat like WPA was Player Win Averages, described by brothers Eldon and Harlan Mills and covered in *The Hidden Game of Baseball*,* although their system involved some arbitrary scoring of win probabilities that we can now calculate more precisely. Win Probability Added, unlike a lot of sabermetric stats, tells you in its name exactly what it's trying to measure: how much did a player add to his team's probability of winning a game—or all the games he appeared in over a week or a month or a season?

This flips the sabermetric dogma of distilling the signal player contributions out from the noise of everything else happening on the field on its head: for WPA, we want that context. A home run when your team is down 8–0 only very slightly increases your chances of winning the game, and if it comes with two outs in the ninth, the change is going to be effectively nil. A home run that breaks a tie game increases your team's chances of winning the game, and the later in the game that this happens, the bigger the increase will be.

If this sounds like an attempt to measure clutchiness, you're right—the Mills brothers conceived it that way when looking for evidence of clutch hitting ability. That has not panned out, as WPA has

---

* See John Thorn and Pete Palmer, *The Hidden Game of Baseball* (Chicago: University of Chicago Press, 2015), p. 272.

very little predictive value; a player's WPA in one period of time isn't a good predictor of what it will be in a subsequent period of time, such as from one year to the next. But as a descriptive statistic—hey, this is what actually happened, so get your head out of the spreadsheet and watch the game—WPA is about as good a measure of a clutch hit, at bat, pitch, or inning as you can find.

Calculating the Win Probability Added of a specific appearance, which could be an at bat or an inning of work, requires knowing two numbers and subtracting one from the other. Before the appearance, what were the team's chances of winning that game, based on the score, the inning, the base-out state, and how often teams in MLB history have won games in which they faced that score in that inning and base-out state? And after the appearance, what were the team's new chances of winning that game, given the same variables? Subtract the first number from the second number and you get the Win Probability Added, which will be positive if the team's chances of winning the game increased (the hitter doubled, the pitcher threw two scoreless innings) and negative if their chances decreased (the hitter grounded into a double play, the pitcher walked two men and gave up a single). For a player, add up the WPA figures from all of his at bats or innings pitched over the course of a season and you'll get a total number that shows you, in context, how much he helped or hurt his team given the timing of his production.

WPA is symmetrical for a single event: if the batter makes an out that drops his team's chances of winning from 48 percent to 46 percent, then the pitcher gains that .02 in WPA as well. Per Fangraphs' description of the metric, "At the end of every game, the winning team's players will have a total WPA of +0.5 and the losing team's players will have a total WPA of –0.5." The stat is also park-adjusted, since the value of a run scored or prevented will vary depending on whether you're in a high-scoring environment or a low-scoring one.

While WPA is context driven, it has limitations. WPA ignores defense entirely, hanging all run prevention credit or blame on the pitcher like some of the more problematic pitching stats. For this reason, WPA is more helpful in conjunction with other stats and information rather than by itself as a measure of a player's ability.

WPA serves two main functions. One, as I mentioned above, is that it is a useful measure of the impact of what actually happened on the field. The probabilities (chances) are based on historical data, the best way for us to estimate how much a specific play or event or series of events altered the potential outcome; if you were a bettor or an investor, this is exactly how you'd want to calculate the change in odds. The other is in understanding how much a player's performance *and the way in which he was used* impacted his team's won-lost record in a season. To rack up a strong WPA for a season, it's not enough to play well; you have to play often and find yourself in situations where what you do makes a difference in game outcomes. That's a function of where you hit in the lineup and who's around you, or when your manager sends you out as a pinch hitter, or, for a relief pitcher, whether you get to pitch in high-leverage situations (later in games when the score is close or tied).

On August 8, 2016, the Cincinnati Reds—who, in case you didn't know where this was going, had one of the worst bullpens in recent memory—took a 4–0 lead into the bottom of the ninth inning against the St. Louis Cardinals. At that point, before the Cards' first at bat of the ninth, the Reds' win expectancy was 98.5 percent; that is, teams up four runs with three outs to go have gone on to win their games about that frequently. After a hit and two outs, leaving the Reds still up 4–0 and a single out from victory, their win expectancy had risen to 99.6 percent. And then:

Event	Reds' Win Expectancy
Walk	98.7%
HBP	95.6%
Single, 2 runs score	91.1%
Single, 1 run scores	83.8%
Walk	73.9%
Walk, 1 run scores	34.7%
HBP, 1 run score	0.0%

All data via Fangraphs.com

Five of those seven events involved the hitter receiving a "free" pass to first base via a walk or a time hit by pitch, but the win expectancy of each event was different. The last walk, where Brandon Moss walked with the bases loaded to force in a run, resulted in the biggest shift in win expectancy (WE), a delta of 39.2; the batter hit by pitch to force in the winning run actually produced less of a shift in WE because you can't get any lower than 0 percent chance of winning (although if you could, this Reds bullpen would have found a way). We don't talk about "clutch walks" or "clutch times hit by pitch," but that is what happened here—the last three batters in particular drew walks or were hit by a pitch in high-leverage (clutch) situations and thus raised the Cardinals' chances of winning substantially without swinging their bats.

The MLB leader in WPA in 2015 was Anthony Rizzo, first baseman for the Cubs, at +7.15 wins above average, a full win above what Bryce Harper, the most productive hitter in the majors that year, provided to the Nationals. That's a function of context, since Harper outproduced Rizzo in individual stats but didn't have the opportunities Rizzo had to affect game outcomes and/or didn't produce as well in those opportunities. Among pitchers, the Dodgers' Zack Greinke, who led the majors in ERA thanks to a very low BABIP, led at +6.79.

But where WPA gets interesting is when you look at the values relievers rack up because of how they're deployed. The MLB leader in WPA among relievers in 2015 was Pirates closer Mark Melancon at +5.39, more than all MLB starters but Greinke and NL Cy Young winner Jake Arrieta. That credits Melancon for a job well done . . . but also credits Pittsburgh manager Clint Hurdle for using his best reliever so frequently in high-leverage situations. That means that WPA is telling us two things at once: the opportunities the player had to affect the outcomes of the games in which he played, and how well or poorly he played in those situations.

As a description of what actually happened in games, WPA is useful, but as a measure of individual skill or a tool to predict the player's performance going forward, it is useless. There's no correlation between WPA in one season and the next independent of the player's own underlying performance—a good hitter is a good hitter, no matter the score, the inning, or who's on base. If you're in a front office, trying to determine how much to pay a player, or what to trade to acquire a player, WPA shouldn't enter into your thinking at all. Its value is limited to fans and writers who want to understand the story of a game, for which it's better suited than most traditional statistics, like the pitcher win, the save, or the now-discredited Game-Winning RBI, a garbage stat introduced by the Elias Sports Bureau in 1980 and quietly discontinued after 1988. WPA gives us a better way to think about what happened, but doesn't help team executives in their quest to more accurately value a player or predict his future.

13

The Black Box:

How Baseball Teams
Measure Defense Today

Given how flawed many of the long-accepted fielding stats are, it shouldn't come as shock that, when it comes to fielding, the old numbers don't give us much to work with. Unlike other flawed numbers that are only telling us part of the story, stats like fielding percentage are actually deceiving us, which makes them of very little use.

And so, when it comes to fielding stats, we need to start over entirely, but the question is where. If I could somehow wipe fielding percentage and errors from your brain and then ask you to tell me how we might assess a fielder's value, what would you say?

I think a reasonable first answer might be this: does he make the plays he's supposed to make? This is the most basic thing we expect of any player on the field. If a ball is hit to him that we would expect him to field—that is, to convert into an out, either making the play himself or beginning a play for another fielder to complete—then he'd better field it. If he can't do that, we'd probably consider him a below-average fielder, and we'd expect a fielding statistic to dock him for the plays he should make but doesn't. So we'd need to track all the plays our fielder should have made, see how many of them he did make, and then compare it to some baseline of players at that same position—how often they made those same plays themselves.

If you go a little deeper, you might also consider the plays the player does make that most players don't. We tend to think of these as highlight plays, but they don't have to look like Web Gems to actually be great defensive plays. Andruw Jones is one of the ten or so best fielders in baseball history, but many of his best plays wouldn't make a highlight reel because his range was so good he wasn't diving to make these highly valuable catches. So now we have to look at all of the plays that our player made that most players at his position don't make, and see how often he made them and what happens when a fielder doesn't make each of those particular plays.

This is the fundamental logic between the new defensive stats you see on sites like Baseball-Reference and Fangraphs and the proprietary defensive metrics teams use themselves for their own player valuations. The play *not* made can be damaging, and the extra play that is made can be extremely valuable. Any attempt to value a fielder's contributions on the field or to try to estimate his true defensive talent level must include these plays, which none of the "old" defensive metrics accurately counted.

Before the advent of play-by-play data that showed where balls in play first hit the ground or were fielded, putouts, assists, and errors were all we had, and anyone trying to come up with a better way of valuing fielding had to find a way to glean some kind of information from that data.

One of the earliest alternatives to fielding percentage was Range Factor, developed by Bill James to try to put some kind of numerical value on a player's range by measuring the frequency of plays he made. Range Factor was simply putouts plus assists divided by games or, better, putouts plus assists times 9 divided by innings played, making it an ERA-like rate stat scaled to nine-inning games.

A player who made a lot of plays would thus score higher, and we would presume that such a player had more range.

Palmer and Thorn tried a novel approach with Fielding Runs, which they described in a chapter of *The Hidden Game of Baseball* called, appropriately for its time, "Measuring the Unmeasurable." Their statistic, which is a linear-weights approach to fielding data, still relies on the same raw information of putouts, assists, and errors, while also considering double plays for infielders, and then compared individual players' results to estimates of the league average for each position. Unfortunately, because of the problems in the raw data, this fell into the old dictum about garbage in/garbage out; their results pointed in the right direction, as did Range Factor, but there was too much nonsense in their inputs (for example, using games played rather than innings played, which wasn't available) to give fielding runs the precision they reached with batting or pitching runs.

While John Dewan was working for Stats Inc. in the 1980s, he developed Zone Rating, the earliest attempt to divide the field of play into zones of responsibility for the fielders. The concept is simple—we'd certainly expect the shortstop to field a ball hit to the place where the shortstop usually stands, and if we mark off that spot and the area right around it, we can say he's responsible for balls hit into that zone. Dewan divided the field into zones of responsibility for each player, then looked at how many balls were hit into each zone for each fielder, and how often the fielder turned those balls into outs. The concept was correct, representing a substantial leap forward over anything based on traditional stats, but Dewan didn't have the data required in the 1980s or '90s to get meaningful results from Zone Rating. Dewan eventually cofounded Baseball Info Solutions, a new data-collection firm that, among other things, provided more specific details on where balls were hit into play, and even employed people to watch defensive plays and subjectively grade them as "misplays" or "good fielding plays." Before the advent of more specific play-by-play data, showing locations for balls in play and for fielder positions, this was as precise as advanced defensive metrics could get.

The advent of new data has changed the approach once again. As of 2016, when I'm writing these words, there are two major, publicly available defensive metrics that attempt to answer the question of how many runs a defender saved or cost his team compared to an average fielder at the same position. One is Ultimate Zone Rating (UZR), developed by Mitchel Lichtman and available on Fangraphs' site. The other is defensive Runs Saved (dRS), developed by Baseball Info Solutions and available on Fangraphs and Baseball-Reference. While the two rarely align perfectly—which highlights one of the key difficulties in evaluating defense—they typically agree on direction; that is, if UZR says a player is well above average, dRS will probably say the same thing. Over multiple seasons, they're more likely to agree on a player, simply because large sample sizes tend to reduce the effect of outliers in the subjective aspects of these stats.

Because these stats are publicly available, they immediately become Important Things, perhaps even Numbers You Are Not Allowed to Question. This is silly, although it's a tenet of behavioral economics that when someone slaps a number on something, that's what we assume that something is worth; it's integral to commerce, where we'll all automatically assume a product is more desirable or of higher quality just because its price is higher. And it's important to bear in mind what UZR and dRS are actually telling us.

There's a key difference between measuring the value of what a player did and what his actual or "true" talent might be. A career .320 hitter who goes 0-for-4 did not suddenly lose his hitting ability in that game, but the 0-for-4 is an accurate statement of what he did in those four trips to the plate. The same idea applies to defensive metrics, but in my experience is often forgotten: a player is not his UZR. His UZR (or his dRS) estimates the value of what he did in the field, with some adjustments. It does not tell you what his underlying ability* is, and without a lot of mathematical chicanery I

---

* When I talk about a player's underlying ability, also sometimes called a "true talent level," I mean the thing that team analysts would love to isolate in the player—what he's really capable of doing in a perfectly neutral, randomness-free environment. If I could tell you Joey Bagodonuts' true talent level as a hitter was .300/.400/.500, you'd know what he was worth in dollars or players, and you could plan your roster more effectively around him. You'd ex-

won't bore you with here, we can't draw a straight line from a UZR number to that underlying ability unless we make assumptions so big they could swallow Mount Everest whole and still have time to consume K2 for dessert.

Instead, what we want to do with defensive metrics is the same thing we do with stats for offense and pitching: get the most accurate possible picture of what each player did on the field. The difference between fielding stats and other stats is that a proper accounting of defense involves something more speculative: deciding when *a* player didn't do something he should have done. We really don't do anything of the sort with hitters or pitchers; we try to isolate responsibility, but we don't get into the less comfortable realm of "well, he swung through that hanging breaking ball, but he really should have hit it halfway to Mars." That's part of scouting, but isn't and probably should not be any part of even advanced hitting statistics. With fielders, however, we have to consider what didn't happen, because part of the difference between a good fielder and a bad one is the play the good fielder makes on a ball the bad fielder never even touches.

Lichtman describes the philosophy of Ultimate Zone Rating as trying to tell us two things: for any ball that's hit or put into play, did any fielder who had any chance to catch that ball do so, and what were the chances of a league-average fielder at that position making that same play? It turns out that this calculation is not as easy as it seems, although improved data on balls in play in the last few years have made the results more useful.

"How often would an average center fielder have caught that particular flyball?" seems like a straightforward question, but to answer it, you need a lot of flyballs to that specific point on the field—hit the same way, at the same speed. That's awfully limiting, even if we had lots of historical data showing the precise spot on the field where a flyball landed or was caught. Instead, analysts like Lichtman and the

---

pect variation around that line, because we live in a universe filled with randomness, but you would at least know the baseline, and you could make more accurate projections with that as your starting point.

folks at Baseball Info Solutions (BIS) use some approximations to give them enough of a sample of past balls in play so that saying "an average center fielder catches that ball 80 percent of the time" has some actual meaning.

For UZR, that means dividing the field into a number of zones, about 10 feet by 10 feet, for where a ball hit in the air landed or was caught, and then rating each ball by how hard it was hit (soft, medium, or hard) and, for flyballs, whether it was a line drive or a true flyball. For groundballs, the system comes up with a vector for each ball hit into play, a combination of an angle (dividing the 90 degrees from the third-base line to the first-base line into eighteen five-degree wedges) and a speed estimation (soft, medium, or hard again). Then Lichtman's algorithm can look through a historical database of ten years of balls in play to find other balls that resemble the one we're looking at.

For example, a medium-hit line drive to a zone in the left-center gap might be caught 20 percent of the time by the center fielder, 10 percent of the time by the left fielder (some of whom are there because that's where you put the guy who can't field), and 70 percent of the time by nobody, falling in for a hit. A softly hit groundball to the left side, 10 degrees from the third-base line, might be fielded 40 percent of the time by the third baseman, 5 percent of the time by the pitcher, and 55 percent of the time by nobody. With that many dimensions—location, hit type, estimated velocity, and angle for groundballs—we're getting enough precision to distinguish between different types of balls hit into play without getting so specific that we're comparing that ball hit into play today to one catch that Jim Edmonds made eight years ago and nothing else. The larger the sample of past balls in play we get to use for comparisons, the more confident we can feel when rating the current play in question.*

---

* Improved data coming from MLB's Statcast product, available to major-league teams, provide precise exit velocities (the speed of the ball off the bat), hang time for balls hit in the air, launch angle off the bat, and more, which will allow us to be more precise in grouping balls in play into buckets for our database of comparisons, and then for determining how often a new ball in play would be caught by an average fielder. I'll discuss this product more in a later chapter.

There are two major problems with the UZR/dRS approach beyond the lack of precision in historical data. One is that these approaches must assume that all fielders start in essentially the same positions on the field—that every center fielder is positioned in the same spot for every hitter, behind every pitcher, regardless of the score or inning. If you thought, "Well, that's stupid," you're incredibly rude but not far off the mark; we can all think of situations, like the final batter of the 2001 World Series, where a manager chose to bring in the infield, or play outfielders in the so-called no-doubles defense (which is better referred to as the "more singles" defense), all with an eye toward preventing certain outcomes. If you try to grade a center fielder on a routine flyball when he was playing very shallow to try to prevent a bloop single from driving in a run, you're going to see he failed to make a play that center fielders make nearly 100 percent of the time, and you'll think he blew it.

These metrics also can't distinguish between a player who makes a lot of plays because he's fast and a player who makes a lot of plays because he positions himself well before the ball is hit. Cal Ripken Jr. is considered one of the best defensive shortstops in history, something that is backed up by the rudimentary defensive statistics we have for his playing career, even though he was a well-below-average runner and in his era was the biggest man ever to play shortstop on a regular basis. (Ripken was listed at 6'4", 200 pounds. At the time Ripken retired, no player at least that tall and weighing at least that much had ever played a single game at shortstop. Corey Seager and Carlos Correa, both of whom debuted in 2015, are both listed at 6'4", 215.) Ripken was well known for his pre-pitch positioning based on who was on the mound, the pitch the catcher called for, and who was at the plate. According to his biography at SABR's website, he would frequently attend the pre-series meetings pitchers and catchers would hold to review the opposing batters and discuss how to pitch to them. This observation and knowledge of where a hitter would be likely to hit a certain pitch allowed Ripken to position himself better before the ball was even put into play; he led the American League in assists seven times, and recorded the third-most

assists in major-league history, thanks to his positioning acumen . . .
and the fact that he didn't miss a game for seventeen years.

In UZR, Lichtman only compares balls hit by left-handed batters to those hit by other left-handed batters, and balls hit by right-
handed batters to those hit by other right-handed batters. He does
make some small estimations based on certain batter archetypes, including very-low-power batters who might lead opponents to bring
their outfielders in, and speedy hitters who face infielders playing
slightly closer to home plate to increase their chances of throwing
the runners out on groundballs. Those are necessary adjustments
but also inexact.

The second problem is a very modern one, that of the defensive
shift, perhaps the single most noticeable change in how baseball
is played that we've seen in the last decade. (I refer specifically to
"overshifts," where a team might play three infielders on the right
side of second base against a left-handed pull hitter.) Balls hit to
shifted fielders end up in the trash bin; there's no value in crediting
a third baseman who was shifted to short right field with fielding a
groundball there when it was 120 feet from his normal position. BIS
does track teams' usage of shifts and how often batters face them,
but a ball hit into a shift doesn't give us any useful information on
the fielders involved except as one point of evidence that the shift
was a good idea.

Once we've figured out how often a fielder in question makes a
certain play, then we need to figure out what that play is worth. A
groundball through the hole on either side of the infield is not as
damaging as a hard-hit line drive up the right-center gap; the first
is almost always going to be a single, and the latter will almost always go for extra bases. Although this sounds intuitive, it's where
advanced defensive metrics throw people off the most, because the
value we're talking about here isn't tangible: we know what a hit or
a home run is worth, more or less, but here we're often talking about
a hit that didn't happen, a hypothetical value that I think makes a lot
of fans uncomfortable because we've all grown up (myself included)
judging players on tangible numbers describing discrete events we
saw and can count.

Here's Lichtman's explanation, taken from his UZR Primer found on Fangraphs' site.

Let's say that that same batted ball in the example above was caught by the CF'er on the first play of a game. Since typically someone will catch that same ball only 25% of the time (see above), this particular CF'er will get credit for an extra .75 plays—100% minus 25%. We then convert .75 plays into runs by multiplying .75 by the difference between an average hit in that location and the average value of an air ball out. A typical outfield hit is worth around .56 runs and any batted ball out is worth around –.27 runs, so the difference between a hit and an out is worth around .83 runs. . . . Since our fielder gets credit for .75 extra plays, we give him credit for .75 times .83 runs, or +.6255 runs for that play.

This particular example is straightforward because it involves one fielder; when a ball is hit to a zone where multiple fielders might have some responsibility, UZR splits up the credit or blame based on how frequently we might expect each of those fielders to make the play in question. But the core idea to remember here, even if you're never going to calculate UZR or dRS or anything like that on your own, is this: a defensive play has a value in runs prevented, and that same play, when not made, has a value in runs not prevented.

If you add up all of the values of the plays each defender made and should have made but didn't, you get a total value for his defensive contributions . . . or, to be more precise about it, you get an *estimated* total value. Advanced measures of defense do not provide an exact accounting, but rather an estimate of runs prevented or permitted. If a player has a UZR or dRS for a season of +8 runs, that means we think his defensive performance in that season was worth about eight runs above average. It doesn't mean that he's an above-average defender, or that he saved exactly eight runs above an average fielder at the same position. It gives us a rough idea of what his glove was worth, and the more games or plays we can include in that sample, the more confidence we might have that this number reflects something like his actual talent level on defense.

But what do these numbers and situations actually look like in practice?

Ozzie Smith ranks as the greatest defensive shortstop in MLB history, a beautiful case where what our eyes tell us (those backflips!) lines up with the hard data we have on performance. Smith recorded more assists than any other player in MLB history at any position but one, shortstop/second baseman Rabbit Maranville, who played from 1912 to 1935, when hitters put the ball in play substantially more often than they have in the modern era. Smith leads all shortstops in assists even though he played fewer games at the position than Omar Vizquel, Derek Jeter, or Luis Aparicio, and recorded the eighth-most putouts among all shortstops as well, behind seven guys who played before World War II. Baseball-Reference uses TotalZone, a metric that uses historical estimates on where balls where hit into play along with the recorded putouts and assists, to roughly value the defensive performances of players prior to the advent of play-by-play data, and Smith comes out as the most valuable defensive shortstop and fourth-most-valuable defender at any position in history, saving about 239 runs over the course of his nineteen-year career.

Smith's reputation matched up with the defensive stats, and he was a productive hitter for a shortstop in an era where shortstops rarely hit at all, so his Hall of Fame case was extremely strong and he was elected by the BBWAA in his first year on the ballot in 2002, appearing on 91.7 percent of ballots cast, clearing the 75 percent threshold required for election. His enshrinement marked only the second time the writers had elected a player primarily known for his defensive abilities to the Hall, after the 1984 induction of third baseman Brooks Robinson, the most valuable defensive player at any position in MLB history.

There's certainly something satisfying about having the best defenders at key positions—Smith at shortstop, Robinson at third, even Bill Mazeroski, selected by the Veterans Committee, at second base—in the Hall of Fame. The greatest eligible center fielder, Willie Mays, is in; the only center fielder above him in TotalZone's ratings is Andruw Jones, who will hit the ballot after 2018. Jones's case is complicated by the fact that he was effectively done as a big-league regular at age thirty and played sporadically and poorly for several years, eventually playing his last two seasons as a professional in Japan at ages thirty-six and thirty-seven. He was a far better player than Kirby Puckett—who sailed into the Hall of Fame on his first ballot but is one of the worst players the writers have ever elected—and yet Jones probably has a comparable case to Jim Edmonds, who failed to reach the 5 percent minimum in his first and thus only year on the BBWAA ballot.

Name	G	PA	HR	R	RBI	SB	AVG	OBP	SLG	Off	Def	WR
Andruw Jones	2196	8664	434	1204	1289	152	0.254	0.337	0.486	116.3	281.3	67.1
Jim Edmonds	2011	7980	393	1251	1199	67	0.284	0.376	0.527	317.7	73.3	64.5
Kenny Lofton	2103	9235	130	1528	781	622	0.299	0.372	0.423	181.3	139.4	62.4
Kirby Puckett	1783	7831	207	1071	1085	134	0.318	0.36	0.477	204.9	−28.4	44.9

Edmonds played fewer games but held his value deeper into his career, and if you consider the inexact nature of defensive statistics it's fair to think of Edmonds and Jones as more or less equivalent, at least in terms of a Hall argument. If you put Jones in, you probably should have Edmonds in, but since Edmonds received almost no support whatsoever on the ballot, it would be a surprise to see Jones fare substantially better.

Jones's appearance on the ballot after the 2017 season won't be the one to spark the big debate, however; that will fall to Omar Vizquel. As I've shown when discussing the flaws with fielding percentage, Vizquel was a very good player who has become comically overrated by fans, coaches, and media alike. Indeed this has progressed to the point where many simply say that the defensive metrics around him are "wrong" because, in fact, they don't support the preconceived notion that Vizquel was a latter-day Ozzie Smith. Here's the hard truth: he wasn't. He was a good defender, but was maybe half of what the Wizard of Oz was with the glove. While old defensive stats like fielding percentage revealed Vizquel's shortcomings, TotalZone and UZR make it even clearer:

	Smith	Vizquel
Games	2511	2709
Putouts	4249	4102
Assists	8375	7676
Double plays turned	1590	1734
TotalZone runs prevented	239	134

So despite Vizquel playing a little more than a season's worth of games more than Smith did, Ozzie made more plays than Omar did—a lot more, enough that TotalZone gives him an edge of over 100 runs prevented compared to Vizquel over the courses of their careers.

Neither player was any great shakes with the stick, either; Smith was a career .262/.337/.328 hitter, while Vizquel ended up at .272/.336/.352, playing most of his career in a higher-offense era than Smith did, so Smith's offense ends up more valuable than Vizquel's by more than 100 runs over their careers. And Smith was a far better base stealer, with 176 more stolen bases than Vizquel had but just 19 more times caught stealing.

But the crux of the arguments for Vizquel as a Hall of Famer is that he was close to Smith's level on defense, when all of the available information says that he wasn't. Vizquel may have been a joy to watch, and writers who covered him in Cleveland and San Francisco have nothing but praise for him as a player and as a person. His performances on the field, however, simply do not justify his reputation, and if elected—as I suspect will happen on his first or second year on the ballot—he'll become one of the worst players enshrined in the Hall of Fame.

Speaking of first-ballot Hall of Famers, in July 2016 Cooperstown welcomed Ken Griffey Jr., whose appearance on 99.3 percent of ballots set a new record—and, by the way, none of the three voters who omitted him has had the courage to come forward. Junior was clearly a Hall of Famer by any standard, but the narrative of his career doesn't quite match the facts, either—to wit, his insistence on continuing to play center field in the last ten years of his career meant that he stopped being a valuable big leaguer after age thirty, and his defense was so bad in his thirties that he had several seasons where he was actively hurting the team just by playing.

Griffey Jr.'s career through age thirty was one of the best in history, marred only by injuries that seemed to stem from how hard he played in the field. He was known for highlight catches in center, and up to age twenty-seven or so his defensive numbers were outstanding, with 88 runs saved above average by TotalZone through that season. After his age-thirty season in 2000, he had 438 homers, a .296/.380/.568 triple-slash line, and 76 Wins Above Replacement (per Baseball-Reference); had he quit right there, he'd have been worthy of enshrinement in the Hall, and he appeared to be on pace for one of the five or ten greatest careers of all time.

His defensive numbers started to slip in his late twenties, and he should have moved out of center field right around age thirty or thirty-one, his first two years in Cincinnati after he'd spent the first eleven years of his career in Seattle. From 2001 to 2006, his last six years as a regular center fielder, his defense was worth 73 runs *below* an average center fielder by TotalZone. We have UZR figures available from 2003 forward; between 2003 and 2006, UZR has him 66 runs below average (plus another two runs below average in 2008, when the White Sox traded for him and delusionally returned him to center). He destroyed significant value with his play in the field, and because no team was willing to force him out of center field until about five years too late. For most of those seasons his bat would have been below average for any position he might have been able to play. Combined with Griffey's decline as a hitter to a .260/.350/.483 line from 2001 until he retired, he generated only about 7.5 Wins Above Replacement of value for the last half of his career, one-tenth of what he was worth in the first half. What could have been one of the greatest careers of all time stalled out after Griffey turned thirty.

*   *   *

While for some players and positions these advanced defensive metrics are useful for the academic debates around the Hall of Fame, when it comes to catchers, their use is much more immediate. Indeed, for catchers advanced metrics are becoming more and more vital in game-time decisions, and this comes despite the fact that UZR and other similar stats do not apply to catchers because catchers don't have range or zones in the same way other players on the field do. Catcher defense is a sum of parts that include controlling the running game, receiving, framing pitches, and game-calling, only some of which is measurable with the data we have right now.

The defensive value of catchers has posed many specific problems over the years, given the complex nature of the catcher's job: receiver, game-caller, and primary obstacle to base stealers. A catcher receives a putout on each strikeout, which is one of the most absurd statistical oddities in traditional stats and makes any stat based solely on putouts and assists useless for the position. Passed balls count against the catcher, but wild pitches do not, even though the difference between the two is a subjective decision by the official scorer.

Base-stealing value itself isn't as easy as it may first appear, because of confounding factors around when opposing runners attempt to steal. Certain pitchers hold runners well, or have great pickoff moves, so runners might as well be nailed to the first-base bag. Other pitchers just don't bother with the running game, like the Mets' Noah Syndergaard in 2016. Opposing baserunners stole 48 bases in 57 attempts with Syndergaard on the mound that season, both of which were the highest in the major leagues by huge margins, because Syndergaard didn't do anything to try to hold runners. The Mets may not have had Johnny Bench behind the plate, but their catchers' caught-stealing rates were worse than they might have been if Syndergaard had worked to keep runners from stealing. (Even worse than Syndergaard was Yankee reliever Dellin Betances, who is the worst-fielding pitcher I've ever personally scouted; Betances threw 73 innings in 2016, and baserunners were a perfect 21 for 21 in base-stealing attempts with him on the mound.)

The throwing prowess of a catcher can also suppress base-stealing attempts: If you know a catcher can really throw, then you're probably not going to take the chance on getting thrown out. Longtime Cardinals great Yadier Molina, who represents a sort of gold standard for catcher defense in fact and in reputation, has a career 42 percent caught-stealing rate—that is, runners have only succeeded in 58 percent of attempts—in his career in the majors, about 50 percent higher than the league average during those years. Defensive metrics will credit him with the plays he's made, but public metrics don't consider the plays *not* made—runners who just gave up rather than try to run against him. Molina has seen about two-thirds of the attempts that a league-average catcher saw in those years. Your advance scouting reports on the Cardinals will tell you to run on Molina at your own peril, and that should be to Molina's credit somehow, even though any value assigned to him is ultimately an estimate of something that didn't happen.

Then there's the controversial but indisputably real subject of catcher framing, the process by which catchers can affect umpires' ball or strike calls just by how they receive those pitches.

Measuring catcher framing is perhaps the newest catcher-specific defensive metric. The first public research on catcher framing appeared on the sabermetrics blog Beyond the Box Score in 2008, by Dan Turkenkopf, who subsequently went on to run the analytics department for the Milwaukee Brewers. Pitch-framing was long one of those black-box topics in baseball, where everyone acknowledged that it existed, without actual proof of its existence or its degree, due mostly to our inability to measure it. By 2008, we were starting to get the data required to evaluate just how much value a good framing catcher could provide his team—or how much a bad framer could cost his team—and the results of such research have thoroughly altered the ways in which teams value and pay their backstops.

Framing is a euphemism for what is actually happening behind the plate: Catchers who frame well are stealing strikes. Good fram-

ers have the ability to take pitches that are, in nearly all cases, within
two inches of the perimeter of the strike zone and get them called
for strikes more often than the average catcher can; poor framers
do the opposite. Home plate umpires are asked to do an impossible
job, to call balls and strike from behind the catcher when their view
is perforce obstructed by the catcher, and to determine where the
ball was when it crossed the plane of home plate rather than where
it was when the catcher caught it. Umpires make plenty of mistakes
on ball/strike calls—even though, as a percentage of total pitches
called, their error rates are surprisingly low, around 3 percent—and
it turns out that good catchers can affect those borderline calls to
their advantage.

If the idea of stealing strikes sounds wrong or jarring to you, well,
you're far from alone. There's no other situation on the field where
we accept tricking the umps as a part of the game, much less as a
player skill worth compensating. If an outfielder were discovered to
have a special ability to trap balls in play so that they appeared to be
caught on the fly for outs, we wouldn't stand for this. We don't allow
pitchers to doctor the baseball to make it move in unusual ways—a
matter of player safety as well as of fairness. But the idea of a good
pitch-framer is well ingrained in the game, so when analysts like
Turkenkopf and later Mike Fast of Baseball Prospectus (and now the
Houston Astros) started to put large values on the best and worst
framing performances, no one batted an eye.

You'll hear various maxims around baseball like "the best pitch
in baseball is strike one" or that "the most important pitch is the
one-one pitch," the latter referring to the pitch thrown when the
count on the batter is one ball and one strike. There's some real truth
in there, despite their pithy nature, because the expected outcome
of an at bat shifts dramatically with the count. When the first pitch
of an at bat was a strike, hitters in 2016 hit .223/.266/.352, and
when the first pitch was a ball, hitters hit .271/.382/.457. When the
1-1 pitch was a strike, hitters in 2016 hit .178/.229/.279, and when
the 1-1 pitch was a ball, hitters hit .249/.386/.418. Those are enormous gaps. Catcher-framing stats work off those gaps, estimating

the value of a ball called a strike (or vice versa) because of the way the catcher caught the pitch based on the count at which it occurred.

Fast's September 2011 piece at Baseball Prospectus, "Removing the Mask," built on Turkenkopf's work and showed that pitch-framing mattered in a huge way; Fast's research, covering the seasons 2007 to 2011, showed Jose Molina's framing was worth 35 extra runs to his team per 120 games caught (about a full season for a starting catcher), Jonathan Lucroy ranked second at 24 runs per 120 games, and the worst catchers in that span cost their teams about 25 runs per 120 games caught. Just going from a league-worst framer to an average one would be worth about two and a half wins to your team, using the rough guideline of about ten runs scored or prevented adding up to a win of value. (That equivalency will vary over time, depending on the run-scoring environment, but it's not going to vary enough to change the conclusion here that framing matters.)

Fast's research landed him a job with Houston and changed the market for valuing catchers. Catchers who could frame were suddenly in demand, and catchers who couldn't saw their markets start to shrink. The Tampa Bay Rays acquired Molina, a truly awful hitter, from Toronto, and he caught in 281 games for them over the next three years despite a .213/.271/.286 triple-slash line. Over that span, his framing was worth 70 runs prevented to Tampa Bay, according to Baseball Prospectus's framing statistics.

Tampa Bay's GM, Andrew Friedman, left the Rays to become the president of baseball operations for the Los Angeles Dodgers after the 2014 season, and hired Farhan Zaidi, formerly an assistant GM for the Oakland A's who was also in charge of much of the team's statistical research, to be the Dodgers' new GM. One of their most significant moves in their first off-season at the helm of the Dodgers was a massive trade with the San Diego Padres that included catcher Yasmani Grandal, who had worn out his welcome with Padres pitchers for his poor receiving and game-calling. Grandal happened to be an outstanding pitch-framer, and his framing saved the Dodgers 25.6 runs in 2015 and 27.5 runs in 2016, also according to BP's framing stats.

Baseball Prospectus's Harry Pavlidis and Jonathan Judge have continued to improve their framing metrics, introducing a new version before the 2014 season that they called RPM framing, with RPM standing for "regressed, probabilistic model." This is heavier-weight statistical work that smooths out the data by looking at the probability of each pitch type in each location being called a strike, taking umpire tendencies on those pitches into account, and then regressing those career totals to the league average, a statistical technique designed to reduce noise or randomness in the sample.

BP's results at that time weren't too surprising; for the period 2008–13, the best framers were Brian McCann, Jose Molina, and Jonathan Lucroy, while the worst were Ryan Doumit, Gerald Laird, and Chris Iannetta. Doumit retired after 2014 and hadn't caught even half of his team's games since 2010, while Laird played just one game in 2015 before calling it quits. Iannetta continues to get opportunities to play regularly behind the plate as of this writing, although for this I can offer no explanation. BP further updated their model before the 2016 season and it remains the best framing metric available in the public sphere.

Pavlidis and Judge continued their work on quantifying the value of catcher defense with a pair of presentations at the annual saber-metrics conference called Saberseminar, held every year in mid-August in Boston. Their work looked at the question of catcher game-calling (which would include calling pitch types and locations) and whether we might be able to infer any such skill from looking at pitch-by-pitch data for various catchers while they were behind the plate. This was a preliminary look and it appeared that the impact that they found was much smaller than that of pitch-framing, but it also demonstrates how the torrent of new data available to teams and analysts is changing the way we look at the game. Now we can question conventional wisdom—perhaps refuting it, but also perhaps confirming it—in ways that were impossible a decade earlier.

And in the end, the same can be said, not just for catching stats but for defensive stats as a whole. Fielding was long a total unknown for analysts and front office executives trying to ascertain the true value of a player's performance, and then it gradually improved as better play-by-play data became available for the majors and eventually for the minors as well. Analysts still had to make some estimates, so these metrics never had the level of accuracy we expect from, say, batting statistics; we're estimating how often a fielder makes a certain play, how many runs the play would be worth if it weren't made, and even things like how hard the ball was hit or where the fielders involved were standing at the start of the play.

While the data are getting better with the help of MLB, many of the emerging defensive metrics remain proprietary. Several analysts told me that UZR and dRS represent the best fielding metrics available to the lay public, so I'll continue to use them to talk about player values. But the divergence between what teams know and what is available to those of us in the public is emblematic of the rise of Big Data within baseball; valuing fielding has been seen as a sort of Hilbert's problem in baseball for several decades, a critical question to answer if teams wanted to value players accurately, but a question in search of the right data to allow anyone to solve it. This remains an ongoing effort within front offices, one that has accelerated with the advent of new, precise data on fielder positioning—that is, where everyone's standing when the play starts—that's available to all thirty teams but, alas, not yet available to the public.

The knowledge gap is also emblematic of a greater gap between what the average fan can follow. In many ways, baseball is becoming a more technical sport to understand. It's still a simple game to watch and enjoy, but as you'll see later, in Part Three, teams are now advancing in data analysis at a speed we haven't previously seen in the sport, introducing not just new metrics but entirely new ways to think about player performance.

14

No Puns Intended:

Going to WAR to Value the Whole Player

If you've been confused by recent debates about baseball players—whether it's trades or MVP Awards or the Hall of Fame—that refer to stats like WAR (Wins Above Replacement), this is the chapter for you. That doesn't mean this chapter is about WAR specifically, and it's certainly not going to be a defense of the construct—WAR itself isn't a stat, but a way of putting other stats together—but it is going to explain why we might want to look at players in the way that the various flavors of WAR let us look at players. And if you want to understand these debates, or think about players the way front offices do, you need to understand how we even got to this point, where WAR could dominate debates over player value even when we don't agree on what the best WAR is.

When I say that WAR isn't a stat, but a construct, I'm trying to get a couple of pieces of information across in the most concise fashion I can. Measuring player value is an idea. There are many ways to implement this idea, depending on how you measure the individual parts of a player performance, how you weigh them against one another, and what adjustments you include for the player's environment or other outside factors. WAR has become like Kleenex here: Kleenex isn't the only kind of tissue, and WAR isn't the only way to measure a player's total value, but the terms have lost their specific meanings over time.

Wins Above Replacement means roughly what it says: this player produced this many wins of total value above a replacement-level (baseline) player. It doesn't tell you how to measure any of that. You can use whatever formula for wins you want, and whatever kind of replacement-level player calculation you want, and call the difference WAR. You could try to calculate a pitcher's WAR with his win total; you'd get ridiculous results, but as long as you compared it to a replacement level, well, that's kind of Wins Above Replacement. (I threw up in my mouth as I typed that.) You have to compare the player's production to something, and that something isn't zero; it can be an average, but the overwhelming preference of analysts and sabermetricians is to compare it to replacement level, a number based off the average that represents the "free" talent available to teams in the form of triple-A players. The value a player generates above that free talent is the value he delivers to his team, in wins or, ultimately, in dollars.

If someone says to you they don't like WAR or use WAR, or they think WAR is a garbage stat, they're telling you they don't *understand* WAR. WAR is a construct, a bare-bones blueprint for comparing a player's total value to an objective baseline level tied to playing time. If you ask analysts working for MLB teams how they calculate the total value of a player's production, the answers you get will sound an awful lot like WAR. Their calculations are more precise than the public ones, but the core concept is the same.

Set WAR aside for a few moments and just imagine you're the general manager of a Major League Baseball team. It's November 1, and free agency is about to start. Your owner has told you that you have $30 million in extra budget to spend to acquire new players this off-season, by whatever means you choose. That's over and above what's already committed to players currently in your organization. What should your goal be?

If you said "to make your team better," well, duh. That's always the goal. But the goal this time around has a constraint, too: you have a fixed amount of room in your budget. You could increase that by trading away existing players, but you'd also lose their contributions. However you look at the problem, you have a boundary on how much you can do.

So instead, your goal has to be more specific, acknowledging that constraint explicitly. I would phrase the goal as "to improve the team as much as possible given the maximum payroll," or, even more specifically, "to add as many wins to the team in the next season as possible," assuming that you're not trying to rebuild, of course. You want to add players who'll add wins. You want to add the best players $30 million can buy you. And that probably means buying players, whether it's via free agency or trade, who'll be worth more than the price you pay to acquire them. You want to pay a player $10 million and have him be worth $20 million, or $25 million, or more.

How do we determine the dollar value of a player? It's simple math, even though I'm sure some of you are already getting all hoity-toity over the idea of putting a dollar figure on a man's worth. It's nothing personal, just business. You need to figure out how much baseball value he's likely to produce, and then figure out how much that value is worth to your team, in dollars. The second part of that is always going to be team-specific: the marginal value of a win—that is, the increased revenue a team can expect from one more win on the field—depends on the team's market, elasticity of its attendance, place in the standings, likelihood to make the playoffs (the single most valuable win you can get is the one that puts your team into the playoffs), and so on. We can't really know that part as fans.

But we can know, or more correctly estimate, the value of a player's total production by valuing all of the individual things he does on the field and then adding all of those values together. For a position player, that would mean valuing his batting contributions, his base-running contributions, and his fielding contributions. For a catcher, we should probably also consider his pitch-framing—his ability to steal strikes by how he receives borderline pitches, a strange way to contribute value but one that is real and quite significant—although some aspects of catching, like game-calling, remain difficult or impossible to quantify.

Analysts also consider the value of a position player relative to his position, because the average shortstop does not hit as well as the average left fielder or designated hitter. It is easier to find a player to play a position on that latter end of the defensive spectrum than a player on the end that includes the more demanding positions. Exact position values will fluctuate slightly year to year, but I think of the spectrum this way:

Positions Hardest to Easiest
SS, C
CF
2B, 3B
RF
1B
LF
DH

You can compare a player to the "replacement level" for his position, which is what WAR does, or you can compare the player to the average for his position, as long as you bear in mind that an average player is actually still quite valuable because somewhere between a third and half of the teams probably get less than average production from that spot. (That's the mathematical average, as opposed to the median, above or below which we'd find exactly half of the teams.) Before we can even do this simple comparison, though, we have to decide how to value everything a hitter does at the plate.

What is a home run worth?

It seems like a simple question, with a simple answer: A home run is worth one run. If a player hits a home run, he scores, every time, without fail. That's worth one run.

But the home run also has the power to score every runner who's already on base at the time that it's hit. That could be zero runners, one, two, or three. Clearly a home run can, in many situations, be worth more than one run, because it can drive in a runner from any base. A runner on first isn't that likely to score in the abstract, but a home run ensures that he does.

Figuring out what a home run is worth is part of the larger way that analysts measure total offense. Each plate appearance for a hitter is a discrete event, and each event outcome—an out, a hit, a walk, and so on—has a specific value. If you assign a value to each outcome for a hitter and add them all up, factoring in the ballparks where the hitter played, you get a total value for his offensive contributions.

The method for doing this is known as "linear weights": you take the weight (value) of each outcome and add them all up, linearly, without fancy multiplicative effects or exponents or other I-was-promised-there-would-be-no-math voodoo. It is quite simple, using a formula that gives us a form of hitter value in runs:

Batting Runs = value of a single * number of singles PLUS
value of a double * number of doubles PLUS
value of a triple * number of triples PLUS
value of a HR * number of HR PLUS
value of a walk * number of walks PLUS
value of a HBP * number of HBP MINUS
value of an out * number of outs made

Some formulas also add in weights for stolen bases and times caught stealing, while others separate that into a separate formula for baserunning, but the concept remains the same. We're trying to value a player's offensive production by valuing all the individual things he does and then adding them up. You can also adjust the resulting numbers to reflect the park in which the hitter played his home games—hitting 30 home runs at the launching pad of Coors

Field is not as valuable or as difficult as hitting 30 at pitcher-friendly Petco Park, so an advanced offensive metric should reflect that. It doesn't have to be more complicated than this because making it more complicated doesn't give us any more accuracy.

Statistician George Lindsey was the first to publish a method of valuing offense like this, way back in 1963 in the academic journal *Operations Research,* in a paper titled "An Investigation of Strategies in Baseball," a paper that had no known effect on MLB at the time (shocker) but did prove highly influential to the generation of baseball analysts and writers outside the industry. These included Bill James, Steve Mann, and John Thorn and Pete Palmer, the latter two of whom brought their linear-weights formula to a wider audience in the seminal 1984 book *The Hidden Game of Baseball.* (The book is so important that I jumped at the chance to write the foreword when the University of Chicago Press reissued it in 2015.) Palmer and Thorn later used their formulas in the *Total Baseball* encyclopedias, which were published from 1989 to 2004.

The Palmer/Thorn linear weights formula, called Batting Runs, derives from Palmer's simulations of MLB games from 1901 to 1978, which must have been a significant undertaking given the technology available to him at the time. Their version was:

$$Batting \ Runs = .46*1B + .80*2B + 1.02*3B + 1.40*HR + .33*BB + .33*HBP + .30*SB - 0.60*CS - .25*(AB - H) - .50*(OOB)†$$

Don't get hung up on the coefficients in that formula; you're not going to be quizzed at the end of the chapter, and they're out of date anyway. But notice what they do tell us about the relative values of these events:

- A home run is worth 1.4 runs, which means its power to score other runners on base is worth 0.4 runs on top of the one run it's automatically worth because the batter scores.

---

† OOB equals outs made on the bases, which might otherwise fall into a baserunning stat.

- Whereas slugging percentage values a homer at four times that of a single, this Batting Runs formula has that ratio at three, meaning that slugging percentage actually overvalues home runs—and all extra-base hits, in fact.

- A single is worth about 30 percent more than a walk. This makes sense, since a single advances all runners and can advance some runners more than one base, while a walk can only advance runners who are forced to move up.

- A batter who comes to the plate four times and hits three singles has produced more value than the batter who comes to the plate four times and hits one home run. The first batter has produced 1.13 runs of value (.46*3 –.25*1), while the second batter has produced .65 runs of value (1.40*1 –.25*3). This may sound counterintuitive—how could a batter homer and yet produce less than one run of value on the day?—but it reinforces my earlier argument that a batter making an out has actually destroyed value, reducing the team's chances of scoring in that particular inning.

The individual coefficients change over time as the run-scoring environment changes—for example, a home run is worth more in years when offense is down than when it's up—but the concept remains the same. A hitter does things. Those things have value. Add up the values of the things and you get the total value he produced.

Somehow this became controversial, because that's not How We've Always Done Things Around Here, Son, but over the last ten years, it's become standard within the industry to look at players this way, and that change has gradually (albeit not completely) come through to the media and to a portion of the overall fan base. There are still people shouting on TV and radio about nerds and newfangled statistics, but their numbers are declining and they are increasingly becoming punch lines.

Palmer and Thorn used stolen bases and caught stealing in their master formula and, in *The Hidden Game,* broke them out into a

separate Base Stealing Runs number. The indispensable site Fangraphs has updated this formula in by adding Ultimate Base Running (UBR), which also includes the value baserunners create or
destroy with their actions on the base paths—such as going from
first to third on a hit, or failing to take an extra base, or scoring/not
scoring from third on a flyball. Fangraphs combines its weighted stolen base values with UBR and a smaller factor, wGDP, that weighs
a hitter's ability to avoid or propensity for hitting into double plays
compared to the league-average rate of doing so, to get a total Base
Running Runs number that is the most complete measure publicly
available for a player's running value.

To give you some sense of what a good Batting Runs total would
be, here are the leaders, using Fangraphs' formula (excluding baserunning), for 2015, along with their avg/obp/slg triple-slash line:

	BR	AVG	OBP	SLG
Bryce Harper, WAS	74.3	.330	.460	.649
Joey Votto, CIN	58.6	.314	.459	.541
Mike Trout, LAA	57.1	.299	.402	.590
Paul Goldschmidt, ARI	51.9	.321	.435	.570
Josh Donaldson, TOR	44.3	.297	.371	.568

These Batting Runs numbers are "park-adjusted," meaning that
they've been modified slightly to reflect the hitters' home ballparks.
Goldschmidt plays half his games in Chase Field, a relatively good hitter's park (it's about one thousand feet above sea level), while Trout
plays in one of the majors' best pitchers' parks in Angel Stadium.

And, just for kicks, the worst hitters in MLB in 2015:

	BR	AVG	OBP	SLG
Chris Owings, ARI	−30.6	.227	.264	.322
Jean Segura, MIL	−25.7	.257	.281	.336
Alcides Escobar, KC	−25.6	.257	.293	.320
Wilson Ramos, WAS	−21.9	.229	.258	.358
Alexei Ramirez, CWS	−20.3	.249	.285	.357

In a little bit of baseball slapstick, the Diamondbacks made a big trade in the off-season to replace Owings . . . with Segura.

All five players on this list play in the middle of the field, with Ramos a catcher and the others all shortstops by trade, meaning that they play positions where teams will often sacrifice some offense to gain value on defense—or will accept awful offense because they can't find anyone more capable to fill those positions. This is why shortstops and catchers are highly valued in the market for players— the draft, international free agency, MLB free agency, and trades. There are never really enough to go around, and that's how you end up with Alcides Escobar having one of the worst offensive seasons in the majors . . . on the team that won the World Series that same year.

For a pitcher, we have a couple of ways to approach the problem of value, depending on how much you want to consider the benefit (or harm) a pitcher gets from the defense behind him or just plain ol' luck. A pitcher's fundamental job is to get outs; the more hitters he retires, the better for his team, right? If a pitcher retired every batter he faced, he'd be the best pitcher ever. So we could simply base our valuation of a pitcher's performance by how many hitters he faced, how many he retired, and what the hitters he didn't retire ended up doing—hits, extra-base hits, walks, hit batsmen, and so on.

I slid right by something in that last paragraph, though. Is a pitcher's fundamental job to get outs, or to prevent runs? If a pitcher allows 12 hits in a shutout, did he do his job? If a pitcher retires 27 of 29 hitters but gives up two runs in a complete game, did he do a better job than the first guy? Disentangling pitching performance from defense and luck while also considering how much to weigh sequencing remains a contentious subject, because there is merit on both sides of the argument.

By sequencing, I mean the order in which things happen to a pitcher; flyout, walk, walk, homer, groundout is not the same as homer, walk, walk, groundball double play, flyout. Those two sequences have the same five events, but the first one scores three runs with two outs recorded while the second one scores one run with three outs recorded. Sequence matters. And to some extent there's a skill involved in this; there are pitchers who are worse with runners on base because it requires them to pitch from the stretch or slide-step rather than the windup. Some pitchers lose a mile an hour or so on their fastballs from this; some just have a harder time maintaining their mechanics (and thus command) when in the less comfortable delivery.

But sequencing isn't always very predictive. We can look at a pitcher's walk rate as a percentage of batters faced, and it'll tell us how likely he is to walk batters going forward. The same is true of his strikeout rate, which implies his contact rate—and since pitchers by and large tend to give up fairly consistent batting averages on balls they allow in play, we can somewhat predict the rate at which he'll allow hits in the future, too. Home run rates show more variance, but for many pitchers they stay within a small range around those pitchers' flyball rates (the percentage of balls in play they allow that are classified as flyballs rather than groundballs or line drives). What those rates together don't tell us is whether those negative events will be clustered together or not; we can estimate how many runs the pitcher will allow over a large enough sample, but even a full season isn't enough of a sample to smooth out all of the noise we might find in a pitcher's performance. And even if it were, defense matters— how good the fielders behind a pitcher are and how well they were positioned—because no pitcher can do his job in a vacuum. Two pitchers could generate the same groundball to shortstop, but the one in front of Andrelton Simmons sees it converted into an out while the one in front of Derek Jeter sees it go past him into center field. Life ain't fair, but our stats should be.

Because there is no consensus on which of these two approaches is actually the better way to value a pitcher, I'm going to continue to discuss both for the remainder of this chapter. You can find WAR based on a pitcher's runs allowed on Baseball-Reference, and WAR based on a pitcher's performance on a per-batter basis on Fangraphs, although anyone could calculate WAR one of these ways or using some kind of hybrid or smoothing approach to split the baby (if, say, you wanted to calculate a new WAR for Salomon Torres).

Regardless of method, we want to value pitchers based on what they prevented, whether that something is a run or a hit. Sticking with the run-based approach for the moment, a pitcher with a 5.00 ERA is obviously less valuable than one with a 3.00 ERA, but how do we determine just how much less? If they have the same number of innings pitched, we can look at the difference between their earned runs allowed and say that the second pitcher prevented N more runs than the first one. So if both pitchers threw 180 innings, the pitcher with the 5.00 ERA gave up 100 runs while the pitcher with the 3.00 ERA gave up 60 runs, and we could say that the second pitcher prevented 40 runs when compared to the first one. That's the value he provided over what the first pitcher provided (or destroyed, since a 5.00 ERA is kind of terrible unless you pitch your home games on the moon).

This approach puts an implicit cap on the value a reliever can provide, because relievers today typically max out around 80 innings a year. An average starting pitcher who throws about 200 innings will be worth more than most of the relievers in baseball, even the best ones, because he gets another 120 innings in which to prevent runs—that is, to provide more value. This is why starters are paid more in free agency, are worth more in trade, and, in my personal opinion, are better choices for the All-Star Game than all but the absolute elite of the relievers.

To give you some sense of how relievers measure up to starters, let's look at Matt Moore, who was the closest thing to a perfectly league-average starter in MLB in 2016. Moore's ERA was 4.07 and his FIP was 4.17; the major-league ERA for the whole season was 4.18 and its FIP was 4.19. (Moore was traded in July from the AL's Tampa Bay Rays to the NL's San Francisco Giants, so he spent slightly more time in the DH league, which tends to have higher run-scoring.) Moore threw 198 innings across 33 starts, and both major sites calculate his Wins Above Replacement at 2.2.

There were 132 relievers across all of MLB in 2016 who threw at least 50 innings, the bare minimum I'd consider a full season's worth of work. How many of those relievers were more valuable than good ol' League-Average Matt Moore? Baseball-Reference says twelve.

Fangraphs says seven. Either way, it means an elite reliever, performing well into the top 10 percent of all relievers in that season, is only
worth as much in run prevention as a league-average starter.

Many more relievers than that posted ERAs or FIPs below
Moore's, but they only threw a third as many innings—and there's
value in just throwing league-average innings to a major-league team,
because league-average pitching is hard to find. The distribution of
baseball talent is such that you will find fewer pitchers in any season
who perform at an above-average level than below average, because
guys who perform below the average tend to lose their jobs, often
to other guys who also perform below the average but at least do it
with a different name on the back of the uniform. Average is never
an insult in baseball—it makes you better than most, and teams are
willing to pay a lot of money for a player who can be average and
handle the workload of a full season.

If I told you you had a choice of two pitchers, one who would
be dead average for 200 innings and one who would be just a shade
above average for 66 innings, which would you take? What if the
second pitcher were comfortably above average? Well above average? Elite? Somewhere those two lines intersect, where you'd rather
have the reliever and figure you'll make up the missing innings
somewhere else, but even without resorting to numbers, you should
know intuitively that the reliever has to be a lot better in his shorter
workload to match the value of the 200-inning starter. It turns out
that a full-season starter whose run prevention (ERA, FIP, pick your
poison) is at the 50th percentile is more valuable as a full-season
reliever whose run prevention is at the 90th percentile.

However, even a run-based approach should probably look beyond innings pitched, because the inning isn't really the right unit
here. An inning means three outs, but doesn't always mean the same
number of batters—and doesn't even mean the pitcher himself retired three batters. An inning must have three batters at a minimum,
but can have up to six batters without a run scoring. We measure
batters on a per plate appearance basis, because it's obvious that
that is the correct fundamental unit for a batter—it's one discrete

event for him. For a pitcher, however, it's the same thing: Each batter he faces is *also a discrete event*. Yes, we think about a pitcher by how many innings he pitches over the course of a season, or even within a game, but an inning is an atom, and we can break an atom down further into smaller parts that help explain how matter behaves and even what matter is. If baseball has its superstring, it's the plate appearance.

If we evaluate pitchers on a runs-prevented framework, which Palmer and Thorn called Pitching Runs, there's still disagreement over how best to isolate a pitcher's contribution (which I discussed in the chapter on ERA), and even then there are different ways to skin the proverbial cat of pitching valuation.

There is one basic tenet in common among all methods of valuing pitchers: it's about runs prevented. The pitcher threw some innings and gave up some stuff—hits, walks, homers—that led to some runs. How many runs would an average pitcher have given up in those innings?

If I tell you a pitcher gave up 4 runs for every 9 innings he pitched in a season, is that good? Well, if the league RA9 (run average, or runs allowed per 9 innings) is 3, then no, it's probably not good. But if I tell you that same pitcher pitched half his home games in Denver, a mile above sea level, or on the surface of the moon, then okay, maybe it's not so bad. If that pitcher played in front of the best defensive unit in baseball history, though, maybe it's not so good after all. And so on. Context matters, which is why all good baseball metrics use a set baseline, like the average, and compare players to that.

So a good pitching value metric starts with runs allowed, which you can then compare to a baseline level of runs allowed for an average pitcher or a replacement-level pitcher to determine how many runs the pitcher prevented. You can simply use the pitcher's actual runs allowed, which is the method used by Baseball-Reference.com (which I used very heavily in writing this book), or you can estimate his hypothetical runs allowed given his performance on a per-batter basis, which is the method Fangraphs uses. I see merit in both methods, and I look at both sites when considering a pitcher's value, be-cause each number tells me something—and so does the difference between the two.*

Once you settle on your RA9—again, the pitcher's runs allowed per 9 innings—you have to try to tweak it for the environment, which includes adjusting it for the ballparks in which the pitcher pitched. I mentioned the sad soul who throws half his starts in Denver at Coors Field, but other pitchers have to pitch there, too, with pitch-ers in the Colorado Rockies' division, the NL West, pitching there more often than pitchers in other divisions. Baseball-Reference also adjusts the RA9 by the strength of the opposing offenses the pitcher faced, and assesses a small penalty to relievers, whose average RA9 is typically about .15–.20 runs lower than the average for starters. Yes, it's a lot of adjusting, but I can't just hand-wave it away, because it's necessary to get some level of precision in our result.

Take the RA9 that comes out of all that adjusting and compare it to the league average RA9. That difference, multiplied by the pitcher's innings-pitched total and divided by 9, gives you an esti-mate of the number of runs the pitcher prevented over the course of that time period, which is now called Runs Above Average but might as well be called Pitching Runs or Runs Prevented, as it all amounts to the same thing: this is what the pitcher was worth, mea-sured in runs.

Let's look at more tables! Temper your excitement, please; it's a little unbecoming. First, here are the top five pitchers in the NL using the actual runs allowed approach of Baseball-Reference:

---

* Baseball-Reference's method tells you the numbers on the scoreboard—did the pitcher prevent runs in real life. Fangraphs' method tells you what the pitcher did on a per-batter basis and strips out stuff that may have been out of his control—defense, bullpen support, bad luck—and some stuff that might have been in his control, such as pitching worse from the stretch or allowing more hard contact than he should have. The difference between the two tells you how much information, which is probably a mix of noise and signal, is removed when you go from B-R's method to Fangraphs'. A pitcher whose value on Fangraphs is higher than it is on B-R might have had some bad luck or poor support, and maybe didn't help his own cause much. You might expect such a pitcher to see his superficial stats improve going forward.

Pitcher	RAA (Pitching Runs)	ERA	IP
Zack Greinke, LAD	54.5	1.66	$222^{2}/_{3}$
Jake Arrieta, CHC	53.2	1.77	229
Clayton Kershaw, LAD	42.2	2.13	$232^{2}/_{3}$
Dallas Keuchel, HOU	40.0	2.48	232
David Price, DET/TOR	34.8	2.45	$220^{1}/_{3}$

Now, the same ranking, using Fangraphs' approach, which is based on a pitcher's walks, strikeouts, and home runs allowed, and uses a league-wide BABIP (batting average on balls in play) to estimate runs allowed:

Pitcher	RAA (Pitching Runs)	ERA	IP
Clayton Kershaw, LAD	71.2	2.13	$232^{2}/_{3}$
Jake Arrieta, CHC	62.1	1.77	229
David Price, DET/TOR	55.9	2.45	$220^{1}/_{3}$
Max Scherzer, WAS	55.3	2.79	$228^{2}/_{3}$
Chris Sale, CWS	54.5	3.41	$208^{2}/_{3}$

Sale has been an underrated pitcher for most of his big-league career, as he plays in a fairly homer-friendly ballpark at New Comisk—I mean, US Cellular Park, and has generally not played in front of good defensive units. His FIP, the base runs-allowed figure Fangraphs uses to calculate its RAA here, is 2.73, so they're saying that his defense/bullpen/bad luck cost him about two-thirds of a run in his ERA.

Also notable is that Kershaw went from third in the majors to first, a swing of 29 runs prevented in value. Imagine that you're a general manager asked to decide how much to pay Kershaw for the upcoming season. You have two analysts working for you. One says Kershaw was worth 42 runs prevented in 2015, and the other says he was worth 71. Do you just fire them both and pull a salary out of a hat?

The debate between these two methods of valuing pitchers is part philosophical and part analytical. Many people dislike the idea that pitchers have no control over the results of balls put into play, and it's possible, given improved data that MLB is providing to teams via its Statcast product, that we'll find out they have a little more control than we'd believed for the last decade. But for forecasting, you'll get slightly better results using an approach based on the pitcher's "peripheral" stats, as Fangraphs does, than you will using an RA- or ERA-based approach.

But what's good for forecasting isn't necessarily good for valuing past production. Zack Greinke's 1.66 ERA was the lowest any starting pitcher had posted in twenty years, the lowest in a nonstrike season in thirty years, and the eighth-lowest of any starting pitcher since the live-ball era began in 1921. (Two of the seasons above him on the list were Bob Gibson and Luis Tiant in 1968, the "year of the pitcher," when MLB raised the height of the mound.) Whether we think Greinke was lucky, or helped by his defense, or aided by a demon summoned from the sixth circle of hell, the 1.66 ERA means that while he was pitching or responsible for the runners on base, very few guys actually scored. You'd pay more to get Greinke's 1.66 ERA than Kershaw's 2.13 ERA, even though you'd bet on Kershaw being better than Greinke in the following season (which turned out to be the case in 2016).

If it sounds like I'm refusing to take sides here, well, I am. I see merit in both ways of looking at player value and I use both methods myself when writing about big leaguers. If pushed to use one over the other, I'd take the peripheral-based approach that Fangraphs uses, but I recognize its imprecision as well and would hate to lose the information that the RA-based approach contains.

Of course, I did have to take sides on this issue in a very public way once, and it put me in the middle of a controversy I really wanted no part of.

In 2009, I voted on a BBWAA postseason award for the first time, and was given a ballot for the NL Cy Young Award, which in that particular year was quite competitive, with incumbent winner Tim Lincecum turning in another great year, but two Cardinals

pitchers, Adam Wainwright and Chris Carpenter, also having outstanding seasons, along with Atlanta starter Javier Vazquez and Arizona starter Dan Haren. Those five guys were clearly the top five
pitchers in the league, but how you ranked them depended a lot on
how you viewed the job of the pitcher and separated that out from
the contributions of his defense.

At the time, the Cy Young ballot contained just three spots for
names—shortly afterward the BBWAA added two more spots, probably in response to this situation—so I listed Tim Lincecum first,
Javier Vazquez second, and Adam Wainwright third. That order-
ing reflected a defense-neutral way of valuing their contributions,
which in that particular year discounted the Cardinals' pitchers performances a little relative to the other three names. Where it became
controversial, however, was around the omission of Carpenter, who
led the NL in ERA that year—with only 192 innings pitched, less
than any of the other four pitchers I mentioned above and a lower IP
total than any starting pitcher who won the Cy Young Award in any
full season since the award began in 1956.

If you followed the previous section, though, you can see why
that lower workload moved Carpenter off my ballot of the top three
pitchers. Pitching is about run prevention, yes, but the more you
pitch and prevent runs, the more value you deliver. Carpenter had
a lower ERA than Vazquez, but about the same FIP, and Vazquez
provided his team with another 27 innings of above-average pitching over what Carpenter gave St. Louis. Since Carpenter's innings
total was so low by historical standards, too, I didn't think my ballot
would garner any notice at all, figuring a lot of voters would omit
Carpenter for that reason, while Vazquez, who finished second in
the NL in strikeouts behind Lincecum, would grab a few second-
and third-place votes.

That . . . is not what happened. I was the only voter to include
Vazquez on any ballot at all, and one of only two to leave Carpenter
off my ballot entirely. This sparked a lot of silly outrage from a subset of Cardinals fans, many of whom couldn't do simple math and
claimed that I'd somehow cost Wainwright the Cy Young by list-
ing him third (putting him first and Lincecum second on my ballot

would not have changed the overall result). It also had the peculiar result of handing Vazquez a $70,000 bonus for finishing fourth in the Cy Young voting, even though he had appeared on just that one ballot. I've still never met Vazquez in person but I think I'd let him buy me a cup of coffee at Gustos the next time I'm in San Juan.

As for whether my ballot was "right," I just don't know. I think we'll be debating the separation of pitcher value from defensive contributions for some time to come, and it's quite possible that I'll look back on that ballot at some point and wish I'd listed the pitchers in a different order. Or not.

Regardless of whether you're valuing a hitter or a pitcher, the final piece of the WAR calculation comes from a player's value in the field. I discussed fielding value in a previous chapter, saying that whatever metric you use, whether it's a public one like dRS or UZR or a proprietary one developed by a team using MLB's own data, you're going to add up the values of the plays the fielder made and that he didn't make, comparing them to the probability of an average fielder making those plays. A shortstop who makes every play an average shortstop makes and then makes ten extra plays to his left and ten to his right will grade out a few runs above average, because those twenty plays would amount to "singles prevented." An outfielder could get the same bump in fewer plays, because an outfielder who catches a ball that is rarely caught is probably preventing extra bases.

Once you have all of the components of a player's value, you can simply add them up and get a total number of runs of value produced or prevented relative to the average player. If you divide that number by the number of runs of value needed to produce one additional win at the team level—it's usually right around 10, but does vary slightly as offensive levels change—then you can express the player's total value as Wins Above Average rather than Runs Above Average, but they say the same thing. For position players, we compare their production to the production of other players at the same specific positions, as the expected offensive output for a shortstop or catcher is far below the expected output for a first baseman or a designated hitter.

WAR, however, uses a different baseline, one that trips up a lot of fans and media because it is a novel concept not found outside of baseball. WAR stands for Wins Above Replacement, and rather than using a league-average player for that position, it uses a "replacement-level" player, a calculated level of production equal to what you'd expect a typical player recalled from the minors to be able to provide to a major-league team for the minimum salary. In other words, if the major leaguer whose value you're examining were to get hurt, and his team had to call up some random triple-A player to fill the spot, you'd expect to get replacement-level production, which would mean a WAR of zero.

This isn't perfect, and to some extent, it's widely used because it's what we have, and it's what teams use in their own internal metrics. (And perhaps because it's a lot easier to talk about someone's "war" than to talk about his "waa.") When readers attempt to argue with me over the concept of a replacement-level player, I point out that it's just a baseline, and you can use a different baseline if you wish without getting different results—it won't change the way you rank players' production, but will change what their relative values appear to be. We speak of a player who was worth 6 WAR being worth twice as much as the player who was worth 3 WAR, but that's not necessarily true; if we used the league average as a baseline, those numbers might drop to 4 and 1, respectively.

My real argument on replacement level, despite my misgivings over it, is that you have to pick *some* baseline and stick with it. The level used by Baseball-Reference and Fangraphs is arbitrary, and it might not be the best choice of baseline, but as long as it's transparent, then we can work with the results it gives us. Those sites both use a .294 team winning percentage, which translates to about a 48-114 record, as its replacement level, meaning that a team full of replacement-level players would be expected to post a .294 winning percentage over a full season. (So, yes, the 2003 Detroit Tigers, who went 43-119 and were by far the worst major-league team I've ever seen myself, were worse than replacement level.) A team with Mike

Trout, who has averaged just about 10 WAR per full season in the majors, and 24 replacement-level players would be expected to go 58-104.

Adding up the WAR numbers for all players on a team won't always match a team's win total (plus the 48 wins as a baseline), but it should get us close in most cases and over a large enough sample we'd expect them to coincide. The performance of a single team in a single season can be affected by performances in high-leverage situations, by managerial tactics (for better or for worse), strength of schedule, and so on, but if you look at hundreds of team-seasons, you'd expect their WAR totals to approach their win totals over 48—or else you need to reexamine the weights you're using for batting, pitching, or fielding runs.

Offense, defense, baserunning, run prevention—that's everything that goes into WAR, so when I say that WAR isn't a stat, but a construct, I hope now you can see the difference. WAR is just a way of adding up the various measurable components of a player's performance, setting a standard baseline, and using it to compare player value across seasons, leagues, even across eras. When writers mock WAR (and do so with headlines that should prompt Edwin Starr to sue for defamation), they think they're mocking a single stat when they're actually mocking the idea of valuing players at all. If you don't think you can value a player, I guess that's fine, but the entire industry has decided that it disagrees.

For a team's general manager or president—don't get me started on baseball title creep—to decide how much to pay a player, or how much to give up in trade for a player, he has to know what the player's past production has been worth, and will probably ask his analytics department to provide a projection for what that player's future production is likely to be as well. Each team will value production slightly differently, especially for the less definitive areas of valuation like fielding or pitching, but you can't begin the conversation about whether to pay Joey Bagodonuts $12 million a year or $14 million a year unless you at least know what his production last year was worth, or the year before that, or what your analysts say he's likely to be worth next year.

General managers face two major constraints when it comes to signing or acquiring major-league players: money and roster spots. Each team has its own payroll budget, a function of its market size, TV rights fees, and owner wealth. And each team has a 25-man active roster for major-league players, with a 40-man roster with those 25 players plus those on the major-league disabled list and minor leaguers with enough experience to require their inclusion on it. That means every decision about players—signing one, releasing one, trading one or several for one or several, and so on—occurs in the context of what else you could do with that money and that roster spot. (The same is true, with different constraints, in the draft.) If you, the GM, want to make these decisions in a rational way, you need to have a system that puts a single value on a player's past production or on a player's projected future production. You may call the system whatever you want, but it will end up as Runs or Wins Above Some Baseline. Without such an objective system, how could you decide which player to add or drop, or where to spend your limited resources or roster spots?

Teams operated in an informational vacuum for nearly all of MLB history, including the first thirty years of free agency, and the result was unsurprising—free agents were frequently mispriced and were largely paid for past performance they weren't likely to repeat. Today's MLB front offices aren't just using the WAR figures you find on public websites, they are calculating their own total values for players via proprietary formulas and using the results to make better decisions. Mocking the mere concept only serves to separate the Luddites in the media and audience from those who believe they should at least understand how front offices operate before they think of critiquing those decisions.

This is how the industry works today, and if you don't like it, build a better formula yourself.

PART THREE

---◆---

Smarter Baseball

15

Applied Math:

Looking at Hall of Fame Elections Using Newer Stats

The 2016 World Series may have been an inflection point in the history of baseball analysis, as two of the most overtly analytically focused front offices met in a series that saw both clubs dispense with much conventional wisdom on player usage—especially in how they deployed their pitchers—and led to the end of the longest championship drought in American professional sports.

The Chicago Cubs, who defeated the Cleveland Indians in seven games, had not even appeared in the World Series since 1945 and hadn't won the title since 1908, but ended both streaks thanks in part to the adoption of various analytical tools by their front office and field coaching staff. Led by President of Baseball Operations Theo Epstein, who had previously led the Red Sox to two World Series titles (including one that ended their own eighty-six-year drought) as their general manager, the Cubs overhauled their organization to build a top-flight analytics department, hired the analytically minded Joe Maddon as their field manager, and changed the team's entire philosophy on drafting and acquiring players. They became the majors' best defensive outfit in large part due to their use of advanced data to determine where to position fielders for each batter, recording arguably the best team performance in converting balls in play into outs (relative to their league) since World War II.

In the postseason, the impact of statistical analysis and just the new information that has become available to MLB teams in the last few years was even more stark. Not only have these defensive shifts become commonplace, but both managers, Maddon and Cleveland manager Terry Francona, treated the pitcher win and the save like the fetid anachronisms they are, pulling starters before they'd reached the five-inning threshold and using their best relievers too early for save situations. Cleveland entered the postseason with two of their three best starters on the disabled list, yet came within a few outs of winning its first World Series since 1948, thanks in no small part to Francona's tactical maneuvers and the performance of their best reliever, Andrew Miller. We'd seen glimpses of this kind of managing previously—in 2014, the Giants won game seven of the World Series when starter Madison Bumgarner came out of the pen on short rest to shut the Royals down—but never to the extent we saw in the 2016 postseason. The gap between managers who used new information and insight and those who didn't was obvious even to casual fans. The game itself may not have changed, but the way it's played and managed has changed forever.

The statistical revolution that started around the time of the publication of *Moneyball* has altered the fabric of the game at a permanent and fundamental level. In the 2016–17 offseason, the last two significant holdouts to embracing statistical analysis as a core part of their baseball operations departments, the Twins and the Diamondbacks, began building such capabilities. There is no returning to the days where gut feelings and guesswork ruled baseball decision-making, and the revolution has only made teams thirsty for more data.

While all of these statistical advances, as well as those on the horizon, will continue to reshape the game for years, their effects will be felt in very different ways at all levels—from the scouts in the field looking for talent, to the players in the actual games, to the way that writers (God help us) vote on their Hall of Fame ballots. Taking that last point first, I'll spend some time as most baseball fans online do: using modern statistical tools to engage in long and utterly futile debates over who belongs in the Hall of Fame.

WAR, however you choose to calculate it, is the right tool for a job like evaluating a player's career. The Baseball Writers' Association of America votes each winter on which players to elect to the Baseball Hall of Fame in Cooperstown, New York, but until very recently such votes were based either on emotion and gut feeling or on the kind of incomplete or downright misleading traditional stats I discussed in Part One. The guidelines for Hall of Fame voters are vague, and there are long, ongoing discussions even among serious voters and other writers about what it means to be a Hall of Famer. Are we talking about the player's value at his peak? His longevity? Consistency? A little of everything?

If nothing else, though, we can talk about some of the more egregious mistakes in BBWAA voting history, and even look at some of the current debates around whether there's any place at all for a modern closer in Cooperstown, using these advanced stats, including WAR, to provide the debate with an objective foundation.

Lou Whitaker was one of the best infielders of the 1980s, and at the time of his peak, he and shortstop Alan Trammell were widely presumed to be on track for the Hall of Fame—although such presumptions are often built on the belief that the players won't decline quickly in their thirties. (Just ask fans of Dale Murphy, who was about as clear a Hall of Famer through age thirty as you'll find, but was finished as an average regular by age thirty-two.) At the time of Whitaker's lone appearance on the Hall ballot in the 2000–01 offseason, he ranked fourth all-time in home runs by a second baseman, behind Hall of Famer Joe Morgan and future Hall of Famers Ryne Sandberg (elected in 2005 on his third ballot) and Joe Gordon (named by the Veterans Committee in 2009).*

---

* Rogers Hornsby played 1,541 of his 2,139 career starts as a second baseman, with another 350 coming at shortstop, so he's first in homers among players who played primarily second, while Sandberg has the most home runs hit as a second baseman.

Whitaker also ranked fifth at that time in doubles by a second baseman, behind four Hall of Famers, with 420. I don't care for RBI as a measure of hitter performance, but voters do—and did even more in 2000 than they do today—and Whitaker was fifth all-time among second basemen in that category as well, and fourth in runs scored, and fourth in walks drawn, and sixth in hits. Among second basemen with at least 3,000 plate appearances in the majors, he ranked 20th in batting average at .276, 12th in OBP at .363, and 8th in slugging at .426. These are all stats you could have found on the back of Whitaker's baseball card, and other than his batting average the rest all make a strong case for his election. He was one of the five greatest second basemen in history when he first appeared on the ballot.

That first appearance was also his last, unfortunately. The 2001 Hall of Fame class included two players inducted in their first year of eligibility: Dave Winfield, who appeared on 84.5 percent of the 515 ballots cast, and Kirby Puckett, who appeared on 82.1 percent. Whitaker appeared on just 15 ballots, 2.9 percent of the total, even though he had a better career than Puckett or Winfield. Because he failed to meet the 5 percent minimum to stay on the ballot, Whitaker's name did not appear again.

In fact, Whitaker appeared on fewer ballots than pitcher Dave Stewart (38 ballots), whose 3.95 career ERA would be the highest of any pitcher in the Hall; Davey Concepcion (74 ballots), whose .322 OBP would be the fifth worst in the Hall and whose .357 slugging percentage would be the fifth worst from the live-ball era; and Jack Morris (101 ballots), whose 3.90 career ERA would *also* have been the highest in the Hall . . . and who was a huge beneficiary of the defense provided by Whitaker and Trammell behind him.

Trammell at least received a modicum of support over fifteen years on the ballot, the maximum permitted under the rules at the time of his retirement, eventually reaching 40.9 percent in his final year of eligibility. I believe both Trammell and Whitaker should be in the Hall, but Whitaker's case is the more important one because of how badly the BBWAA screwed up in his one shot at glory. And I have a grim theory on why it happened.

*   *   *

Lou Whitaker was an outstanding offensive second baseman in an era when second basemen didn't hit a whole lot. In his best season, 1983, American League second basemen as a whole hit .268/.325/.369, and Whitaker hit .320/.380/.457. His worst season came in 1980, his third year in the majors, and even in that campaign he posted a .331 OBP, exactly the league average for all AL hitters that year. He started strong, winning the Rookie of the Year Award in 1978 at age twenty-one; had a solid peak from 1983 to 1989, with five All-Star appearances and a .359 OBP in those seven seasons; and never really declined, just playing less often into his late thirties but still hitting well, even posting a .293/.372/.518 line at age thirty-eight as a platoon player against right-handed pitching.

Whitaker's career Wins Above Replacement total of 75 puts him well above the bar for Hall of Fame second basemen:

Player	WAR
Eddie Collins*	123.9
Joe Morgan*	100.3
Charlie Gehringer*	80.6
Lou Whitaker	74.9
Ryne Sandberg*	67.5
Roberto Alomar*	66.8
Willie Randolph	65.5
Chase Utley+	63.7
Robinson Cano+	60.5
Joe Gordon*	57.1
Billy Herman*	54.7
Bobby Doerr*	51.2
Nellie Fox*	49.0
Johnny Evers*	47.7
Bill Mazeroski*	36.2

* Hall of Famer

+ Active as of April 2017

In fact, Whitaker leads all eligible position players who aren't currently either in the Hall or on the ballot in WAR. By that one particular measure, he is the best position player left out of Cooperstown, and as you can see on the previous table, that same measure says he's quite a bit better than many players who are already in.

Even if you wish to argue that WAR isn't the right way to go about this—I think this is its best use, but admit its imprecision—Whitaker stacks up well against the eleven Hall of Famers who played almost exclusively at second base in their careers:

Stat	Whitaker's Rank Among HoF 2B
AVG	8th
OBP	6th
SLG	8th
HR	4th
2B	6th
BB	3rd
Hits	7th
RBI	6th
Runs	5th

He clearly fits in with what the BBWAA and the Veterans Committee have decided qualifies a second baseman for enshrinement in Cooperstown, and he also makes the case using more advanced statistics.

Stat	Whitaker's Rank Among HoF 2B
wOBA	8th
wRC+	6th
Batting Runs	5th
Fielding Runs	5th

The Fielding Runs ranking is worth mentioning. In the chapter on how we go about analyzing fielding today, using UZR as an example of how to work with play-by-play data for better evaluation of fielding production, I spent a little time discussing methods of going back to look at historical fielding performances. For every Hall of Fame second baseman other than Roberto Alomar, that's all we have, since the data required to calculate UZR, dRS, and their ilk did not exist until after the other ten players plus Whitaker had all retired.

Whitaker was an above-average defensive player for just about his entire career, and what data we do have bear this out. TotalZone has him saving 77 more runs than an average second baseman over the course of his career, more than Alomar, Morgan, Sandberg, and Doerr, as well as Collins (whose career started in 1903 and probably isn't a good comparison for any modern player). Whitaker made more plays per nine innings in the field than Sandberg, Morgan, or Alomar, and among Hall of Fame second basemen only Fox and Mazeroski, both considered elite defenders, turned more double plays.

As an aside, Mazeroski's selection by the Veterans Committee was a bit controversial for adherents of statistical analysis, because his bat was just not good enough for consideration, let alone induction. He was, however, a truly outstanding defender at second, ranking just three runs behind Joe Gordon for the all-time lead in Total-Zone's runs saved at that position, and turning more double plays— 1,706, which works out to 0.8 per game in which he played—than any other second sacker in history. I'm perfectly okay with having him in the Hall, as he remains the gold standard for defense at a skill position, even if his bat is somewhat light and the real reason he's in the Hall is a certain home run he hit in October 1960.

Whitaker was very good, for a very long career, at a position that really has not historically led to many good, long careers. (The conventional wisdom is that second basemen are at higher risk of serious injury than most other positions because they serve as the "pivot" on the double play and often can't see the runner barreling toward them.) Traditional stats favor him; a very slightly more sophisticated look using some modest sabermetric stats favors him.

So what gives? Why did Whitaker merit only a handful of votes and one year on the ballot, when he's clearly qualified for the Hall, and when during his career he was seen as a future Hall of Famer? (An Associated Press story on August 3, 1993, began with "If history is any gauge, Lou Whitaker will be enshrined in the Hall of Fame one day." Another AP story, on January 12, 2000, listed Whitaker among notable first-timers for the next year's ballot along with Puckett, Winfield, and Don Mattingly. *Sports Illustrated*'s Tim Crothers wrote in April 1995 that the Detroit duo's last double play "might be scored Trammell-to-Whitaker-to-Cooperstown.")

My personal hypothesis—untested and untestable—is that Whitaker did not fit expectations for a player of his time. Middle infielders were supposed to be small and speedy, not powerful and, well, not-speedy, as Whitaker wasn't slow but was a little below average on the bases without big SB totals. He wasn't flashy on defense. He wasn't a good quote and was not that well liked by reporters, who ultimately become Hall of Fame voters. And by the time Whitaker hit the ballot, the prototype of the middle infielder had changed; Jeff Kent hit .334/.424/.596 with 33 homers as San Francisco's second baseman in 2000 and won the NL MVP award.

But Whitaker was also an African American player reaching the ballot at a time when the Hall of Fame electorate was overwhelmingly white. Exact records on the racial makeup of the electorate do not exist, but over the last few years I've tried to determine how many African American Hall of Fame voters there were when Whitaker was on the ballot, and I have found fewer than ten. When I reached out to several voters in the winter of 2013–14 to ask about Whitaker's failure on the ballot, I heard the word "uppity" used to refer to his character, which unfortunately is a word only applied to people of color. African American players who played well with the media, like Winfield and Puckett, had no trouble with the voters, but those who were seen as difficult or aloof, like Whitaker or Jim Rice (a weak candidate who reached the Hall on his 15th and final ballot), fared poorly with voters.

Oh, and as for Puckett, he didn't even have Whitaker's production to get himself into the Hall on the first ballot. Whitaker had a higher OBP and more homers along with far better defensive value.

But Puckett was seen as a nice guy—inaccurately, as it turned out, with Puckett facing multiple accusations of sexual assault after his induction—and had the narrative of a career cut short by glaucoma. (Puckett died of a stroke in 2006, at age forty-five.) While such factors shouldn't influence voting, there is no question that they do; it's just a question of to what degree. If Whitaker wasn't great with the media during his career, though, it shouldn't matter one iota to his Hall candidacy. Both he and his double-play partner Trammell belong in Cooperstown.

Kevin Brown was the neutrino of the Hall of Fame ballot in 2011, passing through the entire process without hitting anything and barely even getting support from nonvoters (like myself) who have argued in favor of overlooked, qualified candidates like Bert Blyleven, Tim Raines, and Whitaker. But a fairly cursory look at Brown's career in comparison to the pitchers already in the Hall and even many of his contemporaries shows he too had a strong case for induction, and should have appeared on many more ballots in his one year of eligibility.

Brown threw 3,256 innings in the big leagues, with a 3.28 ERA, even though he spent almost his entire career pitching in the highest-offense era in baseball history. Brown's first full season was 1989, offensive levels in baseball spiked in 1993, and when he retired in 2005 they hadn't begun to come down. He made six All-Star teams, finished second in the Cy Young voting once and third two years later, and, if you care about such things as voters do, won more than 200 games. Yet in his one year on the Hall of Fame ballot, 2011, Brown garnered just 12 votes, 2.1 percent of the total, falling short of the threshold to remain on the ballot for even one more year. He received fewer votes than Juan Gonzalez, a one-dimensional slugger who was all over the Mitchell Report and was done as a regular at age thirty-two.

The nonbaseball reasons for Brown's flop on the ballot are a bit beside the point here, but for the sake of completeness I'll mention that he was considered an odd, unlikable guy, was not a good quote or especially friendly to the media, and was somehow blamed for the fact that the Dodgers gave him the first nine-figure contract in baseball history, a seven-year, $105 million deal that went south in year three when he started to break down physically. I don't think any of that *should* matter one whit for his Hall case, but I'm realistic enough to know that it does matter.

Brown's Hall case, just based on what he did on the field, is surprisingly strong—I say surprisingly because I didn't appreciate just how good he'd been until well after he'd retired. (Perhaps I too was taken in by the unfavorable media coverage.) Baseball-Reference's WAR formula gives him 68.5 for his career, which puts him 31st all-time among pitchers. Fangraphs' version gives him 76.5, good for 24th all-time. There are currently 77 pitchers in the Hall of Fame as of August 2016, so if Brown is even just top 40 in baseball history, he pretty clearly belongs in Cooperstown.

Brown's career was a little short by Hall standards, but that reflects the trend of lower innings totals for starting pitchers as well as his own injury troubles in his thirties, and there are still plenty of starters in the Hall, even from previous eras, with lower total workloads than Brown had. Here are five starters already enshrined to whom Brown compares favorably, with Brown's stats included for the sake of comparison:

Pitcher	WAR (B-R)	IP	ERA	FIP	ERA+
Kevin Brown	68.5	3256.1	3.28	3.33	127
Dazzy Vance	62.5	2966.2	3.24	3.18	125
Catfish Hunter	36.6	3449.1	3.26	3.66	104
Jim Bunning	60.3	3760.1	3.27	3.22	115
Bob Lemon	37.5	2850.0	3.23	3.79	119
Tom Glavine	73.4	4413.1	3.54	3.95	118

ERA+ compares the pitcher's ERA to the league average; an ERA+ over 100 means the pitcher's ERA was better than average, and under 100 means that he was worse. I include it here primarily because Brown pitched in a much higher-offense era than the other names on the list.

I hesitated to even include Catfish Hunter, whose rapid election to the Hall was one of the worst such votes in BBWAA history. He was a colorful character, he threw a perfect game, and his successful arbitration case against the Oakland A's over a contract violation made him the first real free agent in modern baseball history, landing him a five-year, $3.35 million contract with the Yankees and opening the eyes of other players to how much money they were really worth. But his performance on the field wasn't close to Hall of Fame caliber; he was an average pitcher for a moderately long career who threw his last full season at age thirty and his last pitch at age thirty-three. If we just used his career alone as the standard for all pitchers, the Hall of Fame would have the population density of Bangladesh.

Did Glavine's inclusion surprise you? His on-field case is nowhere near as good as his first-ballot induction—he appeared on 92 percent of ballots—might lead you to believe. Glavine was never a great pitcher, but he was a good pitcher for a very long time, especially today, an era when his kind of durability is becoming less and less common. He won two Cy Young Awards, but one of them, in 1998, should have gone to someone else:

Pitcher	WAR	ERA	FIP	IP	W-L
Tom Glavine	6.1	2.47	3.50	229.1	20-6
Kevin Brown	8.6	2.38	2.38	257.0	18-7
Greg Maddux	6.6	2.22	2.81	251.0	18-9

The world was still flat in 1998, so the pitcher with the most wins took home the Cy Young Award despite having a higher ERA in a lower innings total than both Brown, the best pitcher in the NL that year, and Maddux, Glavine's own teammate!

Brown, meanwhile, finished third behind Glavine and one of his own teammates, Trevor Hoffman, who threw all of 73 innings as San Diego's closer that year, posted a 1.48 ERA, and somehow got more first-place votes (13) than any other pitcher that year, including Glavine. Brown threw 184 more innings than Hoffman, and allowed 56 more earned runs, which would be a 2.73 ERA just on the excess, and yet thirteen clowns thought Hoffman was the better pitcher even though he worked the equivalent of about a month and a half of work from Brown.

One more comparison for Brown illuminates the sheer folly of the Hall electorate, because while Brown slipped off the ballot after one year, a far inferior pitcher, also never a candidate for Miss Congeniality, spent the full fifteen years on the ballot and seems likely to sneak into Cooperstown one day via the Veterans Committee:

Pitcher	WAR (B-R)	IP	ERA	FIP	ERA+
Kevin Brown	68.5	3256.1	3.28	3.33	127
Jack Morris	43.8	3824.0	3.90	3.94	105

Jack Morris was a thoroughly average pitcher who gained a lot of wins by spending his entire career on good teams, mostly with Detroit in the 1980s, then adding three seasons with World Series winners in 1991 (Minnesota) and 1992–93 (Toronto). Morris's ERA of 3.90 would be the worst of any pitcher in the Hall. He was never the best pitcher in his league or close to it. He never finished higher than fifth in the American League, where he spent his whole career, in ERA or WAR, and only led the AL in any significant category once, leading in strikeouts (and innings) in 1983. He should never have gotten close to the Hall of Fame, but he did, peaking at 67.7 percent in balloting in 2013, falling short of the 75 percent park required for enshrinement.

Morris and Brown were on the Hall ballot together in 2011, and while Brown appeared on only 12 ballots, Morris appeared on 311. At the time, the BBWAA did not make ballots public unless the writers chose to do so—a terrible policy that allowed some clowns to hide their stupidity or personal grudges behind the veil of anonymity. While thankfully this is changing beginning with the 2017 ballots, which will all be made public, this change will not be retroactive, so don't count on finding out who, if anyone, voted for Brown but not Morris. Regardless, we do know that at least 299 people voted for Morris and not Brown, a completely indefensible position.

Morris threw 568 more innings than Brown, a little over two seasons' worth of pitching, but he gave up 472 more earned runs than Brown did, and that's even with the strong defensive tandem of Whitaker and Trammell playing behind him for most of his career. That's an effective 7.48 ERA in Morris's innings "advantage"; would Brown have improved his Hall case any by throwing another 500 innings of awful performance?

Brown was snubbed for most of his career by the writers, who ultimately hold the power over seasonal awards and the Hall of Fame—with the former affecting the latter, too—and thus can take out their dislike of a player on him many times. That seems to be what happened to Brown, one of the best sinkerballers of the modern era and a great pitcher who should have won one or possibly two Cy Young Awards and, at the least, would fit right in among pitchers already in the Hall of Fame.

One thing you might have gleaned from this book or from my writing about baseball for ESPN is that I don't hold high regard for the total value of relievers' performances. This often comes up in Cy Young discussions, where some hot-taker decides to push a closer with a fluky-low ERA for the Cy against starting pitchers who'll carry three times the workloads—ignoring the fact that most closers are failed starters who moved to the bullpen because they couldn't stay healthy or couldn't turn over an opposing lineup three times as starters. The obvious implication is that I wouldn't support the Hall candidacies of relievers, and by and large that's true, with one large exception from the modern era.

The Hall of Fame has very few pure relievers, period. There are only 23 pitchers in the Hall who made at least 100 relief appearances in their careers, and most of those were starters by trade; 18 of the 23 finished with more games started than relief appearances. Only 7 pitchers in the Hall made at least 200 relief appearances, including starter-to-closer-to-starter John Smoltz, and starter-to-closer Dennis Eckersley. Bruce Sutter is the only Hall of Fame pitcher with zero games started in the majors; Rollie Fingers started 4 games, Rich "Goose" Gossage 16, and Hoyt Wilhelm 52.

Sutter is the only truly modern short reliever—referring to the length of his outings, not his stature—in the Hall at all, and he was one of the dumbest selections in BBWAA history, named not because of his performance, which shouldn't have gotten him as far as Utica, let alone Cooperstown, but because of how he was used. When people talk about the advent of the modern one-inning closer, they start with Sutter. He won a Cy Young Award he didn't deserve in 1979; J. R. Richard had a better season in three times the workload, which turned out to be his last full season before a stroke ended his career in May 1980. Sutter had just ten full seasons in the majors and two partial ones, and finished his career with only 1,042 innings pitched—not just the lowest total of any full-time pitcher in the Hall, but 650 innings less than the next-lowest total, fewer than Babe Ruth threw (1,221), fewer than Addie Joss (2,327), who died at age thirty-one and didn't even complete nine seasons in the majors.

By Wins Above Replacement, Sutter is the worst pitcher in Cooperstown, coming in 0.5 WAR below Rollie Fingers and 12 WAR below Catfish Hunter. Sutter's election is a modern embarrassment, an overvaluing of the save stat combined with the dysfunction of the current system; he was elected in 2006, the only player to earn enough votes that year, which sort of demonstrates that timing can indeed be everything. Had he been on the ballot with other, more qualified candidates, he probably wouldn't have squeaked by with 77 percent of the vote that year and may very well have fallen short entirely.

Sutter's main problem as a candidate for Cooperstown is that he just didn't pitch enough. It's hard to do anything in a thousand innings to justify your inclusion even against modern starters who have lower workloads relative to starters from before 1990; Sandy Koufax, whose career ended at age thirty due to arthritis in his left elbow, reached 2,324 innings, and Pedro Martinez, handled gingerly for most of his career due to his slight frame, still reached 2,827 innings. Sutter couldn't even reach half that, and most modern closers can't do so, either.

Trevor Hoffman became eligible for the Hall of Fame after the 2015 season and appeared on 67.3 percent of ballots that winter. The following year he reached 74%, making it inevitable that he'll be elected to the Hall in the next vote. Hoffman was, with some reason, considered the best one-inning closer in the National League for about a decade. He's one of only two closers to cross the 600-save mark, limping across that threshold and grabbing a very temporary hold on the all-time saves mark in his final season in 2010, where he posted an ERA just under 6.

Hoffman pitched in 18 separate seasons, only missing a significant chunk of one of those due to injury, and yet barely creaked past Sutter in the innings-pitched department with 1,089. His ERA of 2.87 ranks 14th among pitchers with at least 1,000 innings who pitched after World War II (eliminating all of the pitchers whose ERAs reflect time pitching in the low-offense, dead-ball era before 1921):

Rank	Player	ERA	IP
1	Mariano Rivera	2.21	1283.2
2	Clayton Kershaw	2.39	1732
3	Hoyt Wilhelm*	2.52	2254.1
4	Whitey Ford*	2.75	3170.1
5	Dan Quisenberry	2.76	1043.1
6	Sandy Koufax*	2.76	2324.1
7	Ron Perranoski	2.79	1174.2
8	Bruce Sutter*	2.83	1042
9	John Hiller	2.83	1242
10	Kent Tekulve	2.85	1436.2
11	Jim Palmer*	2.86	3948

(*continued on next page*)

Rank	Player	ERA	IP
12	Andy Messersmith	2.86	2230.1
13	Tom Seaver*	2.86	4783
14	Trevor Hoffman	2.87	1089.1
15	Sparky Lyle	2.88	1390.1
16	Juan Marichal*	2.89	3507
17	John Franco	2.89	1245.2
18	Rollie Fingers*	2.9	1701.1
19	Bob Gibson*	2.91	3884.1
20	Dean Chance	2.92	2147.1

The man atop this list can wait just another moment while I dispense with Hoffman, as he deserves his own discussion. Hoffman's performance, even before we discount it for the time he spent pitching in San Diego's two incredibly pitcher-friendly stadiums, Petco Park and its predecessor Qualcomm Stadium, is just not that remarkable for a modern reliever. Quisenberry fell off the Hall ballot in one year. So did Hiller. So did Tekulve. Messersmith lasted two years but only appeared on three ballots each time. Sparky Lyle lasted four years, peaking in his first run by appearing on 13.1 percent of ballots. In fact, Hoffman's career totals, without the saves, look a lot like that of a good starter who blew out early in his career:

	IP	ERA	ERA+	WAR
Hoffman	1089.1	2.87	141	28.0
Pitcher X	1319.2	3.27	142	33.3

Pitcher X lasted only seven years, spending his whole career with a team that played in one of the majors' best hitters' parks. He won a Cy Young Award in his fourth year in the majors, then finished second in the voting in the next two seasons. The following year, he made one four-inning start on April 6, went on the disabled list with a serious shoulder injury, and never made it back to the majors. I've never heard anyone suggest that Brandon Webb, who didn't pitch in the required ten seasons to even appear on a ballot, deserves some sort of consideration for the Hall of Fame, yet his body of work is at least equal to that of Trevor Hoffman.

I told you that story so I could tell you this one, however, as Hoffman's eventual election appears to be a fait (or fault) accompli. But there is one modern reliever whose case for the Hall stands up to even the fairly strict scrutiny to which I'd subject all Hall candidates, based on his body of work in the regular season, boosted by his body of work in the postseason, and, I think, made even a bit easier for voters because of the player's outstanding reputation for character on and off the field.

Mariano Rivera was another failed starter, promising but frequently injured in the minors, and posted a 5.51 ERA in 1995, his rookie season with the Yankees, making ten starts and nine relief appearances. The following year, the Yankees made him their setup man, often allowing him to handle the seventh and eighth innings ahead of Proven Closer™ John Wetteland, a combination that helped the Yankees win the World Series that fall and ensured that Rivera would never start another game in the majors. From 1996 until his final season of 2013, Rivera threw 1,216.2 innings, all in relief, with a 2.03 ERA—and did nearly all of it by throwing just one pitch, a cut fastball that hitters on both sides of the plate would just pound into the ground. Rivera was hard to hit, and even harder to take deep—he gave up just 60 homers after that first season—and he had outstanding control, walking 245 batters (excluding intentional walks) in his entire career, fewer than one every five innings.

Even with that first season of poor performance included, Rivera's career puts him well above that of the best of his peers among short relievers. The chart above shows that his ERA is the lowest for any pitcher with at least 1000 innings from 1947 onward, and it's not particularly close. (Also, how freaking good has Clayton Kershaw been? He could retire right now and have a strong Hall of Fame case just on half a career of work.) Other relievers have been better in short stints, but no reliever in this era of the one-inning closer, roughly defined as 1980 to now, has been as good as Rivera for as long as Rivera was:

Reliever	WAR	IP	ERA	Runs
Mariano Rivera	56.5	1283.2	2.21	340
Lee Smith	29.4	1289.1	3.01	475
Trevor Hoffman	28.0	1089.1	2.87	378
Billy Wagner	27.7	903.0	2.31	262
Francisco Rodriguez	24.9	938.1	2.70	307
John Franco	23.7	1245.2	2.89	466

(Fangraphs' version of WAR rates Rivera a good bit lower, at 39.7 for his career, because it normalizes his BABIP rather than assuming or accepting that Rivera's career BABIP of .263 was the result of skill. Over a season or two, we might look at a low BABIP and say that it's luck or randomness, or that it's the result of playing in front of a good defensive unit. Rivera allowed more than 3,500 balls in play in his career, a sample large enough that we can say with a high degree of confidence that we think his low BABIP was the result of skill, or mostly the result of skill.)

Rivera doubles every other modern closer in WAR except Smith, who threw almost exactly the same total number of innings and gave up 135 more runs than Rivera did. As for Hoffman, Rivera's most direct contemporary on the list, Rivera gave up fewer runs in almost 200 more innings pitched. To get from Billy Wagner's career to Rivera's, you need 380 innings and 78 runs allowed, which is roughly equivalent to Sandy Koufax's final season *plus* about 17 more scoreless innings.

There are 75 MLB pitchers in the Hall of Fame as of this writing, and Rivera's WAR total of 56.5 would put him 49th among them. Rivera's ERA of 2.21 would rank 9th, behind Walter Johnson, who pitched from 1907 to 1927, and seven guys who pitched in the deadball era.* Sutter's election can't simply open the door for every reliever who was better than he was to waltz into Cooperstown, but if

---

* A few pitchers near the end of the list are outliers, like Satchel Paige, who spent most of his career in the Negro Leagues; Babe Ruth, who's there for something other than his pitching work; or Candy Cummings, elected because he allegedly invented the curveball.

he's in, Rivera, who pitched more than Sutter and pitched far more effectively, certainly has a case.

Of course, the narrative of a player's career can matter as much as his performance, and Rivera's narrative is a strong one. Mariano Rivera owns the lowest postseason ERA in major-league history, and it's not just a tiny sample: he threw 141 innings in the playoffs in his career and gave up 13 runs, 11 earned, for an ERA of 0.70. No other pitcher in the live-ball era has thrown 100 postseason innings with an ERA below 1.00. Only six pitchers in MLB history have thrown more innings in the playoffs than Rivera did, all of them starters, and the lowest ERA of the group was 2.67, nearly two full runs allowed per nine innings more than Rivera allowed. What he did in October over the course of his career sets him above every other pitcher who had the opportunity to pitch in the postseason.

Many great pitchers never had the same opportunity that Rivera had, or they simply had less of an opportunity, so I've never liked the idea of putting a player into the Hall primarily because of his postseason work or keeping a player out because he struggled in the postseason. Hoffman wasn't great in the playoffs, with two blown saves and a 3.46 ERA overall . . . in a whopping 13 innings, such a tiny sample that it's best to just ignore it rather than hold it against him in any way. Rivera, however, got that opportunity, enough that we couldn't hand-wave it away as a fluke, and excelled. If you felt like his regular-season body of work made him a borderline Hall candidate—while that's not my view, I think it's quite fair given his relatively low innings total—then his playoff résumé should be enough to convince you he's a Hall of Famer.

Among pitchers not yet in the Hall of Fame, Roger Clemens, still on the ballot as of the 2016–17 off-season, is the all-time leader in WAR, with a ridiculous total of 139.4 that has him only behind Walter Johnson on the list of pitchers in or out of Cooperstown. Clemens's statistical case is rock solid, but accusations of performance-enhancing drug use have led some voters to omit his name, enough that he seems unlikely to get into Cooperstown via the BBWAA vote.

The next-best WAR total among pitchers not in the Hall belongs to Mike Mussina, who ranks 19th overall with 82.7 WAR, was never suspected of PED use, and even had the kind of career won/lost record that would typically impress voters (270 wins, 153 losses). But through his first four years on the ballot, he hasn't exceeded 52 percent, which he just reached in the 2016–17 off-season.

Some of the subjective arguments against Mussina are valid if you believe these things matter for enshrinement: he never won a Cy Young Award or came close, he only made a few All-Star teams, and he won 20 games only once in his career, in his final season. That last one is a bit disingenuous, since he won 19 games in the strike-shortened year of 1995, but it's also just stupid because pitcher wins are useless.

The real problem with Mussina's candidacy, in my view, is that he spent his entire career in the high-offense era and voters have a hard time mentally adjusting their thresholds to reflect how tough that environment was for pitchers. Mussina's career ERA of 3.68 would be the second highest of the modern era to land its owner in the Hall of Fame, ahead only of Red Ruffing's 3.80. But Mussina's ERA came almost entirely in the go-go 1990s and early 2000s, when run-scoring in baseball reached all-time highs, so he was above the league average in run prevention every year of his career but one:

Year	R/G	Mussina's RA	Difference
1991	4.49	3.18	1.31
1992	4.32	2.61	1.71
1993	4.71	4.51	0.2
1994	5.23	3.22	2.01
1995	5.06	3.49	1.57
1996	5.39	5.07	0.32
1997	4.94	3.49	1.45
1998	5.01	3.71	1.3
1999	5.23	3.9	1.33
2000	5.28	3.98	1.3

Year	R/G	Mussina's RA	Difference
2001	4.86	3.42	1.44
2002	4.8	4.3	0.5
2003	4.87	3.61	1.26
2004	4.99	4.97	0.02
2005	4.68	4.66	0.02
2006	4.87	4.01	0.86
2007	4.82	5.33	-0.51
2008	4.68	3.82	0.86

That's a very simplistic look at the matter, comparing just the American League's runs allowed per team per 9 innings (R/G) to Mussina's runs allowed per 9 innings. Mussina pitched in the very difficult American League East for his entire career, facing some potent Yankee lineups in the 1990s and Red Sox lineups in the 2000s, without getting any help from his home ballpark in Baltimore or in the Bronx, so if anything this probably understates how good Mussina was relative to the league—but you can see here he was average at worst, above average frequently, and several years was well above average. In fact, he finished in the AL's top ten in earned run average eleven times, in the top ten in Fielding Independent Pitching twelve times, in the top ten in strikeouts ten times, and in the top ten in fewest walks allowed per 9 innings *fifteen* times.

That's why Mussina's advanced stats paint a more favorable picture of his career than his traditional stats do. Wins Above Replacement, regardless of which formula you use, is built around an estimate of Pitching Runs allowed that is adjusted for its era, because the replacement player in question would give up more runs in a high-offense era and fewer in a low-offense era. It moves like the average would move, and if you want to use the average as your baseline instead, please do: Baseball-Reference has Mussina's career Wins Above Average total at 48.6, which would put him behind only eleven Hall of Famers, guys like Seaver and Maddux and Pedro and a couple of dudes named Johnson.

Pitcher	IP	ERA	RA	FIP	WAR
Mike Mussina	3562.2	3.33	3.60	3.57	82.7
John Smoltz	3473.0	3.68	3.94	3.24	66.5

Smoltz sailed into the Hall in his first year on the ballot, deservedly so; he was one of the best pitchers of the last twenty-five years, and had a solid postseason résumé to boost his candidacy. (So does Mussina, but that's not necessary to make his case.) Mussina pitched 90 more innings and, once you account for the differences between their leagues—Mussina spent his entire career in the AL, while Smoltz threw 99 percent of his career innings in the NL, where pitchers hit for themselves and offense can be up to half a run lower per game—he pitched a little bit better than Smoltz did. If you take the league difference into account, Mussina even outpitched Tom Glavine on a per-inning or per-year basis, although Glavine, who was also elected on his first ballot, threw an additional 900 innings.

Mussina did nearly double his support in his third year on the ballot, and cross 50% in the most recent tally, so I'm cautiously hopeful about his candidacy. Now that Tim Raines, who entered his tenth and final year of eligibility after the 2016 season, is safely enshrined, Mussina might find himself the next cause célèbre among stat-savvy baseball fans.

Oh, there are more cases we could discuss here—the media campaign for Jim Rice, one of the least qualified players in the Hall of Fame; the gap between Tony Perez's credentials by traditional statistics and advanced ones; the loud camp (of which I was a part) opposing Jack Morris's candidacy—but that kind of talk could take up a whole book, and it has, by others more qualified than me. Bill James covered it in his *Whatever Happened to the Hall of Fame?* in 1995 and revisited many of the debates in his updated *Bill James Historical Abstract* in 2001. Jay Jaffe has written numerous pieces for Baseball Prospectus and *Sports Illustrated* on the same topic. I won't rehash all of these debates here; my point is that having reliable, context-independent statistics for valuing player performance makes these debates possible. We're no longer arguing about feelings and memories, but about whether this level of production meets the threshold for enshrinement. That's a much more fruitful and less frustrating conversation to have.

16

No Trouble with the Curve:

How Scouting Works, and How the Statistical Revolution Is Changing It

One of the great false dichotomies of baseball coverage today is "stats versus scouts." The claim that these two sides don't or can't get along was a key part of the mythology of the book *Moneyball,* which chronicled the Oakland A's search for inefficiencies to exploit in the market for players, leading them to become one of MLB's earliest adopters of statistical analysis. The problem with the story is that it's not true: scouts and analysts aren't at odds, and just about every MLB front office now expects both departments to work together to improve their decision-making in all aspects of player acquisition, from trades to free agency to the draft. Over the next few pages, I'm going to describe what scouts actually do, dispel some myths about the practice, set up the explanation of what MLB's new Statcast data measures, and show how the nature of scouting has changed as a result of the statistical revolution.

The depictions of baseball scouts in the popular media over the last fifteen years haven't been kind to the scouts or at all helpful in educating the lay audience on their role. The execrable film *Trouble with the Curve,* which starts with a shot of Clint Eastwood urinating and only goes downhill from there, painted some false-romantic notion of scouts as lone wolves driving back roads and identifying future stars with a quick look and a gut feel. (The film was rife with inaccuracies, but perhaps none was as absurd as the idea that Eastwood, playing a local scout, was the only employee from his team to see the player they were considering for the number-two pick in the entire draft. A team picking second would likely have a dozen people go watch every candidate for that pick.) A scout's job is far more methodical than these books and films might lead you to believe, and his output in the form of scouting reports is more detailed and concrete than you'd otherwise think.

The specifics of a scout's report do vary by the type of player he's evaluating. An area scout's report on an amateur player for the draft or to be signed as a free agent out of the Dominican Republic or Venezuela will focus much more on what the player is expected to become, including a long-term projection on his physical development, than a pro scout's report on a prospect in double-A, which still includes some prognostication but will invariably weigh the player's present baseball skills more heavily.

Org charts differ somewhat from team to team, but there is a common structure to most amateur scouting departments (still sometimes referred to by the dated term "free agent" scouting, even though players in the draft are anything but free). Each team will divide up the country into territories called "areas," usually twelve to fifteen or so, including Canada and Puerto Rico since they're also folded into the draft along with the United States. Each area has a scout called—you guessed it—an area scout, who is responsible for seeing all players in his area potentially worthy of a draft pick in that year. This role is probably closest to the scout of myth, driving 30,000 miles every spring to cover his territory and see a bunch of players who might be worth a pick in the 15th round or might not be worth the gas money spent to go see him. These areas can be huge—most teams assign one scout to cover the entire Four Corners region of Arizona, New Mexico, Colorado, and Utah, sometimes giving the same scout responsibility for El Paso and/or Las Vegas as well. Doing this job well requires organization skills, networking, and a commitment to chasing down a lot of players who might never spend a day in pro ball in the hopes of finding a Chris Carter (White Sox, 15th round, 2005), Ryan Roberts (Blue Jays, 18th round, 2003), or Jarrod Dyson (Royals, 50th round, 2006).

Between the area scouts and the scouting director who oversees the department (and, in theory, is responsible for making the actual draft picks) will be one or two layers of scouts known as cross-checkers or "supervisors," some national and some regional. These scouts spend most of their waking hours between Valentine's Day and Memorial Day on airplanes, and they're responsible for seeing the best players in each of the areas they oversee—for example, a national cross-checker's mandate could be to see every player that area scouts have turned in as worthy of a pick in the first three rounds of the draft. These cross-checkers have two main functions: to provide a second evaluation on every player who might merit a high pick or large signing bonus, and to provide comparisons of such players across different areas.

Each scout will submit a written report on any player he (or she—as of this writing the Mariners have the first female area scout in MLB) deems worthy of consideration in the draft, or any player who might be drafted high by another team even if that particular scout thinks the player isn't very good. These reports contain both numerical grades assigned to specific tools or skills the players have, as well as text descriptions of the player's body, mechanics, instincts, and so on. Many players in any draft class will have been seen by only one scout from each team, the local area scout, and so once the draft progresses past the fifth round or so, scouting directors rely more and more on the "pref lists" (short for preference list) each scout has submitted on players from his area.

A pro scouting staff is usually more straightforward in structure—a handful of pro scouts assigned to cover a specific region, league, or set of organizations, reporting up to a director. But most teams also have other employees, with titles like Special Assistant to the GM,

Special Assignment Scout, or Vice President of Doing Something or Other, who will also go out and see targeted players, from players on the team's short list for their first draft pick to potential trade targets close to the July trade deadline, and whose opinions may not appear on formal scouting reports but will carry weight in the front office's discussions on which players to acquire. These voices can be extremely valuable, but can also lead to process breakdowns, such as the team that drafted a player in the supplemental round (extra picks between rounds one and two) about five years ago because scouts who saw the player for one day liked him, while the area scout, who'd seen him a half dozen games or more, rated the player as a fourth- or fifth-round talent. The player in question hasn't gotten out of double-A and is unlikely to ever reach the majors. Scouts make mistakes on individual evaluations all the time, but the problem with that specific selection was the breakdown of the process, giving undue weight to brief looks by more senior scouts and insufficient consideration to the scout who'd seen the player most frequently.

One of the main challenges scouts face is projecting physical development, yet you will hear this discussed very frequently, even in my own writing about prospects, as if it's more scientific or predictable than it actually is. We talk frequently about "projection" and "mature" bodies, a good "frame" or a player "filling out," because these things do happen—that fifteen-year-old player in the Dominican Republic is going to look very different when he's twenty-two—but this might be the least rational part of the scouting process, relying instead on age-old heuristics.

A player who is projectable looks like he will fill out in a good way as he reaches his early twenties, adding muscle to his entire body—not just building up his upper-body strength like a bodybuilder might—to make harder and higher-quality contact (for a hitter) or to throw harder or maintain his stamina deeper into games (for a pitcher). Sometimes they work out as predicted; I saw Tyler Skaggs throw 86–88 mph in high school, but by age twenty-three he was in the majors averaging 92 mph before he hurt his elbow. Sometimes they don't: The Red Sox took Trey Ball, an Indiana high school left-hander, with the seventh overall pick in the 2013 draft, betting on his athleticism and his extremely projectable body, but despite his great work ethic and some physical maturation, he hasn't seen any real uptick in his velocity or his arm speed three years out.

Athleticism is another tool scouts attempt to value and address, and again, although I use the term and discuss it often, I find its definition to be maddeningly nebulous and often misapplied. What we really seek when we seek athleticism is a sort of quicker quick-twitch quality; everyone has quick-twitch muscle fibers that the body uses for rapid movements, contracting quickly but also fatiguing faster than slow-twitch muscle fibers do because they consume more energy. Jumping, sprinting, accelerating an arm to throw—these all make heavy use of quick-twitch muscle fibers. What we're really looking for when we say we want athleticism is evidence that the player is even better at that stuff than the typical player—his first step is quicker, his movements seem more graceful, perhaps he has better body control. You can see why even I, doing this stuff for more than a decade now, still find myself questioning what the term means or whether we're using it fairly.

One other aspect of a player's body that scouts try to evaluate or project is whether the player is likely to get heavy or slow down to the point where he might lose value somewhere, especially on defense. Sometimes this is as straightforward as looking at a player's height and current weight and finding out how many players with that frame and body type have managed to stay at a position (such as shortstop) in the majors. Some scouts want to see what a player's parents look like, given the role genetics plays in determining one's weight and shape, although that could easily be misleading—it's not as if we're trying to guess a player's serum cholesterol here, and most parents don't work out as much as a typical young ballplayer will. Underneath the guesswork, however, is a serious question: If this player's weight increases faster than he can control it through conditioning, or he doesn't work hard enough to maintain his conditioning, will he have to move to a position where his bat is less valuable—or someplace where he has no more value at all?

*   *   *

A player's mechanics, whether it's how he swings the bat or how he delivers a pitch, are absolutely critical to his ability to perform, to make adjustments, and in many cases to stay healthy. Unlike a player's innate physical abilities or his height, a player's mechanics can change—but they often don't. So evaluating a player's mechanics is a significant part of scouting, although different scouts will tell you they place different weights on mechanics compared to results.

For a hitter, the mechanics of his swing determine how soon he can get the head of the bat into the zone, how long the bat stays in the zone, and the launch angle of the ball off the bat. There's more than one way to skin this proverbial cat; Dustin Pedroia and Frank Thomas are two very successful hitters whose swings defy conventional wisdom on mechanics, with Pedroia swinging very uphill and Thomas hitting off his front foot. But scouting is an attempt to both identify general markers of future success and simultaneously identify players who might be outliers, so at least understanding the mechanics of a player's swing is critical even if it's only to say ". . . but I like his bat anyway." And there are certain things that make it harder, while not necessarily impossible, for a hitter to make frequent contact against major-league pitching, from a back-side collapse (where the hitter's back leg bends so much that the bat path is forced upward) to a "hitch" in the swing (a sudden move downward from where the hitter sets his hands) to a "linear" swing (where the hitter doesn't rotate his hips to generate torque and thus can't use his lower half to improve exit velocity off the bat).

Physicist Alan Nathan wrote for the *Hardball Times* site in April 2016 that "flyball distance reaches a maximum at launch angles in the vicinity of 25–30 degrees," with the optimal angle decreasing slightly as exit velocity off the bat increases. In other words, the traditional scouting idea that a hitter needs loft in his swing to hit home runs is somewhat true, but too much loft—more than about 30 degrees above the horizontal—starts to decrease the hitter's chances of driving the ball out of the ballpark. There's a tangible difference between hitting in the air and hitting for power. New data from MLB's

Statcast product have allowed analysts to investigate such questions and give us conclusions like Nathan has.

Pitching mechanics are an even bigger topic of discussion at the moment because of the unresolved questions around what is causing the higher incidence of Tommy John surgeries—an operation to replace a torn ligament in a pitcher's throwing elbow—among young pitchers in recent years. (This rise in elbow tears has come with a drastic reduction in catastrophic shoulder injuries, which are much more difficult to fix via surgery.) Are these injuries caused by overwork, by certain pitches, by rising velocities, by bad mechanics, or by some combination of these and other factors?

When scouts evaluate pitcher mechanics, they are again using some heuristics developed over decades of scouting, although some of those heuristics are aimed at evaluating a pitcher's ability to develop command or control rather than whether the pitcher will stay healthy. Scouts will look at whether a pitcher is on line toward the plate when his front foot lands, whether his arm has to come back across his body during the act of throwing (this is bad), when he pronates (turns over) his forearm and hand in his delivery, how high his pitching elbow gets relative to his shoulder (too high is also bad), how well he rotates his hips to generate torque, and more.

As with evaluating hitter mechanics, evaluating pitcher mechanics is full of rules that are rife with exceptions. Left-hander Chris Sale does many things "wrong" in his delivery, including that high elbow in back, but as of this writing has more than 1,000 big-league innings without a major injury. Tim Lincecum was supposed by many scouts to be a huge breakdown risk due to his size and his delivery, but he reached 1,028 innings through his first five big-league seasons with a sub-3 ERA before he started to lose effectiveness. Spotting the exceptions early—both players were high first-rounders, Sale taken by the Chicago White Sox, Lincecum by the San Francisco Giants—is part of scouting, but scouts can also rattle off dozens of players with similar mechanics who got hurt, couldn't throw strikes, or couldn't keep the ball in the park. Survivor bias ensures we remember the ones who made it more than we remember the dozens who didn't. While I was writing this book, Mariners left-hander Danny Hultzen, the number-two overall pick in the 2011 draft, out of the University of Virginia, was reportedly headed for retirement after years of shoulder problems; he was a very effective starter in college but came back across his body when throwing, which may have contributed to the torn labrum that required surgery in 2013.

(We do know a few things about pitcher injuries that aren't related to mechanics, however. The American Sports Medicine Institute has published several studies showing that young pitchers, including those as young as eight, are at exponentially higher risk of injury if they throw too many innings over the course of a calendar year, or if they continue to pitch while fatigued. They've also recommended that pitchers take at least three months off per calendar year and have worked with Major League Baseball on an initiative called PitchSmart, which recommends pitch counts and innings limits by age for youth pitchers. If you're interested in more on this subject, I recommend Jeff Passan's 2016 book, *The Arm*, which examines this specific subject in great detail.)

The term "five-tool talent" is thrown around more frequently than such a creature is actually found in the wild, in part because many people use the term without understanding what the five tools are. It's also worth bearing in mind that there are five-tool players who aren't that good at baseball, because these tools have as much to do with raw physical ability as they do with game skills. The five tools themselves are hit, power, run, glove (field), and arm, and you can see how it would be easy for a player to have four of those, be okay on the fifth, and get the "five-tool" term slapped on him. Mike Trout, the greatest player of his generation, is a four-tool talent; he has an average arm at best, perhaps even a little less than that (what a scout would call "fringe-average" or just "fringy").

Four of these tools are fairly straightforward. Power usually refers to raw power—how far the man can hit the baseball, independent of how often the man can hit the baseball. Scouts watch batting practice for several reasons, including swing evaluations, but seeing raw power there is another part of it. You'll hear a distinction between raw power and game power because plenty of guys are so-called five o'clock hitters who can put on a show in BP but not in games. Ryan Sweeney, former first-round pick of the White Sox out of a high school in Iowa, had huge raw power that he'd display pre-game, but hit just 23 homers in over 2,300 plate appearances in his major-league career, in large part because his BP swing and his game swing were so different.

Running speed is measured in a few ways; I've never found player times from the 60-yard dash that meaningful because there is basically no instance on a baseball field where any player runs 60 yards in a straight line. The most consistent baseline measurement is the time from when a hitter makes contact on a groundball to when he steps on first base, which can still be a little skewed by how soon he gets out of the box but is about as objective a baseball-related measurement of speed as you'll find.

Arm is throwing strength and doesn't usually consider accuracy. Similarly, glove/field doesn't always consider range so much as the fielder's hands and consistency, although range is the most important part of fielding ability.

The hit tool, however, is the hardest one to evaluate, especially in amateur players. A scout who evaluates international amateurs might be asked to see a fifteen-year-old player in Venezuela and put a grade on his future hit tool for when he's twenty-three or so and ready for the majors. It's the most important tool of the five—if you can't hit you're probably not going to have much of a career in the majors—but by far the one with the highest variance in opinions and the greatest potential to go awry. A hitter may hit, in the sense of making contact, but not make hard enough contact to succeed as pitchers throw harder and harder as the hitter advances through the minors. He may hit until he reaches a point where pitchers start locating their off-speed stuff, and then suddenly he can't hit anymore. And hitters change—he can alter his swing, learn to recognize breaking pitches, tighten his command of the strike zone—in ways that render scouting reports, especially on their hit tools, to the dustbin.

Scouts measure these tools on the traditional if somewhat quaint 20-to-80 scale (or 2 to 8), with 50 representing major-league average, 80 representing the best possible, and 20 the worst. This scale has many origin stories, but as far as I can tell they're all apocryphal and ours is not to reason why.

The incomplete nature of the five tools in describing a position player have led to variations in what scouts are asked to observe and evaluate. When I was with Toronto, we asked scouts to also evaluate a hitter's plate discipline, a term that encompasses ball/strike recognition as well as ability to distinguish different pitch types, along with the other five tools. We could split the "field" tool into range and hands. I've heard scouts refer to a player as a 5 runner out of the box but a 6 runner under way, which sounds like useful information that wouldn't be captured in the traditional five-tool rubric. So while we all like a player who grades out as above average or better in the five tools, it's not a terribly complete picture of the player, nor is it any guarantee of future success.

Scouting a pitcher is a bit easier because of the radar gun: if he throws hard, it's a good fastball, and the radar gun often helps you identify pitches when seeing the pitcher's grip or release is difficult. Scouts will typically put 20–80 scale grades on each of a pitcher's pitches, perhaps adding a field for a fastball's movement as a distinct grade from its velocity. (A fastball that's 100 mph gets an 80 grade for speed but probably doesn't have much movement or "life.")

One of the most common questions I get from readers is about the pitching terms *command* and *control*—what they mean or what the difference is between the two. Defining control is simple: it's the ability to throw strikes, period. It doesn't speak to the quality of those strikes, but simply to throw the ball over the plate within the strike zone—middle, edge, whatever. If you look at a pitcher's walk rate (walks allowed as a percentage of total batters faced, preferably with intentional walks ignored in both totals), you'll get some idea of his control. We also now have easy access to the percentage of pitches thrown for strikes by major-league pitchers and for most games in the high minor leagues as well.

Command, however, is a more nebulous thing, as important as it is hard to pin down. As Justice Potter Stewart famously said in the Supreme Court case *Jacobellis v. Ohio,* "I know it when I see it," although I don't think he was talking about baseball there. Command, roughly speaking, is the ability to put a pitch where you want it, to make it do what you want it to do. I think of it as ownership of the pitch: if it doesn't land where you needed it to land or break the way you needed it to break, you didn't command it. Control is more tangible and rarely goes away without warning, but command wavers.

I was sitting with scouts at Matt Harvey's major-league debut in Arizona on July 26, 2012, chatting with Mike Berger, who is now an executive with the Miami Marlins. As we were talking about something unimportant, he said without breaking stride, "He just lost it." He'd spotted a slight change in Harvey's delivery during his warmups where the pitcher lost his release point, and with it his command. Harvey had struck out ten men through five innings to that point; after that, Harvey walked two of the next three batters and was removed from the game. I was sitting right next to Berger and I didn't spot it, but Mike's got a few years and a whole lot of games on me and he saw it right away. A very tiny change in mechanics meant the end of Harvey's effectiveness for that game.

My personal philosophy of evaluation is that command comes from the delivery: if you can repeat your mechanics, from your stride to your hip turn to (especially) your arm action, then you can have command. I believe it's more physical than mental, although the mental side of the game matters tremendously as well. But you can be the smartest guy in the world, or the calmest, and still not have command because you can't get your hand to the same release point at the same time on every pitch. You can also command your fastball and not your off-speed stuff, and I've even seen pitchers who could command a curveball but couldn't command the fastball, perhaps because they weren't overthrowing the former but tried to go max effort on the latter. And when I'm evaluating very young players, I look at their present deliveries but also try to gauge their athleticism and body control, because as they mature physically and work with professional coaches, they'll have ample opportunity to learn a delivery they can repeat, and more athletic players, in my experience (and thus merely in my opinion), have a better chance to make that happen.

I've never seen an attempt to quantify command that made any sense to me, although it could be possible as the quality of pitch-tracking data improves. You can't just glean it from strikeout rate, walk rate, from some manipulation of those two, from hit rate or BABIP allowed, or any of those things. You just have to know it when you see it.

Grading out the individual pitches has always been highly subjective, of course, except for the radar gun, which is an imperfect proxy for the effectiveness of a fastball. In recent years, some teams have asked their scouts to start to record new information, like how many swings and misses an amateur pitcher (especially a high schooler) gets over the course of a game, perhaps broken down by pitch type. Scouts might also be asked to grade or otherwise evaluate how tight the rotation is on a curveball or slider, or how far a pitcher extends over his front side at release—that is, where his arm is relative to his landing leg when he lets go of a pitch.

MLB's new data stream, called Statcast, takes some of the subjective elements of traditional scouting and puts objective numbers on them, which is changing the nature of scouting at all levels, from the amateur ranks to the majors. We no longer have to guess how hard a hitter makes contact, or whether a pitcher is truly skilled at limiting hard contact; how tight that curveball rotation is, or how much that pitcher's four-seamer really moves. This doesn't eliminate the role of the scout, but it changes it, removing some of the guesswork from the job and, if a front office really integrates the two sides of its operations, freeing up scouts to do the things that can't be measured with radar or cameras, from evaluating his swing or pitching mechanics to getting to know the player's character.

Some teams have indeed chosen to diminish the role of the scout within their departments, asking scouts who watch amateur players to gather as much video as possible of the player during and prior to games, getting biographical information, and administering tests like psychological and vision exams to players. Many teams have used statistical analysis to supply scouts with lists of players to see who might not otherwise have been on their radar—good performers at smaller colleges, or colleges outside of the NCAA's Division 1 level—or to ask pro scouts to focus more on specific players while doing their general coverage of entire minor-league teams.

An opportunity still exists, however, for teams that can best integrate this new information with their scouting resources to answer questions that advanced data can't answer in a vacuum. We know pitcher Charlie Brown has a high spin rate on his curveball, so why is he giving up so much hard contact? Does Brown throw the pitch too infrequently? Are hitters picking the curveball up early enough to lay off it and wait for a fastball? Does it finish out of the zone so often—as was true with Trevor Bauer and Carson Fulmer in college—that better hitters let it go by for a ball? Rather than asking scouts to provide subjective opinions on variables we can objectively measure, we can ask scouts to fill in the gaps between the skill measurements and the results on the field. Scouting is and has always been about projecting what a player will do when he reaches the majors or comes to the scout's team. Simply acquiring every pitcher with a high-spin-rate curveball will bring you some successes, but at high cost. Understanding which high-spin-rate guys are likely to have success against big-league hitters—the ones best able to recognize or hit a curveball—is the way to narrow your target list in a meaningful way.

This also puts the onus on scouts to at least become conversant in the new language of baseball analysis. I'm not suggesting we need scouts to run SQL queries or learn R (although it would probably look good on the résumé), but scouts are going to be asked to identify more specific attributes in players, and they're going to find themselves held more accountable going forward for their scouting reports. I don't see teams asking scouts to apply the metrics themselves, but when they write up players' abilities, teams will be better able to evaluate the evaluations using improved data.

The baseball industry had seen virtually no change in how players were evaluated since Branch Rickey's days with the Cardinals, but since 2000 we've seen the introduction and proliferation of statistical analysis within the sport and among fans and media, which has in turn changed the way teams scout and acquire players, and all of which has led up to the second revolution, one that is currently in progress. This ongoing upheaval was triggered by the introduction of MLB's Statcast product, one that is big enough to merit its own chapter.

17

The Next Big Thing Is Here, the Revolution's Near:

MLB Statcast

We're not telling people things they don't know about baseball; we're going where they are and giving them more information to help them understand it better.

—Cory Schwartz, Vice President of Stats, MLB Advanced Media

In 2015 MLB introduced into baseball a new source of data called Statcast, instantly changing the way that we think about stats and the game. The new data stream that teams receive from MLB Advanced Media (MLBAM) via Statcast is absolutely massive: 1.5 billion rows of data, each of which has about 70 fields, for all MLB games from Opening Day 2016 through mid-September, so something on the order of 100 billion items just for a single season, which means that for the first time teams have had to think about the mere challenge of storing a terabyte of data before they could even begin anything resembling analysis of it.

Statcast combines two separate systems for gathering physical information from the field of play, one radar-based and one optical-based, which MLBAM merges into a single stream of data that provides an unprecedented amount of detail on each pitch or play. That includes stuff you'd expect, like the velocity of the pitch or the result of the play, but also includes a lot of information that was previously either unrecorded or totally unavailable. Such information would include the speed of the ball as it left the bat, now known as "exit velocity," or the spin rate on the pitch in revolutions per minute (RPM).

Information that was unavailable prior to Statcast is even more extensive and opens up new worlds for statistical analysis of player performance. The Statcast record for a single play includes the position of everyone and everything on the field: every fielder, every baserunner, every coach and umpire, and of course the position and trajectory of the ball from when it leaves the bat until when it's picked up by a fielder—and again if it's thrown from one fielder to another. This at least gives teams with the analytical capacity to model plays, create 3-D renderings, and, perhaps most important, get realistic measures of defensive performance, especially range, because for the first time we know where the fielders actually started on each play, rather than only knowing where they were when they reached the ball.

Although Statcast itself began in earnest on Opening Day of 2015, ushering in a new Year One of data for MLB teams and their analysts, the modern baseball data revolution really began in 2006 with pitch tracking and the tool known as Pitch f/x. MLB started offering fans its Gameday product online in 2001, but pitches were recorded manually and the data was not reliable enough for real analysis. (Prior to Pitch f/x, MLB stringers were instructed to mark any pitch called as a strike as being in the strike zone, even if it wasn't even in the same ZIP code, and the same for pitches called balls. Thus, a pitcher could split the plate in two with a belt-high pitch, but if the home plate umpire, Mr. Magoo, called it a ball, the stringer charged with entering the data for MLB would have to enter it into the system as out of the strike zone.) MLBAM recognized that the consumer product would be vastly improved by accurate pitch data—velocity, movement, and pitch type, as well as a computerized strike zone that didn't necessarily agree with the umpires' ball/strike calls.

Although Pitch f/x started life as a consumer product, its introduction meant teams suddenly had real data to work with—and so did independent analysts all over the world, since MLB chose to make the Pitch f/x data stream public. Fans watching at home, following games on MLB.com, or using the league's best-of-breed At Bat app were treated to pitch velocities, types, and locations, data for every pitch that also came through to clubs in "flat files" (meaning text files, unformatted, with fields separated by commas) those teams could use for a whole new field of analysis. Where previously teams had nothing to work with but event data—in this at bat, the batter saw this many pitches, this many strikes and balls, and the at bat ended when he hit the ball to this fielder—now they had detailed data on every pitch. Pitch f/x allowed analysts to start to tease out insights like who really had the most effective slider in baseball, or to what pitch a certain hitter was most vulnerable—and whether that changed by the pitcher's handedness, or whether the hitter was behind in the count.

Where Pitch f/x was a few hundred thousand rows of data per season, however, Statcast is exponentially larger, which is the result of a huge technological investment by Major League Baseball in hardware and software built to capture this information. Statcast collects enough data for a 3-D model of every pitch, using a radar-based system from a Danish company called TrackMan and an optical system from the Long Island company ChyronHego. As soon as the pitch leaves the pitcher's hand, the radar system is looking for the pitch, sending a notification to MLBAM's scoring system and the stringer on-site with the pitch location and scoring information once the pitch is complete. The radar system then tracks the ball (and only the ball) from bat to fielder if it's put into play, since the radar system offers higher fidelity than the optical system.

The optical system follows . . . well, everything else, especially the movements of all of the people on the field, from recording their starting positions to the routes and speeds of all of the people in motion, including fielders, baserunners, and the batter as he becomes a baserunner. The optical system also serves as a backup to the radar system should the latter lose track of the ball at some point, since the optical system is agnostic toward the objects it's monitoring. The system thus tracks all kinds of observable, measurable player actions, such as running speeds, throwing velocity, and fielders' routes to the ball, as well as the aforementioned aspects to the pitch's path to the plate, including velocity, spin rate, and vertical break.

MLBAM rolled out its first Statcast data in 2015, but year one, according to everyone involved, included a lot of time and effort spent cleaning the data and learning how to make the data more reliable in something closer to real time. Because these systems are tracking players at 30 frames per second and are recording measurements that aren't perfectly smooth—your running speed varies depending on whether your feet are in the air or one is on the ground—there can be measurement errors in such data, as well as clerical errors such as tagging a play with the wrong player ID codes.

Many of these issues were of a kind no one really expected, because we'd never encountered them before in the era where things like catcher throws to second base were timed by hand, by scouts using stopwatches. Such throws, which are called "pop times" and generally run between 1.85 seconds and 2.10 seconds for major-league catchers—you'll get higher pop times the further from the majors you get—assume that the infielder receiving the throw is standing at second base. MLBAM found that they were getting absurdly low pop times from catchers not generally known for their throwing prowess because the system didn't distinguish between normal throws and those cut off short of the bag, one example of how the operators had to train the system so it would capture the right data before team analysts could start using them to develop new metrics.

The sheer size of the Statcast data stream and the inevitability of errors within it have created entirely new jobs within the industry that were unthinkable in 2006, when I left the Blue Jays to join ESPN.

While I worked for Toronto as the team's lone statistical analyst, the bulk of my time spent on analytical work was spent gathering data: writing code to scrape college stats off Web pages or to import the flat files MLB would post every morning that included minor-league data, including split data and game logs for players, and then formatting the data so I could import them into a simple desktop tool like Access (for queries) or Excel (so I could sort, print, or share lists with colleagues). There just weren't enough data to merit an investment in a real relational database management system until the Pitch f/x data started to arrive in 2006, after which many teams started to build systems around packages like SQL Server, mySQL, and Oracle.

I've joked with many people as I've written and researched this book that I am no longer qualified for the type of job I once held with the Blue Jays, and the inception of Statcast data has made that more true than ever. Teams that have built or are building architectures capable of handling this new torrent of information are hiring people with graduate degrees in computer science specialties such as machine learning or signal processing. The sheer quantity of data has created entirely new needs within baseball operations departments, from data cleaning to building systems capable of storing and querying medium to big databases that are several orders of magnitude larger than what previous systems were able to handle—quite literally going from a few gigabytes of data to a terabyte of data each year from Statcast, a quantity that threatens to continue to increase.

Sig Mejdal, the Houston Astros' director of decision sciences, told me that "before, while you might have been happy with a person fascinated with baseball who has some good quantitative skills (can work Excel well) and seems socially mature, now you need an advanced degree or advanced college-level backgrounds. And as the size of analytical teams grows, you don't want one more person just like you; you want a person with skills that none of you have, and that's often master's and Ph.D. level skills."

Multiple other executives who oversee analytics departments said they're looking for similar skills and backgrounds; it's no longer sufficient to know a little code and love the sport; now teams expect candidates to have technical experience before they're hired, including some specialized skills like machine learning, the more accurate term for "artificial intelligence," which MLBAM uses to train its system to tag pitch types based on pitch velocity, break, and the known repertoire of the current pitcher.

MLBAM has also hired multiple experts to help root out systemic errors in the data and to help with more esoteric but critical topics like deciding which data to include when, for example, calculating an outfielder's arm strength to show to fans in a tweet or during a game broadcast. If an outfielder makes a hundred throws back to the infield, some of those will be casual tosses because there is no threat of a runner advancing, while others will be throws made at full strength to try to either catch a runner or prevent one from moving up a base. How can we determine which throws to discard from the sample when calculating the average velocity of his throws so we can compare it to other outfielders' throwing velocities? Throwing out data makes anyone who's worked with statistics a little queasy, because you're introducing a new arena of potential bias ("selection bias," which means you're skewing the data by what you choose to include or omit), but the hope of analysts working with Statcast data is that the sheer volume of samples will minimize any bias from data-cleaning efforts.

The Astros even took their search for people with technical skills one step further in the 2015–16 off-season, posting a job opening for a "development coach," an actual coach who'd wear a uniform, but for whom SQL skills were a plus. SQL stands for Structured Query Language and is the most common programming language used to search for data within relational databases. If you have a database of player statistics and want to know how many players age twenty-nine or younger hit at least 20 home runs this season, you'd write a SELECT statement with a WHERE condition that contains the age and home runs criteria. It is as lightweight as programming languages go, but it is still programming, something most working adults in the United States—let alone baseball coaches—never learned at any point in school. Whether this catches on around the industry remains to be seen, but I'll bet it becomes more common

for teams to at least favor coaches who have a basic level of understanding of how databases work, because if you can even craft a
SELECT/WHERE statement, then you automatically know how to
phrase the questions you want to ask your statistical analysts in a
way that they can turn the questions into SQL queries and get you
answers you can use.

With this new complexity, however, comes a world of new opportunities for coaches, executives, and even players to get answers to
questions that previously were either unanswerable or couldn't be
answered with enough precision to help. These answers are already
helping to change the way the game is played on the field, and going
forward will change the way teams construct their rosters, utilize
pitchers, and draft, sign, and develop players.

The lowest-hanging fruit available for people working with Statcast data, whether it's the folks at MLBAM preparing information
for social media or game broadcasts or team analysts working on
player evaluations, is verifying scouting observations that had previously been left to imperfect human measurements. How fast is Billy
Hamilton? (Answer: Faster than anyone else in the majors, but not
as fast as Usain Bolt.) Whose curveball has the highest spin rate?
(Answer: The Angels' Garrett Richards.) What hitter has the highest
exit velocity or the optimal launch angle for power? What is the optimal launch angle, or range of angles, for power anyway? (It turns
out that hitting the ball with some loft is critical, but too much loft
means more flyouts and fewer home runs.)

Statcast's radar-based system from TrackMan makes all of these
ball-related measurements simple; tracking the ball's velocity, spin
rate, and trajectory is part of what the system tracks for pitches. The
only additional element the system adds after the pitch is a tag of
pitch type—two- or four-seam fastball, curveball, slider, changeup,
and so on—based on the pitcher's known repertoire and the other
characteristics it's already measuring. If the pitcher has just three
clearly defined pitches, the system might be able to accurately identify all of his pitches after just two or three "training" starts. Some

pitchers can take more samples for the system to get to the desired 99.99 percent accuracy because their pitches' velocities might run together, which you'll often see for a pitcher who throws a fastball, a cutter, and a slider, since a cutter is best described as a hybrid of the other two pitches. But after a few starts or a handful of relief appearances, any pitcher will be tagged accurately in the Statcast system, allowing analysts to evaluate the expected value of his various pitches based on factors like velocity and spin rate.

One of the most visible statistics to come out of MLB's Statcast product is exit velocity—the speed with which a batted ball leaves the bat. We've all heard about hard contact, or hitters who can "square up" the ball, but this was the first time MLB was able to provide hard data to support or refute these assertions on certain hitters or pitchers. For hitters, the assumption was that harder contact was better—it would lead to more hits and more power. For pitchers, the assumption was that harder contact was worse; the Pitch f/x data stream allowed teams and sites like Fangraphs to rank pitchers by groundball rate or line-drive rate, but didn't distinguish between how hard those balls were hit.

As it turns out, the relationship between exit velocity and results is not direct or linear—that is, hitting the ball harder is not automatically better. There's another variable, launch angle, that comes into play as well; if you hit the ball hard, but hit it down into the ground, then you're going to hit . . . a very hard groundball. That might sneak through the infield, but it's probably going to be just a single if it does, and it's also likely to be a hard-hit out, perhaps even the start of a double play. If you hit the ball hard—even hard enough to undo the seams—but get under it too much, hitting it high in the air, it's likely to come down short of the outfield fence.

There is a range of angles off the bat, measured by the degrees between the ball's trajectory when it leaves the bat and the ground itself, that is most likely to produce extra-base hits, which of course are the most valuable outcomes for hitters. In April 2016 for fivethirtyeight.com, which is co-owned by ESPN, Rob Arthur wrote in a piece called "The New Science of Hitting" that balls hit at 90 mph or greater with launch angles around 25 degrees (with several degrees of range around that figure) were pretty likely to leave the ballpark.

In September 2016, MLB introduced a category of batted balls called "Barrels," which took any combination of exit velocity and launch angle that produced a batting average of at least .500 and slugging percentage of at least 1.500. In simpler terms, it means that balls hit at least that hard and in that range of angles are at least even money to become hits, with many of those hits producing extra bases. In a piece by MLB's Mike Petriello that introduces the metric, he says that only about 5 percent of plate appearances end in a "Barrel," and even the best hitters in the game produce a ball in play like that in only about 10 percent of their trips to the plate. The leaders in the category are names you'd expect: Miguel Cabrera, Mike Trout, and Kris Bryant, three of the game's best overall hitters, are in the top ten, as are all-or-nothing power bats like Mark Trumbo and the two Davises, Khris and Chris.

We've long guessed that harder contact was better, and that hitters needed some loft in their swings—that is, to come up slightly through contact rather than swinging parallel to the ground—to produce line drives and hit for power. Statcast data has not only verified those guesses, but put parameters around them so teams can better identify hitters with the strength to hit balls at least 90 mph and who have the angle in their swing finishes to hit more balls like those MLBAM calls "Barrels." It also gives coaches at all levels a potential goal for working with young players to develop their swings— if a prospect is making hard enough contact but doesn't have the correct angle in his swing, whether too much (producing pop-ups and flyouts) or too little (producing groundballs), that's at least an opportunity for a mechanical change, which could be as simple as changing the hitter's hands in his load or as involved as reworking how he uses his hips to make his swing more rotational.

Statcast data has also probably put a few baseball myths to rest. Did Mickey Mantle really once hit a ball that would have traveled 565 feet? Almost certainly not, since even today's hitters, who are bigger and stronger than those of a half century ago, can't reach that distance. Did Negro Leagues legend Josh Gibson once hit a ball clear out of Yankee Stadium, or one two feet from the top of the facade, in either case hitting a ball that would have gone at least 580 feet? Absolutely not. These legends were always apocryphal, but now we can say with near certainty that they're bogus.

Another new term to come out of the Statcast data stream is "spin rate," referring to the number of revolutions per minute a pitch makes on its way to the plate. Again, this takes a common scouting term—*spin* or *rotation,* referring to the same thing, with "tight rotation" on a breaking ball especially assumed to be superior—and quantifies it in a way that allows teams to make better decisions. As with exit velocity, however, spin rate doesn't work in isolation, as its effect is greater when paired with velocity.

Scouts have long associated spin with breaking pitches—the spin of a curveball, combined with the ball's uneven surface, gives it its break, and depending on how the pitch is released and how hard it's thrown (that is, how fast the pitcher's arm is moving at release), it may break a lot or a little, in one plane or two, "early" or "late" from the hitter's perspective. But all traditional pitches spin, even four-seam fastballs, the pitches associated with the least movement from release to home plate; the only pitches that spin very little are knuckleballs, where the whole point of the grip is to minimize the spin on the pitch.

Spin on four-seam fastballs turns out to be important, as important as velocity and in some cases more so. The industry's fascination with velocity is nothing new, and is easy to understand. One, we all love seeing "100" pop up on a radar gun or a scoreboard; I was in the ballpark in September 2010 when Aroldis Chapman, then a Cincinnati Red, hit 104 on my own radar gun and 105 on the Petco Park scoreboard, eliciting cheers from the theoretically hostile crowd before the operators turned off the readings to stop fans from applauding the wrong side. Two, velocity has been easy to measure for some time now: radar guns are de rigueur for scouts, reasonably priced for teams (about $1,100 for an industry-standard device), and accurate enough to be a major part of scouting decisions from the draft to trades and pro signings.

Spin rate, on the other hand, was never measured at all, and in my experience only discussed on breaking pitches, curveballs, and occasionally sliders, although the latter were more commonly defined by their "tilt" rather than their spin. (Tilt here refers to the angle of break on the slider. Throw it too flat and you get a "frisbee" slider that often just moves right into the hitting plane of a hitter on the opposite side of the plate.) The TrackMan system has allowed teams to measure spin rate accurately for major-league pitchers and, where the system is offered, at certain amateur scouting events as well.

On four-seamers, spin rate can compensate for lower velocity, while higher-velocity fastballs without spin tend to be less effective than those with more spin and a few mph less of velocity. For example, Statcast data from 2016 showed that four-seam fastballs of 95 mph with spin rates at 2,400+ rpm (which, loosely defined, is above average) generated swings and misses about 10 percent of the time, roughly the same as the swing and miss rate for fastballs of 100 mph with spin in the more average range of 2,100–2,300 rpm. Throwing harder is good, but not necessary if you put more spin on the pitch. This has implications for scouting, for developing pitchers, and, in light of recent studies showing that pitchers who throw at the top end of their velocity ranges are at higher risk of arm injuries, perhaps even for finding ways to keep pitchers healthy.

It also explains why some pitchers who throw exceptionally hard don't miss that many bats. Nate Eovaldi, who at the time of writing had just torn the UCL in his right elbow for the second time, necessitating the second Tommy John surgery of his career, has consistently ranked among the hardest-throwing starters in baseball throughout his career, and became a valuable trade commodity in large part due to that one pitch. In 2016, prior to his injury, Eovaldi averaged 97.1 mph with his four-seamer, the highest average velocity of his career, but more than half of his fastballs came in with spin rates under 2,300 rpm. In lay terms, that means they had less spin than the typical four-seam fastballs at that velocity, so while they reached the plate quickly, they were spinning at a slower rate and had less movement. "Straight ball I hit it very much" holds as true in real life as it did for the fictional Pedro Serrano.

One potential application of this data is looking at "expected swinging strikes," as blogger Andrew Perpetua wrote on Fangraphs in September 2016. We can look at all pitches of a certain type, velocity, spin rate, and location in or out of the strike zone and see how often hitters swung and missed at that category of pitch, and then identify pitchers who throw that sort of pitch and work on getting them to throw to that particular area. Or teams could find pitchers whose swing and miss rates on those pitches were abnormally low, hoping that this was just bad luck or randomness making a pitcher less effective than he would be going forward. Or maybe it's just a lot of noise—the point here is that such questions were unanswerable before Statcast, and now analysts have so much data that they can try to answer old questions and even come up with new ones based on what's now being measured.

The most immediate impact of Statcast data on the team side has been allowing teams to refine their defensive evaluations to a degree impossible prior to this new product—grading players' defensive abilities and also improving how they position players for certain hitters or behind certain pitchers. The most substantial change has come about because now analysts can evaluate range based on where any particular player was standing at the moment the ball was put into play.

The idea of "range," like many other player tools or skills I've discussed in this section and in the scouting chapter, has long been a part of how scouts and teams evaluated players, but prior to modern statistical analysis, it was entirely subjective and based solely on what a scout might see in a sample of a few games or even just a few innings. If the scout didn't see a player have to make a difficult play, or simply wasn't bearing down on that fielder at the time of such a play (because he was focusing on the hitter or the pitcher or something else), the evaluation would be incorrect. And even evaluating range on the tiny number of nonroutine plays a player, especially an outfielder, might have to make in a handful of games was probably folly.

Every team analyst I asked about this topic had the same answer; Jason Paré of the Marlins said it was a "game-changer," and James Click of the Rays pointed out that it eliminates many of the assumptions everyone, inside or outside of teams, had to previously make when evaluating defense. Sig Mejdal of the Astros said it was like two people trying to compare the speeds of two runners, but only one person has a stopwatch. "If we've got a stopwatch and we know Usain Bolt runs faster than Justin Gatlin, you aren't right even if you swear Gatlin is better."

Where public defensive metrics like Ultimate Zone Rating and defensive Runs Saved are directionally correct—if a player posts a UZR over two seasons of +15 runs, he's almost certainly an above-average defender—they can't match the precision that teams' proprietary metrics, based on Statcast data, are able to offer. So while every analyst I asked about these public metrics said they're worth looking at and a substantial improvement over any previous attempts to quantify fielding value (which one analyst referred to as "nothing"), teams are going to know more about defensive value than those of us who don't have access to Statcast data.

With Statcast data, now an analyst can gauge whether a fielder is better than his peers, without worrying that where he's being positioned by his coaches is screwing up the results. On each play, Statcast provides each fielder's starting position, the trajectory of the ball, the route taken by the fielder who fielded it (or tried to and failed), that fielder's running speed, and how far off the ground the ball was when the fielder caught it. You can look at a player's maximum range, or typical top speed when making a difficult play. Statcast's own tools allow anyone to make a graphic of all of an outfielder's plays with the starting positions all normalized to a single spot (called a "polar" view), making it look sort of like a spider with a billion legs—but it's immediately apparent how much or how little range a player has from a graphic like that, because you can see how far the "legs" go in each direction away from the starting position.

This insight does more than just tell teams who the good defenders are; it has already helped change the way teams position their current defenders for each batter. If you know your center fielder has good range coming in—on balls that are likely to fall or be caught in front of his starting position—but has a weakness on balls that require him to run backward, away from home plate, then you will likely start him a few feet farther from home plate, compensating for his weak spot and taking advantage of his strength. If you know your shortstop makes a higher percentage of plays to his right—the "hole" between short and third base—but lets an atypical percentage of balls get by him to his left, you might set him up a step or two toward second base to compensate.

Furthermore, Statcast data can help further refine positioning beyond the simple shifts, such as moving a third infielder to play in short right field against left-handed pull hitters, that we've seen in baseball over the last five years. Now the most advanced teams, like the Astros, Cubs, and Rays, are modeling likely outcomes based on the hitter, the pitcher, and the capabilities of the fielders to determine where the ball is most likely to be put in play and to station defenders in those spots. It ruins the symmetry of the standard defensive alignment—Mejdal specifically cited the emotional satisfaction we get from a traditional setup that "looks right and feels right," but that the data say is wrong. It's better to get more outs, even if it looks ugly on paper, than to set up a pretty defense that lets more balls fall in for hits.

Taking all these different new pieces together, Statcast data are the next frontier in statistical analysis. Where the metrics I described in Part Two by and large took the data we already had and figured out how to interpret them in more meaningful ways, Statcast data completely change the player evaluation paradigm. OBP and FIP tried to better isolate how often players did something of value. UZR, Batting Runs, and WAR attempted to value performances in terms of runs or wins added to the team. Statcast gets more granular, giving teams the raw data to evaluate players' specific skills—how hard a hitter hits the ball and at what angle, how fast a player runs in the field or on the bases, how fast a pitcher's curveball spins, how far out in front of his body he releases each pitch.

The old data got us to the atomic level, but Statcast data get us to subatomic particles we couldn't measure before the new technology arrived. Where this takes the industry is baseball's next frontier.

18

The Edge of Tomorrow:

Where the Future of Stats Might Take Us

The sabermetric revolution in baseball has already happened. There are no longer any holdouts among MLB front offices; by the start of 2017, all thirty organizations had established analytics departments, employing multiple people, often with Ph.D.s in computer science specialties, charged with gathering data and using them to answer questions from the GM or the coaching staff, or to look for previously undiscovered value in the market for players. If your local writer is still talking about players in terms of pitcher wins, saves, or RBI, he's discussing the role of the homunculus in human reproduction. The battle is over, whether the losers realize it or not.

The way in which teams use analytics—a catch-all term that covers both the collection and storage of data as well as the use of those data to produce usable insight—has changed over the last fifteen years, to the point now where it is standard for teams to employ departments full of analysts who have distinct jobs and vary in their levels of interactions with the traditional baseball people. The Pirates have had someone travel with the major-league team to road games for several years now, helping manager Clint Hurdle and his staff work on positioning defenders, a major factor behind their three straight playoff appearances from 2013 to 2015. When current Houston GM Jeff Luhnow was the scouting director for the St. Louis Cardinals, he and his consigliere Sig Mejdal introduced a program that took in players' performance data as well as information found in the scouts' reports and ranked all the players in an objective fashion, telling Luhnow, in effect, which player to select each time the team picked. The Astros now use a similar model, as do multiple other teams, following the Cardinals' example; the Angels, long considered one of the less statistically savvy teams, are the most recent club to adopt a draft-room algorithm that turns drafting into an actual process rather than a set of opinion-driven and inconsistent decisions. A decade ago, using analytics in baseball operations represented a competitive advantage; now it is a business necessity, if for no other reason than to understand what your twenty-nine competitors are up to.

As part of writing this book, I interviewed numerous GMs, front office executives, and team analysts, and a major question I asked them all was what they thought the future of analytics in baseball entailed. Their answers had two common themes: MLB's Statcast data stream represents a quantum shift in how the industry uses analytics; and further advances will be incremental, rather than exponential, as all teams have access to the same data and any insights will spread more quickly throughout the game. David Forst, GM of the Oakland A's, said that "Statcast is the ultimate playing field leveler; everyone can have access to everything on the field being measured. How much of your resources you put into breaking down that data and trusting it in your decision-making" will be the separating factor among clubs, instead of just different teams possessing different data.

The Cardinals' GM, John Mozeliak, has managed one of the most forward-thinking front offices in the game since the start of 2008, and summarized the view of many of his peers when he said, "When you think about what tomorrow's going to look like, clearly the margins are getting tighter in terms of taking advantage of something the Cardinals may have had going for us ten years ago versus today." The gains are smaller, and they may not last as long as analysts or scouts change teams or as information leaks out into the public sphere.

One of the more surprising outcomes of my conversations with executives about the future of analytics was how many brought up injury prevention and rehabilitation as an area for future progress. The medical or training departments were typically their own islands, reporting back to the general manager but working largely independently of the rest of baseball operations. Now teams are integrating baseball data with their medical operations to try to predict injuries before they happen and to try to help players come back from injuries more quickly.

A former GM cited it as the biggest area for future advances and potential competitive advantages for teams. "Injury prevention's a big deal. A lot is being done there, with people trying to get a basis for it. If we can eliminate DL days, that's huge. There's more work being done with deliveries, pitch types, and what the impact is" of pitching mechanics or use of certain pitches. Other executives cited looking for pitchers whose velocities or spin rates are declining, using those data as a proxy for fatigue, shutting the pitchers down before they suffered any structural damage to a ligament or tendon. In late August 2016, when the Padres demoted pitcher Ryan Buchter to triple-A, his manager, Andy Green, specifically cited a reduced spin rate as evidence that Buchter was suffering from fatigue.

Another GM mentioned that "having all of this data allows you to track player wellness better and hopefully cuts some potential injuries off at the pass. Even guys' running speed, when they're getting treatment for leg stuff, you see their speed drop down you know to give guys an off day. It might be some of the most low-hanging fruit out there, minimizing DL days, optimizing health and wellness." He mentioned a rise in the number of companies trying to sell systems or tools that attack this goal, although their efficacy is a wild guess at this point. One analytics director, breaking down the roles of the various people in his department, specifically mentioned having a staffer "who's more injury sports science rehab oriented," as opposed to others who focus on the draft or work with the major-league coaching staff on positioning players.

One point that came up repeatedly in these conversations is how the Statcast data rely on a two-dimensional system when, of course, players are three-dimensional objects moving in three-dimensional space. Teams have started to look for analysts with backgrounds in 3-D modeling, including those with physics backgrounds, to try to tease more insight out of what the Statcast data can provide, but the bigger leap forward would come with data that report on three dimensions. Think about how wearable technology could apply to the movements of a baseball player; the market of such "smart" technologies already includes elbow sleeves for pitchers and gloves for batters. If a player is susceptible to hamstring pulls, what if he could wear something on his thigh to track his leg movements and try to identify what's causing these pulls or spot weakness in the muscle before it strains?

Another analyst suggested the possibility of embedding sensors in the ball or the bat to measure things like spin rate—which is technically two numbers, since the ball spins on two axes—more accurately. This would require an up-front investment by the league itself, but that's what MLB did for Statcast, recognizing that the teams would value the data and that some of the information could be turned into content to enhance the viewer's experience. Again, more precise data about the movement of the ball or the bat could open the door to greater insight on how players get hurt and perhaps on how to reduce the odds of them doing so.

Player development is not typically considered when writers or fans think about the impact of statistical analysis on baseball teams, but that integration has already started for many clubs, and several executives highlighted it as an area for further advances. Mejdal specifically cited the work that his colleague Mike Fast, who created the first widely used catcher-framing metric before joining the Astros, has done in helping work with young catchers in Houston's system; even Jason Castro, a longtime big leaguer, saw his framing improve dramatically in 2015–16 due to work with the team's coaching staff and analysts. Mejdal may seem to state the obvious when he discusses using the results of analytical work with players, but this philosophy is just now becoming widespread in the sport: "If you hope to have the best players and the best staff, how could you withhold something that would enable them to be better players and better staff?"

Every MLB team now has the ability to install the TrackMan radar-based system in all of its minor-league stadiums as well; even low-revenue teams like Oakland have done so, meaning there's no excuse for any team to choose not to install it. That means the granular data we see for big leaguers, like spin rate or exit velocity, are now available to teams on their own minor-league players, as well as opposing players on visiting clubs. (Teams have the option to trade their home parks' data to other teams for those teams' data.) So teams can now use this information to identify players with particular skills or who may be good targets for development, such as having a pitcher use a pitch more frequently or trying to change a hitter's launch angle.

The Astros declined to discuss it on the record, but multiple other executives pointed to Houston's emphasis on the high fastball as an example of how new data have changed a development philosophy. In the high-offense era of the late 1990s and early 2000s, teams shied away from flyball pitchers, because they were more susceptible to home runs, and actively sought out groundball pitchers, with Derek Lowe and Brandon Webb both showing that a starter could thrive with just average velocity if he threw a sinker that forced hitters to hit the ball on the ground. This approach had a trade-off—a groundball is slightly more likely to become a hit than a flyball—but keeping the ball in the park made it worthwhile. The Astros appear to have seen, through Pitch f/x and now Statcast data, that pitchers who throw high spin-rate fastballs that don't sink can also be effective, getting more swings and misses on four-seamers up in the zone or even above the zone—a pitch type and location that scared the hell out of everyone just a few years earlier.

Wearable technology or sensors in the bat and ball would also provide a benefit here, as the giant black box of mechanics, whether for a pitcher or a hitter, might start to receive some statistical foundation. Some teams send their pitchers to the American Sports Medicine Institute or similar locations for biomechanical analysis, but the process is expensive, and optimizing a delivery is based on what little we already know about deliveries. (For example, ASMI research has shown that pitchers with short strides toward the plate release the ball higher in their deliveries, which reduces velocity and is correlated with a higher rate of shoulder injuries.) Collecting data on deliveries throughout a system, or even across multiple systems, would allow for a more systematic analysis of who gets hurt and who doesn't, of who gets more spin or sink or break on pitches, of which hitters put more backspin on the ball, and so on. The questions behind that sentence are not new; teams have looked for those players for as long as scouts have driven to all corners of the country to find players. But putting data behind the assertions of what's desirable in a player may upend some conventional wisdom and could improve the way the industry scouts players and develops them.

We've already seen such adjustments appear even at the major-league level. Daniel Murphy went from a nice platoon piece to an MVP-caliber hitter in 2015 and 2016 by increasing his launch angle through changes in his setup and stance, moving closer to the plate and starting his hands in a better position to get the bat head into the zone.

As revolutionary as Statcast will be to all sides of the game, there is a world beyond Statcast, believe it or not. Statcast is the talk of the town right now because it just moved in, and there's plenty of truth in the belief that such an extensive data stream will yield new insights into player performance, particularly in the descriptive realm—better telling us what actually happened on the field and what those actions were worth. Dividing up responsibility between fielders on a tough defensive play, or between a pitcher and the fielders behind him over the course of a game or a season, has long been a game of statistical estimation—educated guesswork, really, based on things we knew to be true at a macro level, because we couldn't measure this stuff at a micro level. Much of the last 150 years in the world of particle physics has been about using mathematics to explain the existence and behavior of particles our instruments could not see; the technology later caught up to the theory, proving that Ludwig Boltzmann was right about atoms, and that Peter Higgs and others were right about the Higgs field and breaking the symmetry of the electroweak force. Baseball analysis isn't particle physics (yet!) but has followed a similar path of hypothesis to discovery as we've moved from generic play-by-play data to Pitch f/x to Statcast.

However, since Statcast does level the playing field, now some teams are looking for competitive advantages in areas not covered by this data. Some are rather obvious; when any MLB team hosts an amateur event, such as the Perfect Game All-American Classic at Petco or the Under Armour All-American Game at Wrigley Field, the club can choose to turn on the TrackMan system and collect Statcast-style data on the players for their own use without an obligation to share them with other teams. If I were running a club, I'd be lobbying to hold as many of those events as I could afford, just to gather more data on potential draft picks.

Moving beyond Statcast data means using other technologies to collect the information, often requiring that the players themselves consent to devoting some time to the measurement process. The most notable public example of this is Boston's use of software that claims to measure hand-eye coordination, a process they call "neuroscouting." The software asks the player, sitting at a computer, to tap a key when a ball appears on the screen in a certain location or with the seams oriented a certain way, and thus tracks reaction times and recognition. The first year the team used the software in the draft was 2011, and their fifth-round pick that year was an undersized high school infielder from Tennessee named Mookie Betts, whom they drafted on the strong recommendation of area scout Danny Watkins—and because Betts had one of the highest scores on their neuroscouting tool that year.

There are already vendors in the "analytics" space offering solutions for this so-called neuroscouting, vision testing, personality or psychological testing, and more, some of which may work and much of which is probably pseudoscience capitalizing on an industry flush with cash and now populated with executives actively seeking tools like these. It isn't hard to foresee, as one team analyst suggested, "measuring facial expressions coupled with body movement to assess body language for quantifying attitude, stress, or emotion within a game; cameras that emulate fMRI's to measure brain activity; measuring heart rate, sweat, DNA, sleep patterns, food and water intake, energy, muscle fatigue, joint torque and angles, you name it." One general manager mentioned that the problem with some of these tests is that we lack any understanding of what the resulting data might mean; citing psychological testing, he questioned whether "stubbornness" should be seen as a good quality, a bad one, or neither.

The last common theme among these answers was the challenge of merely integrating all of these new data, Statcast and otherwise, with the team's existing operations. One GM who had gone through the exercise of setting up his team's first analytics department bemoaned the time required just to build a system capable of handling Statcast data, but also pointed out that they had few internal systems that required the development of new bridges to connect it to the Statcast database.

One longtime executive who's overseen the construction of analytics departments for multiple teams put the opportunity this way: "Anytime there's a new data stream, organizations face the question of when and how to integrate the new data into their decision-making processes. Organizations that go too quickly might rely on data that is inaccurate or compromised in some way. (We saw that time and time again with early defensive data.) Organizations that wait too long might fall behind and find themselves at a competitive disadvantage. Organizations that rely too much on a single new measure might be underemphasizing other important variables. Organizations that don't factor the new data enough in their mix might be missing out on the benefit of the breakthrough. So, generally, I think the next big opportunity is not in a single new data stream or field of research. Instead, it lies in applying new data at the right time and in the right proportion with other variables to best predict future performance."

Several executives on the baseball and analytics sides told me that the skills for which they're hiring have changed substantially in the last few years with the rise of big data, or what one director called "continuous data." Bachelor's degrees in computer science and programming skills were sufficient before the advent of Statcast; now teams are actively looking for master's degrees or even Ph.D.s. Cleaning data from these various sources—spotting obvious errors or anomalies and removing them before they skew any sort of analysis—is a huge part of the job now, which is yet another skill set (understanding how to develop algorithms that can spot these outliers en masse, rather than having to find them by hand) that wasn't necessary five years ago. Middleware might be familiar to many of you, but the idea of developing software to connect two different systems was simply not germane to baseball teams until these new data sources arrived. Getting systems to communicate so decision-makers have access to the data they want when they need them is the first big opportunity.

The second is cultural—getting the baseball operations folks, from scouts to coaches up to the GM, ready to work with the new data and incorporate them into a draft model, player development decisions, or in-game tactics. One team director of analytics said that "one thing we found out early is to make everything visual. Players have a lot of other things going on, so the more you can communicate in one picture, the more they can get it. We spend most of our time thinking about finding ways to visualize things." With so many employees essentially working remotely—scouts on the road, coaches and players at minor-league affiliates that could be halfway across the country—being able to communicate data-driven concepts in clear language is a potential separator skill for people looking to work in baseball operations.

Nobody to whom I spoke said that there's another revolution coming. Statcast was, in their view, the culmination of a series of upheavals in the business that started with the A's run of playoff appearances around the turn of the century, the publication of *Money-*

ball, the decisions by the Red Sox, Cardinals, and Blue Jays to very publicly hire front office people devoted to statistical analysis, and the 2006 introduction of Pitch f/x data. Of course, no one thinks the stathead era in baseball is over; they believe the change is permanent, and that changes in the near future will be incremental rather than exponential. Teams are hiring a new breed of analysts, and they're going to look for scouts and coaches who have the capacity or the experience to work with the recommendations or insights the analysts develop. It will likely be a period of experimentation with new ideas and technologies, some of which may stick, the way we've seen shifting and batter-specific defensive positioning became a routine part of the game. And the gap between what teams know about players and what those outside of front offices know will continue to grow.

Epilogue

When I started with the Blue Jays in January 2002 as a "Consultant, Baseball Operations," later changing to the catch-all "Special Assistant" title, I was the analytics department. The largest part of my job was merely gathering data and putting it in a form I could present to my boss, J. P. Ricciardi, who was committed to having this information available for decisions but came from a baseball background rather than a technical one. I learned Perl, a scripting language well suited to tasks like scraping text from Web pages and searching through them for specific strings, and spent much of my time each spring working on collecting season data from college teams' websites—eventually collecting from more than five hundred such sites each year—so that, first and foremost, we would have these data available in the draft room, and also so that we could identify players we might need to scout.

At the time, only a handful of teams were mining college data to look for hidden value, although after the publication of Michael Lewis's *Moneyball* in 2004, this practice became more common and the inefficiency in that market closed quickly. Prior to that, however, part of my job was to suggest to area scouts those players they should at least go evaluate—even if it was strictly to dismiss them as nonprospects—based on their statistical performances. Most of these players were doing well with skills that wouldn't translate to the majors, such as the pitcher, whose name I've since lost track of, at Fairleigh Dickinson University who had solid numbers but a fastball that sat around 82 mph. But occasionally we'd find a late-round gem; our biggest success was Ryan Roberts, a senior at Texas-Arlington whom we signed for $1,000 in the 18th round in 2003. Roberts accumulated 5.7 WAR over a nine-year big-league career, playing in 518 games—although only 17 of them were for the Blue Jays.

By my last spring with the Blue Jays, I'd developed additional scripts to strip play-by-play game logs from college sites that offered them so we could estimate groundball rates and swinging-strike percentages for pitchers and very basic splits for position players. Within a few years, however, an independent data provider, collegesplits.com, began offering these data and much more (including left/right splits for pitchers and hitters) to teams for a fee, and by 2010 or so at least half of MLB teams were using this kind of information in their draft processes.

The other major part of my job at the time was to work with the data MLB provided for all professional players through delivery of daily flat files and the posting of game logs for every player. I wrote further scripts to deal with all of these, so we could easily identify, say, pitchers who were particularly effective at retiring left-handed hitters, or who had high groundout rates, or hitters whose value might be obscured by tough home ballparks. I spent more time working to collect, clean, and format these data than I did to "analyze" them, because the latter part was so straightforward—applying park effects, for example—while tiny glitches in the format of a Web page could throw a beautifully designed Perl script (if I do say so myself) into disarray.

MLB's Pitch f/x data set just became available in my last year with Toronto, and I left to join ESPN before I got to do much of anything with it. Had I stuck around, my old tools would have been inadequate to the job; where I could store everything in Microsoft Access and export it to Excel for formatting, Pitch f/x had too many rows of data for basic desktop software. That was a job for a database programmer, and I am not one of those. This was the first inflection point, where hiring more than one person to staff an analytics department—and hiring someone with greater technical skills than I possessed—started to make sense.

Before the 2015 arrival of Statcast data, there were already teams that employed departments of six or more analysts, handling Pitch f/x data, college data, and some of the TrackMan data available for high school players from showcase events. Now Statcast data and its sheer size—the aforementioned terabyte of data per season—have led to an even greater rise in hiring; one department head estimated to me that all thirty MLB teams in total employ about two hundred people in analytics departments, from directors to entry-level programmers. I was one of the only full-time employees of any MLB team in 2002 whose job was to work with data; now, there are fifty to a hundred times more such people working for clubs, and I am completely underqualified for the job I used to hold.

As teams get smarter, the gap widens between what teams know about players and what we know about players—and by we, I mean not just the fans, but those of us who cover the industry for a living. Where fifteen or twenty years ago, the idea of even employing a single consultant to provide insight via statistical analysis was unorthodox, today teams employ entire departments of a half dozen or more analysts, some sporting Ph.D.s, to help gather, organize, and process data and queries to improve their decision-making on players. Increasing the accuracy of player projections—that is, what the player's performance is likely to be next year, the year after, or over the life of a long-term contract—has long been a sort of holy grail for front offices, which is why you're seeing so many resources thrown into analytics departments. Projections can never be perfect and should always have confidence intervals around them ("We're 95 percent confident his OBP will be between .340 and .360"), but even marginal improvements in their accuracy can mean millions of dollars in value to a team.

This puts the fan (in other words, you) in a different place today than in 2007 or 1997. It was reasonable in prior eras to think that when it came to player stats, we all knew what the teams knew, and in certain cases we seemed to know more, or simply to consider it more than the front offices in question did. Today there is no question that the teams have more data than we have, and that they are drawing conclusions that we won't know about until much later, if at all. We may certainly still disagree with team decisions on players, but we don't have the same information they do.

I still take hope in the recent statistical revolution and the ongoing changes promised by Statcast and any future data sources. Where once the discussion and coverage of baseball was ruled by superstition and myth, today more fans demand some rational underpinning to arguments over whether the Nationals gave up too much for Adam Eaton, whether Mike Trout is having the best start to a career in baseball history, whether Manny Machado or Bryce Harper will end up the best player from the 2010 draft, and so on. You can still try to write arrant nonsense or spew it on television, but you'll be picked apart for doing so, because the rise of the analysts has led to a more educated fan base.

Every player's stat line tries to tell the story of his season, so if you want to get the story right, you have to use the right stats. Using the old-fashioned, outdated stats I broke down in Part One meant getting the story wrong. They ascribed credit to one player for the actions of another, and sometimes led writers and fans to believe that players had mythical powers like the ability to play better in a clutch situation. We know better now, whether it's how to value what a player did or how to dismiss quackery like clutch hitters and lineup protection.

Understanding more modern statistics, even those as simple as OBP or slugging percentage, allows everyone to better understand what's happening on the field, whether it's going well or poorly, or the moves that teams make off the field. If your favorite team just acquired a player you've never heard of before, you're going to want to know whether he'll help. The better the statistics you look at to answer this question, the more confident you can be in your answer. And now you're better armed to watch the watchmen, to read the work of people who cover the game (like me) and see if we're telling the right kind of stories about the game, or ignoring statistical information that leads to a different conclusion. When a broadcaster tells you that some player "just knows how to win" or is "a great RBI guy," your BS detector will light up like a Christmas tree. When a manager or GM claims that a low-OBP player can lead off because he's fast, you know why speed is a red herring. You're armed to think rationally about a sport that, for most of its 150 or so years, was covered and treated and discussed in the most irrational terms.

This will still be true for the savvy fan even as the information gap I mentioned above grows. You don't need to know or understand the importance of exit velocity or launch angle or spin rate to watch and enjoy a game, or to follow a player or team through a season. This information may help you—for example, it appears that a fastball with high velocity but just average spin rate isn't going to be as effective as the velocity alone might imply, missing fewer bats and leading to more hard contact. And you, the savvy fan (you're welcome), should keep an open mind about new advances; ten years ago we never thought about putting a value on catcher framing, but now it's driving transactions and pushing the worst framers out of regular jobs.

Teams are developing better tools to drive their player projections, regressing performances to mean levels or employing mixed models to try to incorporate random effects into metrics for pitchers, but you don't have to understand any of this to be an educated fan. You only have to accept that the search for knowledge within baseball never ends, so what appears to be a complete story of a player today may turn out to be incomplete tomorrow. I said in the chapter on pitching metrics that my 2009 NL Cy Young vote may end up looking wrong as we learn more about how much credit or blame falls on a pitcher when a ball in play becomes a hit. Using the best knowledge we have right now while remembering that we may know a lot more in the future is the essence of Smart Baseball.

Acknowledgments

I'd like to thank my editor, Matt Harper, for shepherding this project from concept to completion, taking a set of essays and helping me weave them together into something coherent and cogent.

My agents, Eric Lupfer for literary and Melissa Baron for anything else, helped make this book more than just some idea I had in the middle of thirty other ideas I had that never went anywhere. Eric in particular turned the elevator pitch into a written document and then into a formal proposal, one that landed me with HarperCollins faster than I could have hoped for.

Meredith Wills provided some essential research help, especially early in the process, which formed a lot of the foundation of the early chapters on ERA and fielding, although much of the work she did doesn't appear directly in the book. The commentary about catchers whose proficiency at throwing out runners might hurt their apparent defensive value because runners stop attempting to steal against them comes from research Meredith did for this project.

I spoke to many people inside the industry to research this book, folks who made more time for me than I could have expected. The Statcast team at Major League Baseball Advanced Media, including Cory Schwartz, Greg Cain, Tom Tango (he exists!), Mike Petriello, and Daren Willman spent an afternoon walking me through the product's history and capabilities. I felt like a kid walking through a science museum for the first time.

Molly Knight was especially helpful with advice and a critical eye that helped make the final book cleaner and more polished.

There are more team executives who helped than I can list, and some requested that they remain anonymous, but among those I can thank publicly are David Forst, Theo Epstein, Alex Anthopoulos, John Mozeliak, Chris Long, Sig Mejdal, Jason Pare, James Click, Dan Fox, Matt Klentak, John Coppolella, Mitchel Lichtman, and Farhan Zaidi, who'd like me to say that he was especially unhelpful.

My editors and colleagues at ESPN, especially at ESPN.com and Insider, were gracious enough to give me the time I needed to write a book while maintaining a full-time job and regular presence across ESPN's various platforms. I appreciate their constant support and understanding.

My entire career in baseball has been something of a happy accident, and it only occurred at all thanks to J.P. Ricciardi, who gave me my first job in the game (and, among other things, made "Joey Bagodonuts" a permanent part of my vocabulary), and Billy Beane, who helped convince J.P. to give me a shot. I also worked with some wonderful people in my four-plus years in Toronto, and have to single out Tony Lacava and Tommy Tanous for the time they spent with me at games, teaching the most basic aspects of scouting to someone who, for all my comfort with numbers, could barely tell a slider from a changeup when I first got there.

And finally, I'd like to thank my wife and daughter for their incredible patience throughout the writing process, for all the times I was there but not really there, buried in my computer or stuck on the phone, turning out a 275-page book inside of nine months.

Index

About the Author

Keith Law is a senior baseball writer for ESPN Insider and an analyst for ESPN's *Baseball Tonight,* focusing on all types of baseball analysis. Prior to joining ESPN, Law spent four and a half years working as a Special Assistant to the General Manager for the Toronto Blue Jays, handling all statistical analysis, and was previously a writer for *Baseball Prospectus*. He graduated from Harvard College and has an MBA from the Tepper School at Carnegie Mellon University. Law lives in Delaware with his wife and daughter. *Smart Baseball* is his first book.